PROSPECTS FOR
SOVIET AGRICULTURE
IN THE 1980s

CSIS PUBLICATION SERIES ON THE
SOVIET UNION IN THE 1980s

ROBERT F. BYRNES, *Editor*
AILEEN MASTERSON, *Associate Editor*

PROSPECTS FOR SOVIET AGRICULTURE IN THE 1980s

D. GALE JOHNSON
AND
KAREN McCONNELL BROOKS

PUBLISHED IN ASSOCIATION WITH THE CENTER
FOR STRATEGIC AND INTERNATIONAL STUDIES,
GEORGETOWN UNIVERSITY • WASHINGTON, D.C.

INDIANA UNIVERSITY PRESS • BLOOMINGTON

Manufactured in the United States of America

Library of Congress Cataloging in Publication Data
Johnson, D. Gale (David Gale), 1916-
   Prospects for Soviet agriculture in the 1980s.

   "Published in association with the Center for
Strategic and International Studies, Georgetown
University."
   Bibliography: p.
   Contents: Policies and performance in Soviet
agriculture / D. Gale Johnson—Productivity in Soviet
agriculture / Karen Brooks.
   1. Agriculture—Economic aspects—Soviet Union.
I. Brooks, Karen (Karen McConnell) II. Georgetown
University. Center for Strategic and International
Studies. III. Title.
HD1992.J56   1983   338.1'0947   82–48625
1 2 3 4 5 87 86 85 84 83

ISBN 0-253-34619-3

ISBN 0-253-20300-7 {PBK}

CONTENTS

In memory of
Arcadius Kahan

Foreword

This excellent volume represents the first publication produced by a major project on "Factors Affecting Soviet Foreign Policy in the 1980s" at the Center for Strategic and International Studies. Under the generous sponsorship of the Frederick Henry Prince Charitable Trusts, this eighteen-month effort will make a significant contribution to American knowledge of the Soviet domestic situation and its impact on Soviet foreign policy.

The authors' examination of the current status and trends in Soviet agriculture illuminates a critical component of the Soviet economy that poses significant problems for present and future Soviet decision makers. It also represents an important consideration for Western policy makers, because no one knows the degree to which Soviet agricultural and general domestic problems will serve as a constraint on future Soviet foreign activities or prod Soviet leaders to explore new avenues for meeting the fundamental needs of the Soviet people.

Our center has long been interested in the U.S.-Soviet relationship as the key to a stable international system, and we well recognize the importance of the economic component of that relationship. We have also been concerned for some time with the economic dimensions of national security and have periodically focused attention on agriculture as a critical sector. We are delighted that this analysis reflects these broader Center interests in a fashion grounded in the highest scholarship.

D. Gale Johnson and Karen McConnell Brooks have provided the kind of detailed information about the Soviet Union that will be essential for effective American foreign policy in the 1980s. The goal for the project of which this book is a part is to provide such information on a number of topics and on a larger scale. To this end, CSIS has assembled a group of thirty-five scholars from the best universities around the country to synthesize available information and generate new research on the spectrum of Soviet domestic problems. Divided into several working groups, these experts have been discussing concerns such as the political system of the USSR, the role of the military, dimensions of intellectual and cultural life, societal tensions and demographic trends, the problems of Eastern Europe, and the impact of broader external events on the Soviet system.

The entire project has been administered under the extremely able direction of Dr. Robert F. Byrnes, Distinguished Professor of History at Indiana University, who not only has led the research activities and deliberations of the working groups but also has served as a general editor for the Project's publications. The Project's core staff in residence at CSIS has been invaluable in implementing this effort. Its coordinating activities and substantive contributions have been essential in producing integrated and polished products, and special mention should be made of Aileen Masterson, coordinator of the entire Project, whose editorial contributions to this volume helped ensure its timely completion.

The work done by D. Gale Johnson and Karen McConnell Brooks provides a thorough and valuable analysis of Soviet agriculture, and we are proud to have it as the introductory book in our Soviet series.

DAVID M. ABSHIRE
President, CSIS

Preface

This book represents the culmination of three decades of research on the economics of Soviet agriculture. For almost all this time Arcadius Kahan was the key contributor to research on Soviet agriculture in the Department of Economics of The University of Chicago, joining the effort in 1955 and continuing active involvement until·his untimely death on February 26, 1982. He was actively engaged in the research project from which this book has emerged. We are all losers because he was not able to make his full contribution to our work.

But much of whatever may be meritorious in our written efforts owes an enormous amount to long association with Arcadius. He was always willing to help in numerous ways, ranging from sharing his enormous knowledge of facts and data sources to his insights into the subtle functioning of the socialist economic systems of Eastern Europe. Our personal and intellectual debts are very great and explain why we have dedicated this book to the memory of Arcadius Kahan.

The research from which this book emerged was supported by a generous grant to The University of Chicago by the Frederick Henry Prince Charitable Trusts, but it would be inappropriate to stop with our expression of gratitude to a faceless entity such as a trust. William Wood Prince first discussed with us the possibility of our undertaking a study of factors that influence the productivity of Soviet agriculture, and it was through his good offices that financial support was made available.

The book has two main parts and two authors. Each of us is responsible for the part for which authorship is indicated. Obviously we worked together on the research project, sharing our results and written material as well as our questions and problems. Each commented freely upon the work done by the other. During the formative phases of the research we benefited from the advice and counsel of Arcadius Kahan.

ix

Even though there is no joint authorship involved, it is appropriate that the parts be included within the same covers. We have approached the study of Soviet agriculture from somewhat different viewpoints, using different methods and approaches, and we have tried to answer somewhat different questions. We hope that our results complement each other and contribute to a clearer understanding of a very complex subject.

D. GALE JOHNSON
KAREN McCONNELL BROOKS
September 13, 1982

PART I

POLICIES AND PERFORMANCE IN SOVIET AGRICULTURE

D. GALE JOHNSON

CHAPTER ONE

A Short Introduction to Soviet Agriculture

The performance of Soviet agriculture during the 1970s, especially since 1975, has disappointed the Soviet rulers in many different ways. The growth of output has been low, compared to performance from 1950 to 1970 and compared to the growth of demand for food. Although the country was a significant net exporter of grain during the previous decade, poor output performance has required the USSR to import enormous amounts of grain; for the decade ending in 1981-82, net grain imports were 195 million metric tons.

Soviet agriculture is a high-cost agriculture. In recent years the Soviet government has allocated about 27 percent of national investment directly to agriculture. If investment in agricultural input and marketing firms is included, it has devoted more than a third of national investment to agriculture. Yet as both relative and absolute levels of investment have increased, the rate of growth of output has declined. The costs of producing farm products, especially livestock products, and the prices paid to the farms have been increasing at such a rate that maintaining stable consumer prices for meat and milk required annual subsidies of 35 billion rubles (approximately $50 billion at the official rate of exchange) in 1981. Consumers paid no more than half of the cost of their meat and milk; the rest they paid as taxpayers.

At one time I accepted the conventional explanation that the relatively poor performance of Soviet agriculture was due to the fact that most agriculture was socialized, organized into either collective or state farms, and to adverse climatic conditions for much of the agricultural area. However, I believe now that the socialized nature of Soviet agriculture is not the major source of difficulties. Many other aspects of Soviet planning, management systems, and pricing are far more important in limiting agriculture's performance than is its socialized character. Moreover, while climatic conditions in the USSR are clearly inferior to those of the American Corn Belt or what was once the American Cotton

3

Belt, the land resources, including climatic factors, are fully capable of sustaining substantial output growth and high and relatively stable levels of food production.

What are the prospects for Soviet agriculture? Can its output performance be improved? Can investment and other costs be reduced? And, more important, will the government make the policy changes required to realize more fully the potentials of Soviet agriculture? There can be no certain answers to any of these questions. However, we hope this analysis of the Soviet agricultural system and the reasons for its successes and failures will help indicate possible patterns for the decade ahead.

The Soviet agricultural system is one of great complexity, though no more so than that of the United States, the United Kingdom, or Canada. Any brief description of an agricultural system must be highly simplified. I will emphasize major features that differentiate Soviet agricultural organization from those with which Americans are more familiar.

COLLECTIVE AND STATE FARMS

Almost all agricultural land in the Soviet Union is socialized and operated by either collective or state farms. The average size in 1980 was large—6,600 hectares (16,300 acres) for collective farms and 17,300 hectares (42,730 acres) for the state farms. These two types of farms have a total cultivated area of approximately 225 million hectares (555 million acres), some 40 percent larger than the cultivated area in the United States and more than five times that of Canada. Due to the large size of the farms, their total number is quite small: at the end of 1980, 25,800 collective farms and 21,000 state farms. The total sown area in the socialized sector is divided approximately equally between the collective and state farms, with the state farms having 54 percent of the sown area in 1980. Collective farms have about 515 workers and state farms about 550, annual average basis.[1]

In theory a *collective farm* is a producer cooperative managed by a chairman and board of directors whom the members elect. The collective farm is assigned land in perpetuity, though the farm can neither sell nor rent the land. In fact, collective farms possess only limited decision-making authority. Each farm is required to deliver a substantial amount of its output to the state procurement agencies. If sales to the state exceed the amounts specified, the farms receive substantially higher prices for most commodities. The bonus is generally 50 percent of the procurement price.[2] Farms may also sell part of their output in the collective farm markets, where prices more nearly reflect supply and demand conditions, but such sales are possible only after the farms have made planned deliveries to the procurement agencies.

Members of the collective farms receive payment on the basis of the number of days worked and factors that reflect the skill required for the work performed. Until fifteen years ago the members were residual claimants to the income of the collective farms. However, in the 1960s a system of minimum monthly payments was instituted, and the collective farms are required to make such payments on a timely basis. On a farm of low productivity the minimum payments, with some adjustments for skill factors, may be all that is received. On a farm with high productivity, payments can and do exceed the minimum payments by a substantial margin.

The *state farm* can be reasonably accurately described as a corporate farm. Workers receive a wage, and the state supplies the capital and takes most of the profit, if any. If there is a loss, this is covered by a subsidy.

When agriculture was first socialized during the late 1920s, important differences existed between collective and state farms. However, recent trends indicate than an effort is being made to reduce the differences between the two forms of agricultural firms. The institution of the minimum wage for members of collective farms probably had more than one objective, but one effect was to make the collective farm much more like the state farm. The relative importance of state farms, as measured by sown area, has increased greatly in the last quarter century. In 1950 state farms cultivated only 12 percent of the sown area; today such farms cultivate somewhat more than half of the sown area.

PRIVATE AGRICULTURE

Members of collective farms and employees on state farms, as well as large numbers of workers in nonfarm enterprises, are assigned small plots of land for their personal cultivation. The plots range in size from less than half an acre to somewhat more than an acre.

These plots account for approximately 3 percent of the total sown area, but they produce somewhat more than 25 percent of gross agricultural output. In recent years approximately 30 percent of total Soviet meat and milk output has been produced in the private sector. Almost two thirds of all potatoes and two-fifths of the fruit and vegetables are grown on private plots. It has been estimated that private plots produce 12 percent of net agricultural output.[3]

This comparison of the importance of the private plots in sown area and gross or net agricultural output is not intended to indicate differences in productivity between the private and socialized sectors. Most of the concentrate feed for private livestock is produced in the socialized sector, and private livestock graze on the common pasture lands of the collective farms and otherwise unused land, such as along roads and highways.

The importance of the private plots in gross agricultural output is emphasized to indicate that a substantial part of farm output is not directly under the control of Moscow, except in the long run. In any given year, especially when crop production is low, the private sector presents central planners with difficult decisions concerning the allocation of feed supplies.

One indicator of the official Soviet perception that agricultural conditions are unsatisfactory and output growth is lagging, especially with regard to those products most desired by consumers, is the relaxation of some restraints on private agriculture. The numbers of various kinds of livestock that can be raised on a private plot have historically been limited by law and regulation. In 1980 a new decree, "On supplementary measures for improving production of agricultural products in the private agriculture of citizens," allowed families to take on additional livestock if they entered into agreements to sell the fattened animals or milk to the collective or state farms. Agricultural production purchased in this way can be used toward collective or state farm plan fulfillment and in calculating bonuses for management. Available reports are not specific about the source of the added feed, the prices that will be paid for the animals and products, and the procurement prices. A similar plan had been in effect for three years in Voronezh Province, and pigs were sold to the collective farm for 1.5 rubles per kilogram, a price approximately the same as the state purchase price. In this case the concentrate feed was supplied by the collective farm.[4]

PLANNING AND MANAGEMENT
OF AGRICULTURE

The management of Soviet agriculture is highly centralized.[5] Most important decisions are made or influenced by Moscow through five-year plans, annual plans, and specific instructions concerning a wide variety of farm activities. Much management occurs through directives establishing such goals as size of the livestock herd, planting and harvesting dates, and procurement plans. Prices do have some role. As already noted, large premia are paid for above-plan deliveries of many products as well as for the delivery of particular weights and qualities of livestock products.

The assumption or operating principle that seems to guide agricultural planners and officials is that farm managers and farm people generally cannot be trusted to make the appropriate decisions. This view was elaborated in a speech by A. M. Rumyantsev of the Presidium of the Soviet Academy of Science at the International Conference of Agricultural Economics in Minsk in 1970:

> Every collective farm cannot take into account society's real needs in agricultural products. This can be done only by socialist society as a whole. The latter makes the necessary information available to all collective farms in a centralized way, by drawing up its firm plan of purchasing farm products, by placing orders with these farms, and thus ensuring the stability of their production.[6]

In one important sense Soviet agricultural planners are right in assuming that farm managers will not make appropriate decisions. The price system, as designed by the planners and officials, does not provide information and incentives to guide farms in making decisions concerning the products and the resource combinations they should use to minimize costs and to achieve maximum output of agricultural products. If prices do not provide appropriate guides for production decisions, other mechanisms must be used to influence output and marketings. But such mechanisms have their own difficulties, and numerous efforts have been made, with little apparent success, to improve them.

Brezhnev, in presenting the Eleventh Five-Year Plan in November 1981, was particularly critical of the planning and management of agriculture. While it is not certain that current unspecified efforts to reform agricultural planning will be any more effective than numerous previous attempts have been, a brief summary of his views as presented in *Pravda* may be of interest. After quoting Brezhnev as saying "The food problem is, economically and politically, the central problem of the whole five-year plan," *Pravda* noted:

> In drawing up the food program, an important place should be assigned to such major problems as the improvement of the economic mechanism and the system of management—the management of agriculture and of the agro-industrial complex as a whole. And, of course, local management. The collective farms and state farms themselves should have the final say in deciding what should be sown on each hectare and when one job or another should begin. The district level of management should also be strengthened in every way. We must create conditions that will more actively stimulate the growth of agricultural production and an increase in its intensiveness, encourage the initiative of collective farms and state farms and of all elements of the agro-industrial complex, and make them work not for intermediate indices but for high final results.[7]

One of the most important points in the quotation is that "collective and state farms themselves should have the final say in deciding what should be sown on each hectare and when one job or another should begin." It is quite remarkable that the planning and management system permits officials other than those directly engaged in farm production to intervene in such decisions as what to plant, when to plant, and when to harvest, what to feed, and when to breed. Even with an inappropriate price system, some decisions can best be left to those most immediately involved.

RURAL LIFE

A brief description of the Soviet agricultural system does not give the flavor of rural life nor depict the problems the ordinary member of a collective farm or worker on a state farm faces. Perhaps it is appropriate to try to provide some flavor at this point by describing a personal incident and by two quotations.

In June 1981 I attended the Sixth U.S.-Soviet Economic Symposium in Alma Ata in Kazakhstan. Alma Ata is a prosperous city in a major agricultural, industrial, and mining region in one of the most scenic areas of the Soviet Union. At the conclusion of our conference, we were told that we would have a picnic on a collective farm. On a rainy morning, following a rather lengthy period when it had rained nearly every evening, we were put on a small bus to drive to the farm. For the first fifteen miles or so we traveled on an excellent four-lane highway. For the next few miles—certainly fewer than ten—we drove on a paved two-lane road. Then we turned off to a dirt road, actually a mud road which had not been graded. Within no more than twenty-five miles from one of the most modern and prosperous cities in the Soviet Union, our bus became stuck on a dirt road leading to a picnic site prepared for visiting foreigners! The Soviet rural road system can only be described as a disgrace, the result of decades of socialist neglect.

The area where we had lunch and spent the day was a site on a collective farm prepared for us at very considerable expense. Soviet officials rebuked every effort to visit the headquarters of the farm. I could not even learn where or how far away the nearest village was. The only explanation that I received for this rather inhospitable behavior was that the village was probably a very poor one and that local officials did not want us to see it.

The following quotation from a round-table discussion on "Rural Culture and the Writer's Role in its Development" held in 1981 sustains this view:

> In discussing so-called rural culture, we should keep in mind that the material foundation or external trappings of culture cannot be separated from its spiritual context. A certain wise man has said that roads determine the level of a country's culture. By this yardstick, the level of our rural culture is not very high. We have hundreds and thousands of rural villages and very few paved roads. Villagers still rely largely on dirt roads for their contact with the outside world. These roads served very well in the days of horse-drawn vehicles, but for the modern car or truck

they are impassable in bad weather. We've taken the peasant's
horse away from him, without providing anything to replace it as
a means of contact with the outside world. Sometimes rural
people have to use tractors for transportation six months of the
year. They aren't likely to take a tractor to go visiting or to see a
play. True, They do manage to get hold of tractors to go fetch
vodka, to go to market; or to get store-bought bread at the district
center.[8]

While the last sentence of the quotation presents a rather dis-
paraging view of the preferences of rural people, the description
of the road situation provides some evidence of the starkness of
rural life in many parts of the Soviet Union. On the other hand, the
same article provides a sympathetic and, I believe, perceptive description of what has gone wrong as Soviet agricultural and rural
policies have emerged over the past six decades:

The point here is that the whole rural way of life should be
carefully thought out and linked with housing, readily available
means of transportation, the land and the natural environment.
Culture in the countryside is impossible without this sort of
overall harmony.
Let us consider just one element of the whole: rural labor.
The land is a living organism, and the work of the peasant
farmer is, by its very nature, creative work—work which is
based on millenia of human observation of the cycle of nature
and the land, plants, and animals. Agricultural work precludes a
stereotyped, formalistic approach and requires initiative, the
maximum of independence, and the minimum of petty regulation. Yet what we generally do is try to curb the rural person
with every imaginable sort of command, simplify his labor,
break it down into separate operations and strip it of the in-
teraction with nature that is its living essence. Part of the blame
here lies with misguided scientists who have crudely interpreted the notion of eliminating the difference between city and
countryside and, beyond that, turning agricultural labor into a
variety of industrial labor. You cannot organize agricultural
labor, which requires a creative response to the land and natural
conditions, the way you do industrial labor.
Wherever I have seen peasant farmers attached to "their own"
land and freed from the sort of petty supervision that hampers
initiative, I have always found people of lofty culture, vast
knowledge and remarkable skill. They can not only handle but
repair and even rebuild complex machinery. They are very well
versed in agronomy. Many are real selection specialists who

develop new varieties of fruits and berries in their own gardens and orchards. They visit clubs and take part in amateur arts. They vie with one another in trimming their homes and landscaping their yards. It is no wonder people say that you can tell the culture of such home owners from the street.

In contrast, how sad it is to see rural apartment buildings, so-called communal residences, surrounded by impassable mud and bare yards with rickety little tables where zealous smokers sit killing time by playing dominoes. You won't even find a sapling, much less an orchard, around such buildings. This is an example of what happens when the vital ties between the peasant and the land are severed.[9]

Nothing that we shall write can constitute a more striking criticism and indictment of what Soviet policy has done to destroy the web of rural life and work. Nor, I fear, will we come closer to explaining why particular performance deficiencies exist than has the author of the quotation.

CHAPTER TWO

Agricultural Performance
since 1950

In terms of overall output growth, Soviet agriculture has performed well since 1950 in comparison with Western Europe and North America. This was particularly true for 1950 through 1970, when agricultural output in the USSR increased at an annual compound rate of 3.9 percent, compared to 2.0 percent for U.S. farm output and 2.2 percent for Western Europe. However, during the 1970s agricultural output growth in the USSR slowed sharply. For 1970 to 1979–80, the growth rate was 1.2 percent, while the output growth rate in Western Europe and the United States did not decline. Agricultural production in 1978, a record grain production year, was only 6 percent above 1973, an earlier year of record grain production.[1] Thus from peak to peak, so to speak, production grew at no more than 1 percent annually. For the entire period since 1950, the output record remains a respectable one of 3.0 percent annual growth. However, the slowdown in output growth during the 1970s has significant negative implications.

The success in achieving a relatively high output growth rate since 1950 tells only part of the story. Measured by other criteria, the performance of Soviet agriculture during the past three decades has suffered because of three particular difficulties.

A first shortcoming is that output growth has been rapid but has not kept pace with the growth of demand. To meet increasing demand, the Soviet Union has had to depend increasingly upon imported grains and feedstuffs and, more recently, meat and sugar. With the Soviet population growing at a slow annual rate—less than 1.5 percent between 1950 and 1970 and 1 percent in recent years—why has the USSR found it necessary to import food and feeding materials? An important reason is that retail prices of meat and milk in state stores have remained constant since 1962 and hardly changed since the mid-1950s, while money incomes per capita have increased substantially. The government made a political decision to hold constant retail prices of meat, milk, and most other foods, even though procurement prices for livestock products have doubled since 1964. The fixed retail prices do not equate supply and demand and have been maintained only by payment of enormous subsidies on meat and milk production. In 1980, the total subsidy bill for meat, milk, potatoes, and cereals, including bread, may have reached 28 billion rubles, an enormous sum. In 1981 the subsidies increased by 7 billion rubles* to more than a fourth of gross agricultural output.[2]

Per capita meat consumption remains substantially below the level in other industrial countries with approximately the same income levels, even though it has doubled since 1950. On a comparable basis, per capita meat consumption in 1980 was at least 40 percent lower in the USSR than in Poland. It is ironic that the USSR is subsidizing the Poles, who eat considerably more meat than Soviet citizens. Demand for meat has been and remains high; per capita demand has been growing at an annual rate of about 2 percent. Not all of this has been met in the state stores at the official prices; a significant amount of meat is sold in the collective farm markets at prices more than double official retail prices.

A second shortcoming of Soviet agriculture remains the very high costs of producing livestock products. There is frequent discussion in the Soviet press that even high livestock prices do not cover the full cost of production, though the costs as calculated exclude return for land and include only depreciation (no interest) on capital. In 1977, prior to the increase in milk prices in 1979, milk production involved a loss on 47 percent of the farms' costs, wool on 73 percent, and potatoes on 70 percent.[3]

The third shortcoming has been the remarkably high percentage of total investment allocated to agriculture during the 1970s. Agriculture's share of national investment increased from less than 20 percent during 1961–65 to about 27 percent during the Tenth and Eleventh Plans. Total agricultural investment during the Tenth Plan (1976–80) was approximately double that for 1966–70. It appears that during 1976–80 the gross investment to net output percentage in the Soviet Union was double that in the United States. On a reasonably comparable basis, agricultural investment

---

*The official rate of exchange was $1.54 per ruble in 1980, but the rate was $1.35 in June 1981. Both overestimate the value of the ruble.

in the Soviet Union was 35 percent of the value of net output, while it was 17 percent in the United States.

AGRICULTURE IN THE TENTH
PLAN PERIOD

The Tenth Plan for Agriculture (1976–80) had the general appearance of a moderate and realistic plan in terms of achieving in whole or in large part its goals. In another sense, however, the "output objectives of the plan can be described as pessimistic," as I wrote in 1976. I noted that if the plan objectives were met, there would be little or no improvement in per capita food consumption, in terms of either quantity or composition. The only significant planned increases in food consumption per capita were for vegetables, fruits, and melons. Perhaps the most striking figure in the plan was that direct grain consumption as food per capita was to remain unchanged during the plan period after significant declines in recent years.[4] At the per capita income level of the USSR, stable per capita grain consumption would not occur in an economy in which consumer preferences had a significant influence upon food consumption or one in which supply equaled demand at the prevailing prices for all food items.

The meat and milk goals were extremely modest, with planned increases of approximately 7 to 11 percent for the Tenth Plan, compared to the Ninth. The planned increases were very small compared to the potential growth in demand; for meat, per capita demand probably increased by at least 10 percent during the five years, while the planned supply increase was approximately 3 percent. Gross farm output was to increase by 14 to 17 percent and grain output by 18 to 21 percent. The 1976–80 goals are given in Table 2.1.

But performance fell significantly below these modest goals. There was a shortfall in grain production; the increase for the five years was 13 percent instead of 18 to 21 percent. The shortfall in meat production was even sharper. The 1980 goal was 17.3 million tons of meat and edible slaughter fats; actual 1980 output has been reported as 15.1 million tons. The 1980 output of meat and fat was only slightly larger than the 1975 output of 15.0 million tons, and at 57 kilograms per capita meat consumption was the same in the

TABLE 2.1

Output of Selected Agricultural Products, USSR, Average, 1966–75, and Plans, 1971–80

Item	Quantity or Value				Increase Over Previous Five Years			
	Actual 1966–70	Actual 1971–75	Plan 1971–75	Plan 1976–80	Actual 1966–70	Actual 1971–75	Plan 1971–75	Plan 1976–80
	-- Billion Rubles --				-- Percent --			
Gross output:								
1973 prices	100	113	NA	129–132	NA	13	NA	14–17
1965 prices	80.5	91	98.0	104–106	21	13	22	14–17
	-- Million Metric Tons --				-- Percent --			
Grain[a]	167.6	181.5	195	215–220	29	8	16	18–21
Cotton (unginned)	6.1	7.7	6.8	8.5	22	26	11	10
Sunflower seeds	6.4	6.0	7.0	7.6	26	-6	9	27
Sugarbeets	81.1	76.0	87.4	95–98	37	-6	8	25–29
Meat[b]	11.6	14.1	14.3	15.0–15.6	24	21	23	7–11
Milk	80.6	87.5	92.3	94–96	24	9	15	7–10
Eggs (billions)	35.8	51.5	46.7	58–61	25	44	30	13–18
Potatoes	94.8	89.7	106.0	102	16	-5	--	14
Vegetables	19.5	22.8	24.7	28.1	15	17	NA	23
Fruits and berries[c]	NA	7.9	10.4	10.4	NA	36	NA	32

Sources: Economic Research Service, U.S. Department of Agriculture, The Agricultural Situation in the Soviet Union: Review of 1975 and Outlook for 1976, For. Agric. Econ. Rpt. No. 118 (April 1976), p. 29 and Central Statistical Board of the USSR, The USSR in Figures for 1979, Moscow, 1980, pp. 116–17.

[a]Gross weight, including excess moisture and waste.

[b]Including slaughter fats.   [c]Excludes grapes.

two years. For the plan period, annual average meat output increased 6 percent over the previous plan and thus fell below the
low end of the percentage increase for the goal. Table 2.2 presents
data on 1976–80 goals and performance and 1980 goals and performance.

TABLE 2.2

The 1976–80 Plan Goals and Performance and 1980 Plan and Performance,
USSR Agriculture

	1976–80 Plan	1976–80 Actual	1976–80 Actual/ Plan[a]	1980 Plan	1980 Actual	1980 Actual/ Plan
	(mil. metric tons)		%	(mil. metric tons)		%
Gross Output						
Grain	215–220	205	94.3	235.0	189.2	80.5
Cotton (unginned)	8.5	8.9	105.7	9.0	10.0	111.1
Sunflower seeds	7.6	5.3	69.7	7.7	4.65	60.4
Sugar beets	95–98	88.4	91.6	--	79.6	--
Meat	15.0–15.6	14.9	97.4	17.3	15.1	87.3
Milk	94–96	93.2	98.1	102	93.3	91.5
Eggs	58–61	63.0	105.9	66.8	67.7	101.3
Potatoes	102	82.4	80.8	104	66.9	64.3
Vegetables	28.1	26.0	92.5	30	25.9	86.3
Fruits and berries	10.4	9.4	90.4	--	--	--
Wool	0.473	0.461	97.5	0.515	0.462	89.7

Sources: See Table 2.1.

[a]Based on mid-point of 1976–80 plan goals. Actual/plan means actual
output divided by plan output multiplied by 100 to convert to percent.

Milk production fell short of both the Tenth Plan and 1980 goals, though the major problem with milk in the Soviet Union is not the output level but inadequate utilization of available supplies. Egg output met both the Tenth Plan and 1980 goals.

Cotton was the only crop for which the Tenth Plan and 1980 goals were met. For the other six crops besides grain for which we have data for both production and 1976–80 goals, production fell significantly short of the goals. Sugar beet production, which was to increase 25 to 29 percent, fell some 8 percent below the Tenth Plan goal. No 1980 goal was given for sugar beets. Vegetable production was to increase 23 percent for the plan; production fell short of the plan goal of 28.1 million tons by 7 percent for the period, and 1980 production was 14 percent short of the 1980 goal. Production of fruits and berries during the Tenth Plan fell short of the goal by 9 percent.

Sunflower seed production was to have increased by 27 percent for the plan; instead, production averaged 11 percent below 1971–75. Potato production was to increase 14 percent during the plan period; instead, average output was 8 percent below the previous plan period. The 1980 potato crop was the smallest in almost three decades and was only three fifths of the 1980 goal.

The Tenth Plan period was a disastrous one in terms of agricultural performance. Even though there were enormous capital investment and increases in machinery deliveries and fertilizer supplied to agriculture, grain imports increased significantly.[5] During the Ninth Plan, net grain imports totaled 55 million tons; during the Tenth Plan 102 million tons.

One of the most disquieting aspects of the Tenth Plan was that grain fed to livestock increased from an estimated annual rate during the Ninth Plan of 94 million tons to 121 million tons or 28 percent. Over the same span of time, meat and milk production each increased by only a little more than 6 percent. Only egg output increased even approximately in proportion to the increase in grain used as feed and at a 23 percent increase did not quite equal the 28 percent increase in grain used as feed. With meat and milk production in 1980 little above the level five years earlier, the large increase in grain used as feed raises questions about the potential for further increases in livestock and milk production based on increased amounts of grain.

SLOWDOWN IN OUTPUT GROWTH
IN THE 1970s:
TEMPORARY OR LONGER RUN?

The slow growth of agricultural production during the Tenth Plan Period and for the 1970s as a whole may represent either a temporary aberration or a continuation of a downward trend in growth rates since the 1960s. Obviously only time will tell which outcome will prevail.

An indication of the general trend in agricultural output can be obtained by considering growth rates for specific periods. I have chosen periods of six years, in part because important policy changes occurred at or near the beginning of each period, 1952, 1958, 1964, and 1970.

In the first year, 1952, incentives for farm people were sharply increased following the death of Stalin. In 1958 the machine tractor stations were abolished, but simultaneously a change in price policy and procurement prices reduced farm income; 1964 was the last year of Khrushchev's regime and the beginning of a period of improved material incentives and a sharp increase in available supplies of farm inputs, such as machinery and fertilizer. The year 1970 does not quite fit so neatly in this pattern, yet the policy decision to import grain to permit increased livestock production was made not long thereafter. In 1972 when the grain crop was relatively small, net grain imports reached the then unprecedented level of 21 million tons and gross grain imports were 23 million tons.

But let us look at the annual growth rates of agricultural output for each of the six-year periods, with all comparisons based on three-year averages centered on the specified year:[6]

1952–58	6.7
1958–64	1.5
1964–70	4.5
1970–76	1.6

For 1976–80 there was no growth in agricultural output. Thus, for the decade of the 1970s agricultural production increased at the rather modest rate of about 0.8 percent, even though the 1970s were a decade of unprecedented levels of agricultural investment, a doubling of fertilizer availability, and significant improvement in the relative income position of farm people.

It may be noted that quite by accident both the beginning and end years of each of the four six-year periods were years of record grain yields. The growth of agricultural output for 1964–70 was influenced positively by the fact that 1963 was a year of low grain yields, which would have depressed livestock production during much of 1964. However, the effect of the poor 1963 grain crop on 1964 could not have slowed the growth rate for 1964–70 by more than 0.5 percent annually.

The increase in farm output during the 1970s has not been adjusted for the large increase in grain imports. If this were done, the growth of agricultural production in the USSR would have been nil, if not negative.

The rapid growth achieved during 1952–58 was made possible in part by elimination of the oppressive and exploitive policies Stalin established. Farm prices were increased, many several fold. More inputs were made available. The New Lands program made a major contribution to grain production during the last three years of the period. Thus, policy changes contributed significantly to the output record.

For largely inexplicable reasons, 1958 marked a sharp change in the reasonableness of Khrushchev's agricultural policies.[7] One of his most striking changes was abolition of the machine tractor stations. The machine tractor stations served the collective farms and did most of the field operations that utilized farm machinery. The machine tractor stations both owned the machinery and employed the workers who operated it. These enterprises were instituted to maximize the use of given machines, to provide the skilled workers to operate the machines, and to ensure that the farms made the appropriate deliveries of products to the state. The farms paid for the services performed. The incentive structure for the machine tractor station emphasized the amount of work performed and not the quality of the work; there were no rewards for timeliness of operations, for example. Consequently, it was believed that the efficiency and effectiveness of the use of farm machinery would be improved if the machine tractor stations were abolished and the machinery transferred to the collective farms. The effectiveness of the transfer was mitigated by the failure significantly to increase deliveries of farm machines and to make adequate provision for repair services. In addition, the transfer of machines to the collective farms was accompanied by a reduction in the real incomes of farm people. Khrushchev engaged in numerous reorganizations of the bureaucracies in an attempt to regain the tempo of agricultural production growth. None of his measures proved effective.

Khrushchev took some steps that had a negative effect on livestock output. Perhaps the most important measures were restraints on private livestock production. Apparently misled by the rapid expansion of output through 1958, Khrushchev did what has been done before—and since—when it appeared that the agricultural situation was favorable; he placed restraints on the private sector. The opposite also occurs; when things are not going well, restraints on the private sector are loosened. But in 1959 the number of cattle and hogs on the private plots declined by 13 and 9 percent, respectively, and the sown area on private plots fell by 7 percent.[8]

Khrushchev's successors took a number of positive steps to increase both crop and livestock output. Some restraints on private livestock production were relaxed, the prices of livestock products were increased by approximately a third, procurement goals for grain were reduced (thus leaving more grain on farms for feed), machinery and fertilizer output and deliveries were increased, and the taxation of collective farms was significantly reduced.

These measures appeared successful. During 1964–70 agricultural output grew at the respectable rate of 4.5 percent annually. But the benefits of these measures seem to have been of limited duration. Output growth slowed to 1.6 percent for 1970–76. Agricultural output in 1981 was the same or slightly smaller than in 1976, which means that for the period 1970–81 output increased by no more than 10 percent or less than 1 percent annually.

The costs incurred as a result of policies adopted after 1964 have been enormous and the results, especially for the past decade, have been modest. In late 1981, Brezhnev called the food problem the central problem of the 1981–86 plan. Brezhnev came to power at least in part because of the failures of Khrushchev's agricultural programs. One of the earliest acts of the Kosygin-Brezhnev leadership was a major reform of agricultural policy. It is more than a little ironic that seventeen years later the shortcomings of Soviet agriculture, if all factors are taken into account, are even greater than in 1964 and 1965.

The changes in agricultural policy made in 1964 and 1965 were of a magnitude similar to those Stalin's successors made in 1953, and they have been enormously costly. After a period of apparently significant success in increasing farm production, Soviet agricultural output growth has almost stagnated. Khrushchev's agricultural policies were considered a failure, at least in part, because of the need to import substantial quantities of grain following a poor crop in 1963.

Is it likely that the Soviet Union can regain the higher output growth rate of the late 1960s? My preliminary answer is negative, at least for the 1980s. The benefits of higher prices and higher incomes have already been largely realized. Fertilizer deliveries trebled between 1965 and 1980. While further increases are planned, the percentage increase will be relatively small. No policy changes made for the Eleventh Plan could result in a significant change in the rate of growth of farm output or a reduction in the costs of producing farm products.

CHAPTER THREE

The Eleventh Five-Year Plan
for Agriculture:
Goals, Resources, and Policies

The basic features of the Eleventh Five-Year Plan were outlined in broad terms in 1978. It is quite remarkable that with poor crop production levels, stagnation of the livestock output, and enormous grain imports in 1979 and 1980, the plan goals announced in December 1980 differed very little from those proposed in 1978 for the major agricultural products. It was as though 1979 and 1980 were normal or average agricultural years, or as if potential accomplishments during 1981–85 were in no way related to the experience of the years just before.

By mid-1982 significantly less information has been available concerning the Eleventh Plan than was made available much earlier for other recent agricultural plans, and it was not until late 1981, the end of the first year of the plan, that certain detailed information was published. It is not clear why fewer data were made available later than usual. Perhaps the uncertainty and difficulty created by the poor crops in 1979 and 1980 were the cause, but a general pattern of gradually reducing the release of data may also explain this. For example, production and yield data are no longer available by oblast for the RSFSR and the Ukraine, significantly limiting our efforts to understand the factors that have influenced yields during the 1970s, especially during the period since 1975.

PLANNED OUTPUT

Table 3.1 presents information on planned output of major agricultural products for 1981–85 with comparisons to actual output for the two prior five-year plans. (Table 2.2 compares the 1976–80 planned and actual outputs.) For the majority of products, actual outputs were significantly below those planned. The last column of Table 3.1 compares the 1981–85 plan with 1976–80 actual out-

TABLE 3.1

The 1981–85 Plan Goals for Agriculture and Actual Output for
1971–75 and 1976–80

	1971–75[a] Actual	1976–80[a] Actual	1981–85[a] Plan	1976–80 ——— 1971–75 Actual	1981–85 Plan ——— 1981–85 Actual
		-- million tons--			
Grain	181.6	205	239	113	117
Sugarbeets	76.0	88.4	100.0	116	113
Cotton (unginned)	7.67	8.93	9.2	116	103
Flax (000 tons)	456	394	501	87	127
Sunflower seed	5.97	5.32	6.68	89	126
Potatoes	89.8	82.6	89.1	92	108
Vegetables	23.0	26.0	29.3	113	113
Fruits, berries	8.01	9.59	11.3	120	118
Grapes	4.37	5.6	7.6	128	136
Meat (slaughter weight)	13.1	14.9	17.25	106	116
Milk	87.5	93.2	98	107	105
Eggs (bil. units)	51.5	63.0	72	122	114
Wool	0.44	0.46	0.47	104	102

Source: Ekonomika sel'skogo khozyaystva, No. 12, 1981, p. 4.

[a]Annual averages.

put. The increases of 17 percent for grain and 16 percent for meat look quite impressive. However, if the 1981–85 goals are compared to 1976–80 goals, the increase for grain is 10 percent and for meat 13 percent. The current plan goals for sunflowers and potatoes are actually below the goals of the previous plan, and the milk, vegetable, and sugarbeet goals exceed the previous plan goals by less than 5 percent.

ALLOCATION OF LAND

A comparison of actual sown areas during 1976–80 with planned sown areas for 1981–86 indicates no significant planned shifts among the major categories of crops—grain, sugarbeets, sunflower seed, potatoes, vegetables, and cotton (Table 3.2). The grain areas are identical at 128 million hectares. The total sown area is about 217 million hectares. It is unlikely that there will be a reduction in the area of fodder crops, which was 67 million hectares in 1980.

TABLE 3.2

USSR: Yields and Sown Areas of Selected Crops

	1971–75	1976–80		1981–85 Plan	
	Yield[a]	Yield[a]	Sown Area (mil. hectares)	Yield[a]	Sown Area[b] (mil. hectares)
Grain	14.7	16.0	127.9	18.7	127.8
Cotton	27.3[c]	29.3[c]	3.0	--	--
Flax	3.7	3.4	1.2	4.5	1.1
Sugarbeets	217.0	237.0	3.7	272.0	3.7
Sunflower seed	13.2	11.8	4.5	14.7	4.5
Potatoes	113.0	117.0	7.0	131.0	6.8
Vegetables	138.0	153.0	1.7	169.0	1.7

Source: Ekonomika sel'skogo khozyaystva, No. 12, 1981, p. 7. Sown area data for 1976–80 are from U.S.D.A., Supplement 1 to WAS-27, pp. 20 and 26.

[a]Centners per hectare; actual yields except for 1981–85 for which planned yields are given.

[b]Average annual sown area for 1981–85 is derived by dividing average annual output goals by the corresponding planned yields.

[c]Seed cotton

Consequently, there seems no room for even a modest increase in the amount of clean fallow.

However, a rather substantial shift appears in the allocation of land among the grain crops. The 1985 plan goal for grain is 245 million tons, compared to the 205 million tons annual average for 1976–80. During 1976–80 wheat accounted for almost half of total grain production, 48.6 percent. Data presented on the grain output goals for 1985 indicate that the share of wheat is to decline to a little less than 41 percent (Table 3.3).

While wheat production planned for 1985 is almost the same as actual 1980 (an increase of 2 percent), total grain production is planned to increase by almost 30 percent. Corn grain production is planned to double to 19 million tons, while together oats and barley are to rise by almost 50 percent to 87 million tons. The output of pulses, presumably to increase the production of protein for feed, is to grow by 118 percent. The production of rye is planned to increase by more than 50 percent, almost double the increase in output of all grain.

TABLE 3.3

USSR: Growth and Distribution of Grain Production, 1981–85

1970 Price		Million Tons		Million Rubles[a]	
		1980	1985	1980	1985
103	Wheat	98.187	100.0	101.133	103.000
116	Rye	10.205	15.700	11.838	18.212
306	Buckwheat	1.017	1.600	3.112	4.896
306	Rice	2.791	3.100	8.540	9.486
138	Corn (grain)	9.454	19.000	13.046	26.220
82	Oats	15.544	87.000	12.746	18.548
81	Barley	43.450		35.194	52.148
81	Millet	1.873	3.600	15.171	2.916
113	Pulses	6.362	14.000	7.189	15.820
61	Other	.212	1.000	.129	.610
	Total	189.1	245	208.098	251.856

Source: Ekonomika sel'skogo khozyaystva, No. 12, 1981, p. 4.

[a]Respective quantities times 1970 price.

The planned growth in corn production implies an increase in the area of corn havested for grain that approaches the maximum level under Khrushchev, namely an area of 6 to 7 million hectares compared to recent levels of about 3 million hectares. Wherever he may be, Khrushchev may have reason for a wry smile. Within a year after his political demise, the corn for grain area was halved. The reason for the current shift to corn is probably twofold. First, wheat output even during a poor grain year will be significantly greater than the slightly less than 50 million tons of grain used directly as food and, second, those responsible apparently believe that some areas now producing wheat will yield more grain when planted with corn and with oats and barley, as well. One reason for recent low corn production and relatively high wheat output has been an emphasis upon regional self-sufficiency in the production of food grains. Thus, the corn area has been restricted in the few areas where corn has significant potential, such as Krasnodar and some other parts of the Northern Caucasus.* If the corn area expands in the appropriate areas, there will be some increase in total grain supplies. However, there has been no indication of how these decisions are to be made and carried out.

INVESTMENT

During the Tenth Plan agriculture accounted for 27 percent of total investment in the Soviet economy. During the Eleventh Plan the same percentage is to be devoted to agriculture. While agriculture's share of investment is to remain the same as or slightly greater than during the 1970s, the rate of growth of investment in agriculture declined sharply during the 1970s and is planned to decline even further during the Eleventh Plan. During 1971–75 the annual growth rate compared to the previous plan period was 9.7 percent; for 1976–80 the annual growth rate fell to 3.1 percent and a further decline to 1.9 percent is planned for 1981–85. These

---

*Corn grown for grain and winter wheat do not fit well in a crop rotation; the corn is harvested too late to permit seeding winter wheat immediately after the corn harvest. If corn for grain and winter wheat are in the same rotation, there must be some other spring grain, such as barley, grown in a year following the corn. Winter wheat may then be sown after the barley. The two reasons for limited corn production in the best adapted areas have been the regional self-sufficiency argument and rotation.

sharp declines in the growth of agricultural investment closely parallel the patterns in national investment, since agriculture's share in investment has changed little over the past decade.

While it is true that the growth of agricultural investment during the Eleventh Plan will be modest, the absolute level of investment is planned at the enormous level of 190 billion rubles. Some part of this investment goes to enterprises related to agricultural production but not directly to state and collective farms. The figure given includes perhaps 17 billion rubles of investment planned for such enterprises as repair shops, research institutes, and processing firms. The remaining 173 billion rubles is to be divided between productive investment (136 billion) and nonproductive or social investments (37 billion). The nonproductive includes housing, schools, and social and cultural institutions located in rural communities.

The productive investment is to be at an annual rate of 27 billion rubles. Assuming that gross agricultural output will be 130 billion rubles annually, investment would average 21 percent of gross output. In the United States in 1980 cash receipts from farm marketing were $134 billion. Capital expenditures (excluding dwellings) were $18.4 billion or a little less than 14 percent of the output measure used. The output measure used for the Soviet Union is "more gross" than the one used for the United States, because it includes more double counting of feed and seed than is true for the U.S. measure. Feed fed on the farm where produced is not included in the measure of output for the United States, but all feed is included in the Soviet Union. It is quite certain that the agricultural output/capital ratio in the Soviet Union is, at best, a third lower than in the United States.

A broad breakdown of planned agricultural investment indicates the following (in rubles):

Land reclamation (primarily irrigation
   and drainage)   − 41   billion
Developing feed production and processing − 27   billion
Machinery and equipment   − 30   billion
Storage and processing facilities for perishable
   products — state capital investment only   − 4.8 billion
Housing, social, and cultural facilities   − 37   billion

The amounts listed total almost 140 billion rubles, leaving 50 billion unaccounted for. In terms of percentage increases, the current plan calls for large increases for housing, social, and cultural facilities (40 percent), feed production and processing (70 percent), and machinery and equipment (30 percent). A significant part of investment funds not accounted for in the tabulation will go for construction of facilities for livestock and poultry and for expansion of livestock inventories.

LAND RECLAMATION AND IMPROVEMENT

As in the previous plans, the Eleventh Plan calls for significant investment in irrigation and drainage. However, the addition to the area of irrigated and drained lands is planned to be less than actual achievement during the Tenth Plan. There was a substantial shortfall from the Tenth Plan goals in the addition of irrigated land. The amount of drained land was very near to that established by the goal.

The current plan calls for a net increase of 2.1 million hectares of irrigated land and 3.0 million hectares of drained land. Thus, by the end of 1985 there will be something over 19 million hectares of irrigated land and 20 million hectares of drained land, if plan goals are met. Gross additions to both irrigated and drained land have been significantly greater than net additions during the past decade, and this pattern is assumed to exist during the current plan period. According to the information released, abandonment of currently irrigated land during the plan period is anticipated to be 1.4 million hectares, or approximately a third of the gross additions to the irrigated area. The loss of drained land is not so large, but is still about a quarter of the gross amount of land drained.

The planned land improvements, even if carried out, are of limited scale and will have small effect upon agricultural output during the Eleventh Plan. Assuming that all drained and irrigated land is devoted to grain production and that the increase in grain yield (including the effects of other inputs such as fertilizer) is 15 centners per hectare of irrigated land and 6 centners per hectare of drained land, the increase in irrigated area would increase grain production by about 3 million tons, while the increased drainage would add less than 2 million tons. The two together have the potential for increasing annual grain output by 5 million tons by 1986, when all new facilities are operational. But for the average of the five-year plan, the net output effect would be approximately 2.5 million tons per year or a little more than 1 percent of grain output.

The short run output effect of land reclamation seems very modest compared to the planned investment. For the plan period 41 billion rubles are to be spent on land reclamation. This is a 19 percent increase over actual 1976–80 expenditures, even though the planned gross addition to irrigated land is slightly less than during 1976–80, while the gross addition to drained land is planned to be just a little more. The investment in land improvements is planned to account for 20 percent of total agricultural investment for the period.

PURCHASED INPUTS

Soviet agriculture is becoming increasingly dependent upon inputs purchased from the nonfarm economy. These include capital items, such as tractors, trucks, and farm machinery, and current inputs, such as fertilizer, fuel, electricity, and repair services. Estimates presented by Diamond and Davis indicate that while all agricultural inputs increased by a little less than 80 percent between 1950 and 1977, current purchased inputs increased by more than 600 percent.[1] Fixed capital, which includes both buildings and machinery, increased by 1100 percent. Soviet agriculture is following paths similar to those in other industrial countries in increasing the dependence of agriculture upon the nonfarm sector. Consequently, the performance of agriculture becomes increasingly a function of the adequacy of the performance of the nonfarm economy in providing goods and services to agriculture. The growing dependence of Soviet agriculture upon the Soviet nonfarm economy is one of the major sources of its relatively poor performance in recent years.

Table 3.4 presents data on deliveries of agricultural machinery and changes in the stocks of agricultural machines over the two last plan periods and planned changes for 1981–85. The Tenth Plan called for a significant increase in the deliveries of tractors, grain combines, and trucks to agriculture. The goal for grain com-

TABLE 3.4

USSR: Deliveries of Agricultural Machinery

	1971–75 Actual	1976–80 Plan	1976–80 Actual	1981–85 Plan	Stocks 1 Jan. 81
	(in thousands)				
Deliveries:[a]					
Tractors (in thousands)	1700	1900	1800	1870	
Grain combines (in thousands)	449	540	539	600	
Trucks (in thousands)	919	1350	1108	1450	
Changes in stocks:[b]					
Tractors (in thousands)	359	514	246	339	2580
Average annual rate of growth (%)[b]	3.4	4.1	1.9	2.5	
Grain combines (in thousands)	57	120	33	278	713
Average annual rate of growth (%)[b]	1.8	3.3	1.2	6.7	
Trucks (in thousands)	260	NA	211	NA	1607
Average annual rate of growth (%)[b]	4.2	NA	2.7	NA	

Sources: U.S. Department of Agriculture, ERS, USSR: Review of Agriculture in 1981 and Outlook for 1982, Supplement 1 to WAS-27, May, 1982, p. 32 and Ekonomika sel'skogo khozyaystva, No. 12, 1981, pp. 3-10.

NA = Not Available.

[a] Cumulative deliveries for the five-year period.

[b] Changes in stocks over the five-year period.

bines was met. Although the goals for tractors and trucks were not met, deliveries during the Tenth Plan exceeded those of the Ninth Plan by 6 percent for tractors and by 21 percent for trucks.

The Eleventh Plan goals for deliveries seem reasonable; the increases for tractors and grain combines are rather modest. The increase in truck deliveries is large and may not be met. In fact, performance during the first year of the plan period raises serious questions about how well the nonfarm economy will serve agriculture during the current plan period.

But the bottom half of the table, which presents data on changes in stocks of the three farm machines, can only be viewed as discouraging. It is generally conceded that stocks of these three machines are well below what would be optimal for efficient agriculture under Soviet conditions. During 1976–80 agriculture received 1,800,000 tractors, but the number of tractors on farms increased by only 246,000. The number of tractors on farms at the beginning of 1981 was 2,580,000. During the five years tractor deliveries were 77 percent of the number on farms at the beginning of the period, yet the increase in tractor numbers was less than 11 percent. For grain combines the situation was even more disturbing: deliveries of 539,000 machines resulted in an increase in stocks of but 33,000. Deliveries equal to 79 percent of the number of machines on farms at the beginning of the period resulted in an increase in stocks of but 5 percent. During the five years 1,108,000 deliveries of trucks added just 211,000 to the inventory. Clearly the Soviets run very hard to do little more than stand still.

How do these relationships between deliveries and stock changes compare to what occurs in the United States? The comparison is most unfavorable to the Soviet Union. The concept of the scrappage rate may be used to compare what occurs in the two economies. The annual scrappage rate indicates what percentage of the machines on hand at the beginning of the year were no longer in the inventory at the end of the year. For 1971–75 the annual scrappage rate for grain combines was 12 percent in the USSR and 8 percent in the United States. For 1976–80 the annual scrappage rate in the Soviet Union increased to 15 percent. For the earlier period the scrappage rate for tractors in the Soviet Union was 12 percent, compared to 4 percent in the United States. For 1976–80 the scrappage rate in the USSR was 13 percent. The scrappage rates for farm trucks increased some during the 1970s, from 11.6 percent for the first half to 13 percent in the latter half. For 1971–75 the scrappage rate for windrowers in the USSR was an astronomically high figure of almost 18 percent, an average life of little more than five years. The windrower is a relatively simple machine that cuts the grain and places it in windrows, from which

the machine gets its name. It is little more than a slightly complicated hay mower and with reasonable maintenance should have a
scrappage rate of 5 percent or a life of 20 years.

The scrappage rates implied by the 1981–85 plan are 12 percent
for tractors and 9 percent for grain combines. These scrappage
rates may be optimistic. For the year 1980 the delivery of 346,700
tractors resulted in an increase in the inventory of only 7,000;
these relationships imply a scrappage rate of 13 percent. The
scrappage rate for grain harvesters during 1980 was in excess of 16
percent.[2]

It is generally agreed that the usable inventory of farm machines
in the USSR is too small for adequate and timely performance of
numerous farm operations, including both seeding or planting and
harvesting of many crops. One of the important contributions of
what some believe is excessive mechanization of agriculture in
North America has been to permit timely operations and higher
output as a result.

There is general agreement that the near trebling of fertilizer
deliveries to agriculture between 1965 and 1980 was responsible
for a significant part of the increase in grain production. For reasons that are not fully understood, the Tenth Plan for fertilizer deliveries to agriculture was not met by a substantial margin. The
plan called for an increase in fertilizer deliveries of 10 percent
annually; the actual increase was only 3 percent. Actual deliveries
were 82 million tons, for a shortfall of nearly 30 percent. The plan
for 1985 is for 115 million tons, exactly equal to the 1980 goal. The
1981–85 plan has started out badly, since fertilizer delivered to
agriculture in 1981 was less than 2 percent greater than in 1980.[3]
The 1985 goal requires a 7 percent annual growth rate.

POLICY CHANGES

Based on available information, no significant policy changes
have occurred that would be likely to lead to a sharp turn in the
performance of Soviet agriculture. One trend that apparently will
continue is the expansion of the industrialized livestock
enterprises—large, capital intensive feeding enterprises quite di-
vorced from the traditional collective or state farms and thus dependent upon the purchase of all or most inputs, including feed.

These complexes produce about 12 percent of the beef and pork and 4 percent of the milk in the socialized sector. Capital invested per head of livestock on the complexes is double to quadruple investments on collective and state farms, where investment per head is much greater than in the United States under similar climatic conditions. This huge investment has resulted in some reduction in feed used per unit of output, quite modest for milk but perhaps about a third for pork and beef. The labor savings have been modest for milk (about a third) and on the order of 50 to 80 percent for beef and pork.

The most significant production growth rate for the past fifteen years has been for poultry, with an increase of 180 percent between 1966 and 1979, while meat production other than poultry increased by less than 35 percent. The meager amount of information on feeding efficiency of the broiler factories in the Soviet Union indicates that feed use per unit of output is significantly higher than in the United States, probably by at least 50 percent and perhaps double. Efficient expansion of the livestock complexes, including broilers, during the 1980s depends upon the availability of grain concentrates, protein meals, and adequate supplies of protective materials, such as antibiotics. The second will require expanded import levels of protein meals or oilseeds, since recent performance indicates a probable decline in Soviet production of such necessary feeds.

Another modest policy change that might affect performance during the Eleventh Plan Period is encouragement of the expansion of livestock production on private plots if the output is sold to state and collective farms at procurement prices. Farmers are being asked to forego the much higher collective farm market prices for meat in return for access to feed supplies and animals.

A second change introduced for the current plan involves the method of establishing the base for calculating the sales or deliveries for which bonuses are paid. In the past the base had been determined by negotiation between the farm and the procurement agency, and apparently favoritism was involved, if not something more. Under the new scheme the base will be actual deliveries to the state for 1976–80.

A third policy change is to increase base procurement prices by inclusion of prior bonus payments in calculating procurement prices for 1981 and subsequent years. In other words, the average price received for some unstated past period now becomes the procurement price to which the 50 percent bonus will be added, if earned. A fourth policy change involves additional increases in the procurement prices of a number of farm products. The increases in 1981 procurement prices are (in percentage of 1980 procurement prices):[4]

Corn	26	Rye	33
Peas	25-36	Soybeans	35
Vetch	50	Cotton	10
Millet	33	Flax	13-50

Milk prices were increased an unspecified amount. The increase in milk prices followed a significant increase in 1977. The two types of price increases should have some positive output effects, though the increases represent little more than catching up with past cost increases.[5]

A fifth change instituted was that procurement agencies are to be responsible for all transportation and procurement costs starting in 1981. It is not clear how much this will increase the net prices received by farmers, but the savings could be substantial for farms located some distance from procurement points.

Except perhaps for the increased emphasis upon the industrialized livestock complexes, the policy changes introduced recently will have a positive effect on farm output. The calculation of bonuses on procurement on the basis of past deliveries rather than the procurement plan represents an improvement and reduces arbitrary decisions by the procurement agency. The decree encouraging more livestock production on the private plots if the products are sold to the collective farms should have a modest output effect. Finally, the increase in prices for some farm products as of the beginning of 1981 may have done little more than offset past cost increases, but even so represents a positive change.

IMPLICATIONS OF OUTPUT GOALS

In terms of consumer satisfaction, the most important goal is undoubtedly that for meat. The goal of 17.25 million tons for production of meat (including slaughter fat) would provide an average per capita consumption for the plan of 63 kilograms per year, an increase of just 6 kilograms per capita over the 1975 per capita consumption. It represents an increase of just 4 kilograms per capita over the Tenth Plan goal and some 6 kilograms more than annual average per capita production during the plan period. The Tenth Plan Period objective for meat was a modest one, providing for an increase of just 7 to 11 percent in total output and an increase of just 2 to 6 percent in per capita production. The 1985 goal for meat production is 18.2 million tons or a per capita production of 65 kilograms.

But meeting the goals for either the plan period or 1985 will give little relief to the harassed Soviet consumer, who finds almost no red meat in the state stores and hardly any poultry. The small increase in available supply, assuming continuation of present policies of low retail prices because of the subsidies covering the difference between prices paid to the farms and retail prices, would result in no noticeable change to the Soviet consumer who does not have special access to meat, such as at the place of work.[6]

The milk goal is also modest, calling for a 5 percent increase over the 1976-80 actual. While consumers may not always have access to the milk products they desire, total milk production is large, providing for per capita production of about 325 kilograms, compared to approximately 250 million kilograms in the United States. Unfortunately for the Soviet consumer, a very large fraction of the available milk supply never leaves the farm; much of the nonfat milk solids is fed to livestock. A study of consumption in the USSR in 1976 published by the Joint Economic Committee of the U.S. Congress reported that per capita consumption of milk, eggs, and cheese was between 54 and 64 percent of the U.S. per capita level.[7] Perhaps the fact that per capita milk production 30 percent larger in the USSR than in the U.S. results in consumption that is perhaps 40 percent below that of the U.S. indicates that a major part of the shortcomings in meeting consumer demands lies in the marketing and distribution system, not in production.

Egg production is one of the few recent success stories for Soviet agriculture; poultry meat production may be the other. Between the Eighth and the Tenth plans egg output increased by 75 percent and poultry production more than doubled. Over the same decade total meat production increased by but 28 percent; meat production other than poultry increased by just 22 percent.

The most critical feature of the plan so far as livestock production is concerned is the compatibility of the grain and feed goals and the meat, milk, and egg goals. The current plan calls for 16 percent more meat, 5 percent more milk, and 14 percent more eggs. Based on feed requirement estimates, the meat, milk, and egg goal for 1981–85 would require approximately 12 percent more concentrates and 10 percent more total feed than the output of these feed products for 1976–80.

These seem small increases, and they are. If the grain production goal were met, there should be little difficulty in providing substantially more concentrates than were available during 1976–80. However, grain now provides only a little more than a third of all feed. Thus, grain production increases alone are unlikely to make it possible to meet the livestock goals.

The output of fodder crops must increase significantly, and more high protein feeds, such as the oilmeals, must be provided. Oilmeals must be imported if availability is to increase significantly during the current plan period. The plan goals for hay, haylage (hay cut green and fed immediately), and silage are beyond any achievable level.[8] If the 1985 goals for these sources of feed have been used in estimating the available feed supply, the livestock goal will not be met. While it appears that livestock inventories have not been reduced due to the poor grain and feed crops for the four years 1979 through 1982, probably all feed inventories have been depleted. Thus, for the last three years of the plan period, rebuilding grain and feed inventories will compete to some degree with the increase in livestock production. Stock rebuilding could require as much as 20 to 25 million tons of grain.

CHAPTER FOUR

Policy Factors Affecting Production Growth and Costs

One of the major propositions underlying our analysis of past and current performance of Soviet agriculture is that policy decisions play a major role in explaining the relatively poor performance of recent years. While climatic and soil factors cannot be ignored, particular policy decisions or positions constitute the main sources of relatively poor performance. At this point we shall consider rather mundane policy decisions, such as summer fallow or seeding rates for grains, potatoes, and cotton. We are not now concerned with decisions that could be said to have an ideological content, such as the size and number of private plots or the basic incentive structure for workers and managers.

SUMMER FALLOW

In areas of limited rainfall, farmers have found it profitable to make significant use of a cultural practice called summer or clean fallow. Instead of planting a grain crop every year on a particular piece of land, farmers leave land idle every other year or perhaps one year out of three. During the year that it is idle or fallow, they cultivate the land to keep it free of weeds and to create a surface that will maximize the retention of moisture through minimizing run off and reducing evaporation. In this way the amount of moisture available to the crop planted the following year increases significantly and yields are substantially higher. In those parts of North America most comparable to the major grain areas of the USSR, the Ukraine, Urals, Volga, Western Siberia and Kazakhstan, farmers fallow from a third to half the land devoted to grain production.

In 1940 the clean fallow area of the USSR was 26 percent of the grain area of 111 million hectares. The expansion of the grain sown area that occurred in the 1950s to approximately 125 million hectares was all in areas where it would have been reasonable to have a two-year rotation, clean fallow and then grain. However, instead of increasing the area of fallow from the 1940 level of 29 million hectares, perhaps by as much as 10 to 15 million hectares, by 1975 the fallow area had been reduced to 11.2 million hectares or 8.8 percent of the grain area. There was a small increase in fallow area by 1980, when it was 13.8 million hectares or 11 percent of the grain area.

The reduction since 1940 in the share of the grain area in fallow has two negative effects, an increase in the variability of grain production and in the cost of producing grain.

Grain production is somewhat larger with the current limited amount of fallow than it would be if the amount of fallow were determined on the basis of cost considerations or profitability. Under climatic conditions similar to those prevailing in many small grain producing regions of the USSR, wheat grown after fallow yields from 50 to 70 percent more than wheat grown continuously. Where weed infestation is a significant problem, as it is in many areas of the Soviet Union, the output loss from using fallow may be even less than is implied by the data for North America. Summer or clean fallow is used not only to accumulate moisture but to reduce weed infestation. In most areas in North America where data are available for the yield effects of fallow, weed infestation is generally not a major problem because of past use of clean fallow.

A famous—one might say infamous—Soviet agriculturalist, T. Mal'tsev, recently discussed the implications of weather variability for Soviet grain production: "I have always thought the best guarantee against trouble is for each farm always to have a sufficient amount of well-cared-for clean fallow land somewhere in the range of 20 to 25 percent of the farm's total plowland. Increasing sown areas at the expense of curtailing fallow can be very disadvantageous because an unforeseen drought in any given year can cause a terrible problem—or even a whole lot of problems, since everything depends on grain." Then he argued: "The average annual yield will not decrease because we have sufficient fallow, but will increase."[1] No evidence is cited to support the statement concerning average yield or output, but the fact that Mal'tsev's remarks were printed in *Izvestiya* indicates that an important group of bureaucrats and agronomists continue to emphasize the value of an adequate amount of fallow, even though recent policy and practice, at least until the mid-1970s, have been against the position taken. However, there has been a small increase in fallow since 1975, so it is possible that the agronomists are being listened to somewhat, even though the area of fallow needs to be doubled if Mal'tsev's prescription is to be met.

An analysis of crop rotations in the Prairie Provinces and a small part of British Columbia provides estimates of the economic returns and costs of rotations of various lengths. Each rotation included fallow; no rotation without fallow was considered. The rotations varied in length from two to four years. In four of the six regions analyzed, the rotation with the highest net return (income minus all expenses other than land rent, operator labor, and management) was the simple one of fallow followed by wheat. In the two other regions the rotation with the highest return to land and operator labor was fallow-wheat-barley. The two regions where the most profitable rotation was a third of the land in fallow instead of half were those with the greatest amount of rainfall during the growing season. Thus, even under moisture conditions that were relatively favorable, compared to the rest of the Prairie Provinces and the major grain growing areas of the Soviet Union, the most profitable rotation was one with a third of the land in fallow. The same study analyzed rotations that included oilseeds, namely rape and flaxseed. For the rotations that included oilseeds, the most profitable were the two-year rotations of fallow followed by an oilseed.[2]

The yield advantage of growing wheat on fallow rather than after another grain crop was approximately 50 to 55 percent. This means, of course, that the lower costs of a rotation that included fallow and a grain crop more than offset the lower output and gross income in four of the six regions. These results indicate the substantial costs that the Soviet Union incurs in its drier areas in order to obtain a small increase in net grain output (total output minus seed used).

The amount of attention given to clean fallow in the USSR has increased. For example, *Zernovoye khozyaystvo (Grain Production)* published two articles in late 1980. One dealt with the yield advantage of planting winter wheat on fallow compared to planting after corn silage or small grains in the Rostov area.

For two experiment stations for 1968–77 the yields of winter wheat seeded on fallow and after other crops are given for years classified as good and bad years. The yield advantage of fallow in good years was relatively small, namely about 25 percent. In the bad years the yield advantage ranged from a minimum of 160 percent to a high of 400 percent; the high estimate of the advantage of fallow ignores the example given in which the seeding of wheat after corn silage had a zero yield. The absolute yield advantage of wheat on fallow compared to wheat after other crops ranged from 10 centners to 24 centners per hectare, compared with a national average yield for 1976–80 of 16 centners per hectare. Other examples for experimental plots in Rostov showed that the increase in yields per planted hectare for winter wheat after fallow ranged from 44 percent (11 centners) to 120 percent (almost 18 centners).[3]

The second article was based on data from Northern Kazakhstan and considered the advantages of seeding spring wheat on clean fallow compared to other predecessor crops. The article noted the decline in the area of clean fallow in Kustanay oblast from 16.4 percent in 1967–68 to 6 to 8 percent in 1973–79. It noted that the area of weed infestation increased from 3.2 million hectares in 1974 to 7 million in 1978. For the 11 years wheat yields after clean fallow were 13.9 centners per hectare, after corn 9.6 centners, and after continuous cropping 7.3 centners. The yield advantage of fallow ranged from 45 to 90 percent.[4] It should be remembered that the net yield advantage, when the saving in seed is taken into account, would be substantially greater. If the seeding rate were 2 centners per hectare, approximately the national average, spring wheat on clean fallow would have a per hectare net yield of 11.9 centners, after corn 7.6 centners, and after continuous cropping just 5.3 centners. Compared to continuous cropping, seeding all spring wheat on clean fallow would increase the net production of grain.

The article presented results for as many as ten different rotations. One of the comparisons is consistent with the calculations on the net grain production for wheat after fallow and after continuous cropping. The experiments included one rotation of clean fallow, wheat, wheat, and a rotation of continuous wheat. The average grain production per hectare for the rotation that included fallow was 8.9 centners and for the continuous wheat 7.1 centners. These are estimates of output over the eleven-year period and cover output for the entire period; thus the output per hectare of 8.9 centners for the rotation that included clean fallow was the output actually produced in two years but divided by the sum of the area for three years. The study also bore out the cost effectiveness of clean fallow. The average cost of production per centner for the rotation that included clean fallow was 5.4 rubles, while for continuous wheat the average cost was 8.6 rubles.

Despite evidence from both foreign and Soviet sources of the merits of clean fallow for many agricultural areas, Soviet fallow area remains very low. As shown in Table 3.2 the area sown to grain is to be the same in the Eleventh Plan as it was in the Tenth Plan; consequently, no increase in fallow area appears.

In North America there is evidence that certain cultural practices may be an adequate substitute for fallow or even superior to fallow in terms of the amount of moisture accumulated from late summer through early spring. The substitutes for fallow involve careful preparation of the soil, including the use of mulches, proper placement of seed, and extensive use of herbicides to control weeds. These new methods may not be appropriate in the USSR, either because the techniques leave the soil too cold, slowing germination in the spring, or because the machinery needed and the care with which field operations must be undertaken may not be attained due to poor planning and inadequate incentives at the farm level. Summer or clean fallow is a practice that could be carried out under existing circumstances in the USSR, if the planners would provide the appropriate signals or if they permitted farms to make their own decisions. Brezhnev believed that such decisions should be made at the farm level. Thus far, there is no evidence that the bureaucrats agree with him or intend to surrender authority and power.

SEEDING AND PLANTING RATES

Until little more than a century ago it was common to calculate yields as the ratio of output to the amount of seed used, rather than in terms of the amount of output per unit of land. This practice reflected the high cost of seed measured by its importance as a share of output. Output to seed ratios as low as two or three to one were common until well into the nineteenth century.

In comparison with other industrial countries, seeding rates are very high in the Soviet Union, whether the rates are measured in terms of amounts used per hectare of land or as a percentage of output. Estimates made by the U.S. Department of Agriculture and the Central Intelligence Agency indicate that grain seed now equals 15 percent of grain output measured in terms of bunker weight or the uncleaned grain as it comes from the combine. This is true for wheat and all other grains. If the bunker weight is discounted by 10 percent, a minimum average deduction, seed use increases to 16.5 percent of the output of clean dry grain. This would be an output-seed ratio of just six; in the lower yielding areas of the USSR the output-seed ratio is as low as four.

In the United States the ratio of seed used to output of wheat is about 4.4 percent. For all grains produced in the United States seed use as a percent of output is even less than for wheat, due to the low seed requirement for corn, which accounts for 60 percent of U.S. grain output. Corn seed use is less than 1 percent of output. The output-seed ratio for the United States is more than fifty.

High rates of seed use are not restricted to grains. A recent report indicated that in Bryansk Province the amount of seed potatoes used was a third of the annual production of potatoes in an average or normal year.[5] This also noted that the seed use was much lower on the private plots than in the socialized sector. Collective farmers on the private plots plant "one pood per hundredth," meaning apparently approximately 16 kilograms per 0.01 hectare or 1.6 tons per hectare. The seeding rates on collective farms increased from 4.0 tons per hectare in 1976 to 4.7 tons in 1979. It was said that yields were the same on the private plots and the collective farms.

In the United States seed potato use is approximately 2.3 tons per hectare, somewhat higher than the seed use on the private plots in Bryansk Province but about half that on the collective farms. Potato yields are much higher in the United States than in the Soviet Union or Bryansk Province. Seed used in the United States is only 7 percent of potato output, rather less than a fourth of the similar percentage for Bryansk Province or the Soviet Union.

There is evidence of high seeding rates for other farm crops, cotton, for example. Except for grains and potatoes the waste of output from unduly high seeding rates is not great. However, high seeding rates have other important costs, such as the need to thin plantings of cotton and sugar beets, generally by hand.

It is not easy to determine why so much of the output of grain and potatoes is wasted by high seeding rates, or why the labor costs of thinning certain crops are accepted. One reason is that machines and techniques are not available that will distribute seed in a uniform manner. For example, until a particular technique was adopted for separating and coating sugar beet seeds in the United States, it was necessary to thin by hand.

A second reason is that germination rates among the various seeds are so low that high seeding rates overcome these deficiencies. Low germination rates result from poor selection and handling of seeds. No technical reason explains why germination rates in the Soviet Union cannot be as high as those in Western Europe or North America. If this is the reason for the high seeding rates, it is clearly a policy matter. Low germination can result from lack of incentives for the farms or specialized agencies to provide proper seeding or planting, harvest, storage, and distribution of seed materials.

The third reason may be that agricultural planning officials simply do not know what they are doing. Planning officials may also recognize and accept the absence of appropriate machines, the poor quality of seeds, and, perhaps, inadequate preparation of seed beds or planting at inappropriate times (too early or too late), and attempt to offset these defects by requiring high seeding rates.[6]

Given the level of educational qualifications and experience of the directors of collective and state farms and the availability of agronomists either on the farms or at nearby institutions, it is incomprehensible that Soviet planners would consider it either necessary or desirable to establish seeding rates or norms. Planners may claim that the seeding norms are only guidelines and that farms have discretion to seed or plant as they see fit. If this is true, it is difficult to understand why farms accept such enormous waste as current seeding practices involve. Even if the seeding norms are not mandatory, the costs of departing from the norms may be sufficiently high to the decision makers on the farms that they are not willing to take the risk. The incentive structure may provide no benefit for optimum seeding rates, since most bonuses are paid on the basis of gross output and may impose substantial penalties for departing from seeding rates if the yield is low.

A skeptic might argue that the seeding rates are not abnormally high but that the rates are declared high to conceal an overestimate of crop output. The high seeding rates for the small grains could permit a farm to overestimate yields and outputs by as much as 10 percent and for potatoes even more. This explanation has considerable appeal. However, the amount of evidence of high seeding rates is so great that it cannot be ignored. There are numerous references to the seeding rates in both the popular and professional press, visits to farms by many individuals have elicited information concerning high seeding rates, and directives concerning seeding rates are publicly available. Furthermore, high seeding rates prevail in cases such as cotton and sugar beets, where seed is not a significant part of the gross output measure. Consequently, inflation of gross output cannot explain all of the high seeding rates and may explain very little.

LOW FORAGE YIELDS

Yields of forage crops are a function of soils, climate, and cultural practices, which reflect the priority given to forage crops or the amount of resources devoted to development of seed varieties, investment in drainage, time and effort devoted to the control of weeds and other plants that invade fields, the amount of fertilizer used, and the timeliness of operations in planting and harvesting the crops. Even yields of wild hay are subject to the care and attention given the crop and the land.

In the Soviet Union hay is one of the most important sources of feed among the harvested forage crops. While it provides fewer total feed units than grain, hay accounts for approximately a sixth of total harvested feed and about 13 percent of total feed, including an estimate for the feed derived from pasture. Comparisons have been made between the hay yields for major agricultural areas in the USSR and three different North American areas comparable in climatic and soil conditions. The Prairie Provinces of

Canada are similar to large parts of Siberia, Kazakhstan, and the Urals. The three states of North and South Dakota and Nebraska are similar to the Ukraine, the Volga, and Krasnodar. The three Lake States, Michigan, Wisconsin and Minnesota, are appropriate analogies for the central nonblack soil zone. For the central black earth area Manitoba is a very reasonable analogy.

The highest hay yields in the three North American areas are found in the three Lake States, which have climatic conditions quite similar to the central nonblack soil zone of the RSFSR, Belorussia, and the Baltic Republics. With rainfall in the general range of 22 to 28 inches in both the Lake States and the central nonblack soil zone and other similar characteristics, factors other than climatic and soil conditions must explain the sharp yield differences.

Between 1950–54 to 1975–79 hay yields in the Lake States increased by 48 percent, from 4.0 tons per hectare to 5.9 tons per hectare (Table 4.1). In the three Northern Plains States the yields of all hay increased by 55 percent, from 2.2 to 3.4 tons per hectare. The yields for the Northern Plains states include wild hay, which accounted for about 45 percent of the total harvested hay area in the late 1960s, when data on wild hay acreage and production were last collected. Tame hay yielded more than double wild hay. Even so, the yield of all hay in the Northern Plains States in 1975–79 was about 70 percent greater than the tame hay yield in the USSR. Further, the increase in yield from the late 1950s to the late 1970s was significantly higher than in the USSR. Prairie Provinces tame hay yields have increased relatively little since the late 1950s, about 18 percent. Yet, their yields are nearly double the recent tame hay yields for all of the USSR.

In recent years the Soviet Union has harvested 40 to 45 million hectares of tame hay. If the yield per hectare were increased by but one ton, the increase in available feed would be equivalent to 15 to 20 million tons of feed grains; if the increase in yield were 1.5 tons per hectare, the increase in feed would be equal in feed value to about 25 million tons of grain and greater than the average level of grain imports from 1975 through 1980 of 20.5 million tons.

As shown in Table 4.1 the current absolute differences in hay yields between the comparison areas and the USSR are at least 1.3

TABLE 4.1

Hay Yields in North American Areas and USSR

(Metric Tons per Hectare)

Years	Prairie Provinces[a,b]	Three Nor- thern Plains States	Three Lake States[d]	USSR[a]		
				Annual	Perennial	Tame
1950–54	3.90	2.19	4.02			
1955–59	3.23	2.33	4.44	1.21	(1.39)	
1960–64	3.23	2.67	4.95	1.18	(1.37)	
1965–69	3.45	2.80	5.25	1.32	1.37	
1970–74	3.86	3.16	5.76	1.69	1.73	1.70
1975–79	3.81	3.43	5.92	1.93	2.13	2.04

Sources: U.S. Department of Agriculture, <u>Agricultural Statistics</u>, issued annually and Agriculture Canada, <u>Selected Agricultural Statistics for Canada</u>, issued annually, and Canada Department of Agriculture, <u>Quarterly Bulletin of Agricultural Statistics</u>, various issues, and <u>Narodnoe khozyaystvo SSSR</u>, issued annually.

[a]Tame hay only.

[b]Manitoba, Saskatchewan and Alberta, Canada.

[c]North Dakota, Nebraska and South Dakota.

[d]Minnesota, Wisconsin and Michigan.

tons per hectare. This difference is based on including wild hay yields in the Northern Plains States and comparing this yield with perennial hay yield in the Soviet Union. In these three states, the yield of alfalfa hay in 1975–79 was 4.6 tons per hectare, about 2.5 tons more than the perennial hay yield in the USSR. The production of alfalfa hay takes a reasonable level of management in terms of control of the acidity of the soil, timeliness of harvesting, and production of quality seed. But thousands of U.S. farmers have mastered the required level of management, and alfalfa hay, including mixtures, accounts for nearly half of U.S. hay acreage and three-fifths of hay production. The very small difference between perennial and annual hay yields in the Soviet Union must be attributed to poor management and inadequate supplies of such inputs as quality seeds and lime.

The previous paragraphs have presented certain conclusions based on comparisons between the USSR and the Northern Plains States. However, substantial parts of the hay growing area of the USSR are much more like the Lake States than the Northern Plains. An average of yields in the two groups of states is not unreasonable as an indicator of the climatic conditions that prevail in the major hay growing regions of the USSR. The average yield for 1975–79 was 4.7 tons per hectare, more than double the perennial hay yield in the USSR.

Other forage crops besides hay include corn silage and green chop (green corn cut and fed immediately to livestock), feed roots (including sugar beets), and potatoes. Excluding potatoes, these crops have been harvested from about 18 million hectares in recent years in the USSR. Here again even moderate improvements in yields, especially of corn silage, would make an important impact upon available feed supplies.

Without access to much more data than we have, it is not possible to indicate how much the yields of other forage crops have been affected by the low priority given such crops. However, frequent references to low yields indicate that there is substantial room for improvement.

PROCUREMENT PRICES AND
PRODUCTION COSTS

The determination of procurement prices is clearly a policy matter. Just as clearly relationships between procurement prices and production costs are an indication of relative priorities of planning officials. In turn, the level of production costs may reflect policy factors as well as the underlying technological conditions, and, of course, input prices for agriculture are largely determined by officials rather than by any market. Only limited attention will be given to policy factors that have affected production costs, except to note the recent sharp increases in production costs and the prices of production inputs in an economy that has presumably conquered inflation and to give an apparent example or two of either exploitation of farms or extreme inefficiency or, possibly, both.

TABLE 4.2

Production Costs and Procurement Prices, Selected Periods,
1964 to 1980, USSR[a]

	1964–66	1969–71	1974–76	1978–80
	(Rubles per Ton)			
Production Costs				
Grain	46	52	62	71
Cotton	313	404	427	475
Sugarbeets	20	23	27	31
Meat[b]	1085	1200	1495	1908
Milk	155	178	217	267
Eggs (per 1000)	78	73	74	84
Procurement Prices				
Grain	90	97	103	(103)[c]
Cotton	442	555	583	(583)[c]
Sugarbeets	28	28	34	(34)[c]
Meat	994	1467	1512	(1512)[c]
Milk	148	192	212	277
Eggs (per 1000)	79	90	92	(92)[c]

Sources: Calculated from Narodno ye khozyaystvo SSSR, annual issues, and
           U.S. Department of Agriculture, Agricultural Situation,
           Review of 1978 and Outlook for 1979: USSR, Supplement 1 to
           WAS-18, April 1979, p. 29.

[a]Collective farm data.

[b]Unweighted average of costs for cattle and hogs.

[c]Assumed same as 1974–76—no changes had been announced.

The data on the relationships between procurement prices and
production costs given in Table 4.2 indicate that for at least two
decades most crops have had a substantial margin of prices over
costs, while livestock products have had little or no differential
between costs and prices. The cost price comparisons need to be
interpreted with care, with full recognition of their limitation.
There is no return for the use of land in the cost estimates. Since
crops generally require more land services per unit of output than

livestock products do, the economic costs of crop products are underestimated to a greater degree than is true of livestock products. This may be partially offset by the failure to include interest on capital (depreciation is included) if livestock uses more capital per unit of output than crops.

But in spite of serious reservations about the cost data, these data provide strong support for the view that livestock output is generally unprofitable for many farms most of the time. Repeatedly, Soviet officials have argued that farms can affort to produce livestock products at a loss because of the profitability of crop production. This is clearly bad economics. It is almost certainly bad policy as well, because expansion of livestock output, especially meat and eggs, has had such a high priority for the past two decades. It is difficult to understand why profitability of the outputs most desired by the policy makers, or so it is claimed, has been kept at minimal levels. Such a policy certainly does not induce farms to devote their higher quality human and material resources to production of livestock products when these resources can generally earn much more when devoted to several crop products.

Table 4.3 shows in greater detail than Table 4.2 the substantial increase in production costs that has occurred over the past two decades. The table also indicates the cost differences between state and collective farms.

In an economy that claims to have controlled inflation, production costs for major farm products increased significantly during the 1970s. Between 1964–71 and 1978–80 the cost of producing grain on collective farms increased by 56 percent; milk by 50 percent; cattle by 66 percent; cotton by 18 percent; potatoes by 63 percent; sugar beets by 35 percent; and eggs by 12 percent. While farm wages and earnings increased significantly during the decade, labor costs per unit of output either remained stable or declined. Increases in costs were apparently due to the costly means adopted for replacing labor and/or sharp increases in the prices of farm inputs and machinery.

Two examples of the distribution of the cost increases between the 1960s and 1970s may be of interest. Table 4.4 provides such data, as presented by a Soviet author, for grain and milk produced on collective farms in 1966 and a decade later. It is not possible to

TABLE 4.3

USSR: Average Primary Production Costs of Agricultural Products, 1964–66 to 1978–80, for Collective and State Farms

(Rubles per ton)

	Collective Farms				State Farms			
	1964–66	1969–71	1974–76	1978–80	1964–65	1969–71	1974–76	1978–80
Grain	45.7	51.7	61.7	71.3	58.0	57.3	77.7	78.3
Cotton	312.7	404.0	427.0	475.3	286.5	366.7	424.0	499.7
Sugar beets	19.7	22.7	27.0	30.7	25.0	29.3	37.0	41.3
Potatoes	42.0	62.3	82.3	101.3	62.0	78.3	105.3	123.0
Vegetables	80.7	95.7	102.7	115.0	68.0	85.3	94.3	103.7
Cattle	988.0	1191.0	1539.7	1981.0	1109.5	1309.7	1769.3	2165.3
Hogs	1182.3	1208.7	1450.3	1834.0	1164.0	1134.3	1408.7	1619.7
Sheep	648.0	834.3	1061.0	1304.0	637.0	767.0	1066.7	1274.7
Milk	155.3	178.0	217.3	267.3	172.0	190.3	245.0	290.3
Eggs	77.7	72.7	74.0	84.3	78.5	64.7	60.3	62.7

Sources: Calculated from Narodnoye khozyaystvo SSSR, annual issues.

TABLE 4.4

Changes in Composition of Cost of One Ton of Grain and One Ton of Milk[a]

	1966	1976	1976/1966
	(Rubles)		(percent)
Grain			
Direct Labor Payments	14.6	10.3	70.5
Seed	9.1	10.1	120.0
Fertilizer	2.1	6.1	290.0
Amortization	3.8	5.8	152.7
Repair and Maintenance	1.9	3.5	184.2
Fuel and Oil	1.8	2.6	144.4
Other Direct Expenses	6.5	14.3	220.0
General Expenses	4.9	5.7	116.3
Total	44.7	59.2	132.4
Milk			
Direct Labor Payments	65.0	69.0	106.1
Feed	47.7	92.0	192.9
Amortization	8.2	15.0	183.0
Repair and Maintenance	3.6	6.0	166.6
Other Direct Expenses	16.8	27.0	160.1
General Expenses	19.4	24.0	123.7
Total	160.4	233.0	145.0

Source: Ekonomika i organizatsiya sel'skokhozyaystvennogo
proizvodstva, Moscow, Mysl', 1979, pp. 356-357.

[a]Data are for collective farms.

disentangle from the data how the increased costs within a category might have been shared between higher prices and increased quantities per unit of output. The data confirm the statement that higher payments per day worked were offset by increased output per day of labor, or nearly so. With the increased investment that presumably went into livestock production, it is quite surprising that labor productivity in milk production failed to keep pace with the increased wage rates for the decade. The sharp increase in the amortization cost for milk output reflects the increased investment. For both grain and milk the last two categories, other and general, absorb a significant fraction of total costs.

There have been substantial increases in the prices of many farm inputs. In a period specified as "in recent years" the price paid per horsepower for tractors and attachments has increased by 70 percent; the prices of mineral fertilizers by 20 percent; mixed feeds by 100 percent; and the costs of cattle and hog barns by 130 to 300 percent.[7]

The sharp increase in the prices of mixed feed must reflect a change in pricing policies because the basic prices of grains increased very little over the decade ending in 1980. Yet, an article published in late 1981 discusses the policy of procuring grain in such large quantities that some of the grain must be returned to the farms to feed the livestock. The state imposes a differential between the procurement price and the prices farms are charged for the grain sold to them, either in its unprocessed or processed form.[8] The author notes that at harvest period the farms sell grain to the state for 8.9 rubles per centner. Much of the grain is then returned to the farms as feed. The unprocessed grain is sold to the farms at 14 rubles per centner, a cost mark up of almost 60 percent. If the grain is processed into feed, the farms must pay 24 rubles per centner. It was noted that an inter-collective farm plant provided processed feed for 15 rubles per centner, almost 40 percent cheaper than the state.

Another factor in increasing costs has been the deterioration in performance of major farm machines between 1970 and 1976, and perhaps since then. The daily output of work per tractor declined from 7.2 to 7.0 hectares and for combines even more drastically from 7.3 to 6.4 hectares, a decline of 12 percent. The percentage decline in the amount of grain per combine day was at least equal to the percentage increase in the number of combines between 1970 and 1976. Consequently, there was no reduction in the amount of time required to complete harvesting grain, and the losses from a too-extended period of harvesting were at least as great at the end of the period as at the beginning. Those acquainted with Soviet agriculture agree that the length of time required to complete the grain harvest results in substantial output losses in most years.

A further factor causing high costs in agriculture is the system's inability to retain the skilled workers required to operate the rather complex machinery in use. Between 1971 and 1974, 2.6 million tractor drivers and machine and combine operators were trained, but during those years the total supply of such workers in agriculture increased by only 269,000. In 1979, 1.14 million tractor, combine, and auto driver/mechanics were trained for agricultural work, but the number employed on farms increased by only 32,000. Obviously a very large fraction of those trained decided to use their newly acquired skills in other, more rewarding activities. This loss of trained manpower is due not to the weather but to policy choices. If anything, conditions deteriorated during the 1970s.

OTHER POLICY FACTORS

Three additional examples may be of interest. One comes from a lengthy Soviet discussion of fertilizer waste between factory and field, which the author estimated at 9 million tons per year or 10 percent of all fertilizer.[9] He divided the losses into several categories: shipping in suitable freight cars (626,000 tons); losses at the sales agency (1.9 million tons); and losses on the farms due to inadequate storage and handling facilities (6.5 million tons). He noted that at 600 railway stations fertilizer was dumped on the ground and in the open. The author then went on to note that one ton of fertilizer would increase grain output by 1.5 to 2.0 tons; sugar beet or potato output by 6 to 7 tons; and vegetable production by 12 tons.

A second example comes from inability to supply the appropriate implements for new and larger tractors. There is almost no equipment for tractors of 150 to 300 horsepower. At best such tractors were supplied with a plow and a wagon; otherwise, the equipment available was the same as for tractors with as little as a third as much horsepower.[10] One can say, without much exaggeration, that it was an economic crime to produce enormous tractors without producing the equipment that would permit their efficient use.

The third example is the enormous losses of output during harvesting, transportation, storage, and processing of farm products. While numerous reports in the press and research publications concern large losses from the field to the table, a recent report from V. Tikhonov, a prominent agricultural scientist, is almost astounding in its implications: "We lose approximately one-fifth of the gross harvest of grain, vegetables, fruits, and berries during the harvesting process itself, transportation, storage and industrial processing."[11]

Our late colleague, Arcadius Kahan, put the losses of potatoes at substantially more than a third.

The U.S. Department of Agriculture in its estimates of utilization of grain assumes that waste and dockage range from 10 to 15 percent, well below the estimate Tikhonov made. Thus, the loss of output from Soviet production appears substantially higher than most Western production estimates assume.

Each example—loss of fertilizer, inappropriate mix of tractors and implements, and losses of crops—illustrates the low priority accorded the agricultural and food sector and the most serious shortcomings in the functioning of the Soviet economy. The output losses due to these three factors are clearly within the control of man and are not the result of nature.

Another important policy area that should be addressed is the absence of enforceable contracts between the farms and the input sectors, on the one hand, and the procurement agencies, on the other. For example, there are now no penalties for failure to deliver fertilizer on time or in usable condition. Nor do the farms have any recourse if the procurement agency is unable or unwilling to accept its output of a perishable product. Farms must be given adequate recourse against those who impose unnecessary costs upon them. This is an issue that has long gone unresolved, and there seems to be no willingness to tackle it now.

The major weakness of Soviet agriculture is simply that it exists in a socialized economy. These three examples illustrate some of the reasons why Soviet agriculture performs so poorly. None of them has anything to do with the fact that Soviet agriculture is a socialist agriculture.

PRODUCTIVITY OF AGRICULTURAL INVESTMENT

A recent study has compared productive investments in agriculture in the United States and the Soviet Union in terms of comparable or equivalent prices for machinery and construction.[12] For the eight years 1970–77, U.S. agricultural investment totaled approximately $81 billion dollars, while Soviet productive investment in agriculture was more than six times greater, more than $500 billion. Even if one makes no adjustment for the high value of the ruble in terms of dollar for investment and one uses the official rate of exchange of approximately $1.35 for the ruble, Soviet investment was three times that of the U.S. for 1970–77.

The relative amounts invested in machinery and construction are instructive. In the United States the investment in machinery was three times the investment in construction; in the Soviet Union, when investment is measured in rubles, machinery investment was less than half that of construction. Even if adjustment is made for differences in dollar purchasing power of the ruble for machinery and construction, investments in the two categories were roughly equal in the Soviet Union. This comparison does not prove that Soviet agriculture devotes too large a fraction of agricultural investment to construction. However, other evidence on the limited stock of machinery plus the high amounts of capital used in construction per animal are consistent with such an inference.

The same study compared the capital/output ratio in agriculture for the two countries for the period 1950–54 to 1973–77. Over that period, the stock of capital per unit of output remained nearly constant in the United States, but in the Soviet Union more than two and one-half times as much capital was used per unit of output in 1973–77 than in 1950–54 (see Table 4.5).

However, in spite of the substantial increase in the amount of capital per unit of output in the Soviet Union compared to the United States, output per worker or labor productivity increased much more in the latter than in the former. In the USSR labor productivity increased at an annual rate of 4.2 percent between 1951–77, while in the United States the increase was 6.2 percent. Consequently, the difference in farm output per man-day has widened in recent years. In the mid-1960s output per man-day in Soviet agriculture was 7.2 percent of the U.S. level; by 1974–77 the percentage fell to 5.6 percent (see Table 4.6).

The absolute levels of output per worker given in Table 4.6 almost certainly exaggerate the differences between farm output per

TABLE 4.5

Capital Stock and Capital per Unit of Farm Output

(1950-54 = 100)

	Total Capital Stock on Farms		Capital per Unit of Output	
	United States	USSR	United States	USSR
1950-54	100	100	100	100
1960-64	118	247	99	162
1965-69	135	377	105	201
1973-77	167	813	114	361

Source: Douglas B. Diamond and W. Lee Davis, "Comparative Growth in
          Output and Productivity in U.S. and U.S.S.R. Agriculture,"
          Joint Economic Committee, in Soviet Economy in a Time of
          Change, 1979, p. 42.

TABLE 4.6

Value of Farm Output per Man-Day

(1957-59 dollars)

	1964-67	1974-77
USSR	2.63	3.60
United States	36.79	64.86
USSR as a percent of United States	7.2	5.6

Source: Same as Table 4.5, p. 40.

man-day in the United States and the USSR, but there can be little
doubt that the diverging trend in the figures represents something
close to reality. Some part of the difference in farm output per
man-day is due to the greater reliance in the United States on purchased farm inputs than in the USSR. Since the output measure is
for output available for sale or home consumption, the difference
in value added per worker would be less than indicated in the
table. Nonetheless, even with very high absolute and relative in-

vestment levels in Soviet agriculture for the past fifteen years, no narrowing of the gap in labor productivity between the United States and the USSR has occurred.

CONCLUDING COMMENT

For the next decade, the performance of Soviet agriculture will become even more dependent upon the rest of the economy than it has been. Modern agriculture cannot be efficient and productive unless the rest of the economy provides it with high quality current inputs in a timely manner; with farm machinery that will have a long and relatively trouble-free period of performance if properly maintained and used for appropriate farming activities undertaken; and with a responsive service sector to assist in maintaining equipment and machines. Modern agriculture must also be served by a marketing sector that is capable of responding to any reasonable level of output, that provides its services at low cost, and that holds losses and waste to the minimum level economically effective. One of the great advantages of American agriculture is that its infrastructure—input industries, transportation, marketing, research, and extension—is highly efficient and responsive. One of the great disadvantages of Soviet agriculture is that the rest of the economy and the local infrastructure, such as roads, so poorly serve it.

CHAPTER FIVE

Livestock

While climatic and other natural conditions significantly influence crop output and productivity per unit of land, livestock output and productivity per unit of labor, feed, and total resources are relatively independent of natural conditions. Low-cost livestock production is possible under a wide range of climatic conditions, and local production of feed need not restrict the supply of feed for livestock production. Several major industrial countries have long depended upon imported feed concentrates for a significant share of feed consumed by livestock. Consequently, a review of the performance of the livestock sector in the Soviet Union can throw some light upon the impacts of natural conditions and policy decisions upon productivity.

Climatic factors have two kinds of effects upon livestock production. One is the direct effect of climate, primarily temperature, upon the rate of growth and feed intake of various types of livestock. Extremes of temperature can have adverse effects upon rate of gain. The other effect is through availability of pasture and crop residues used as feed. It is true that most of these effects on available feed could be offset by feeding concentrates and hay and other stored forage crops. However, such concentrated and stored feeds are generally more expensive than pasture, and consequently, adverse pasture yields due to climatic conditions could result in a reduction in livestock output. Nonetheless, livestock production is less influenced by climatic conditions than crop production where there is no irrigation.

It is not easy to compare productivities in the livestock sector between the Soviet Union and the United States or other countries. Serious questions can and must be raised concerning the availability and use of feed, which are difficult to estimate under the best conditions. Since some feeds such as silage and other green feeds are not sold or transferred, accurate measurement of availability presents many problems. In the Soviet Union the situation is particularly difficult due to certain conventions and deficiencies in the agricultural statistical system. Their grain data are for bunker weight and thus include a substantial and varying degree of foreign material and waste. Many feed products are subject to substantial waste from the time of harvest to the time of use. Poorly stored silage, for example, can lose as much as a third of its feed value. The Soviet press contains numerous references to losses of a wide variety of agricultural products, and feed products are no exception to the general rule.

There also appears to be a general tendency to set unrealistic goals for certain feed products, such as hay, silage, haylage, and straw. These unrealistic goals may be designed to create a semblance of balance between livestock goals and feed supply. However, unrealistic goals may also result in exaggerated reports of production of such products, reports that are difficult to check or verify. It is hardly in any one's interest to prove that a large shortfall in the production of hay or silage has occurred.

Enough is known about Soviet livestock production to show that significant deficiencies exist and that livestock output could be increased significantly if these were overcome. One important deficiency is the shortage of protein in livestock rations, a shortfall recognized by both outsiders and Soviet specialists. However, those who plan Soviet feed imports have apparently given little consideration to the possibility of reducing feed costs per unit of output by importing more oilmeals and less grain.

Another difficulty is the output of milk per cow, which is little more than two-fifths that of the United States and the Netherlands and hardly more than half of the Finnish level. Milk output per cow in Poland, Hungary, and the German Democratic Republic is significantly higher than in the USSR.[1] Low output of milk per cow means that the feed used for maintenance constitutes a relatively high percentage of total feed consumed. This means that as milk output per cow increases, a greater percentage of the feed is used for current output. Other things equal, a cow producing 4,300 kilograms of milk annually should require about 25 percent less feed per kilogram of milk than a cow producing 2,000 kilograms.

Other shortcomings apparently include inadequate supplies of disease preventives, such as antibiotics, and of materials to control insects that adversely affect production through irritating and hurting animals.

PLANS AND PERFORMANCE
DURING THE 1970s

Before further discussion of the particular problems of livestock production and Soviet efforts to find solutions, it seems appropriate to review the livestock plans and performance for the 1970s with some brief note of the 1960s and late 1950s. Table 5.1 presents data on the output of livestock products as annual averages for the last five plan periods and for each year of the 1970s and for 1980. By almost any criteria, output performance for meat production was very good during the period from 1955–60 to 1971–75. Meat output increased at an annual rate of 3.9 percent. Egg production increased even more rapidly at an annual rate of 5.9 percent, while milk production grew at a rate of 2.9 percent. All livestock output increased at an annual rate of 3.7 percent. This is a measure of the gross output without any deduction for feed consumed; it represents the quantities of livestock products available for consumption.

However, during the Tenth Plan the growth of livestock output slowed significantly (Table 5.1). If production during the Tenth Plan (1976–80) is compared to that of the Ninth Plan (1971-75), the annual rates of growth were as follows: Meat, 1.1, milk, 1.3, and eggs, 4.1 percent. Even though the growth of egg output was reasonable, the growth rate was down from 7.5 percent annually for the Ninth Plan compared to the Eighth Plan.

Performance during the Tenth Plan is even less favorable if one compares 1980 with 1975, the last year of the Ninth Plan. Meat output in 1980 was less than 1 percent greater than in 1975. Milk output was actually slightly lower in 1980 than in 1975. Only egg production had increased significantly—17 percent over the five years for an annual growth rate of 3.3 percent. True, 1980 was not a good year from a climatic standpoint and was the second year of relatively poor grain crops. Nevertheless, it must be quite discouraging to Soviet officials to have imported such enormous quantities of grain during the Tenth Plan and to end the plan period with lower per capita livestock production than five years earlier.

Even the respectable rate of growth until 1975 left the Soviet consumer with a low level of meat consumption, given the per

TABLE 5.1

Output of Livestock Products to Date, Selected Periods
and Annually, 1970-80

	Beef and Veal	Mutton, Lamb, Goat	Pork	Poultry	Meat[a]	Milk	Wool	Eggs
				1,000 metric tons				
1956-60	2,790	915	3,237	631	7,854	57,200	317	1,277
1961-65	3,474	1,050	3,788	748	9,320	64,714	362	1,581
1966-70	5,187	992	4,327	853	11,583	80,553	398	1,935
1971-75	5,985	972	5,394	1,335	14,004	87,446	442	2,782
1976-80	6,833	881	5,860	1,828	14,826	92,660	459	3,140
1970	5,393	1,002	4,543	1,071	12,278	83,016	419	2,204
1971	5,536	996	5,277	1,183	13,272	83,183	429	2,440
1972	5,722	923	5,445	1,237	13,633	83,681	420	2,592
1973	5,873	954	5,081	1,295	13,527	88,300	433	2,713
1974	6,384	974	5,515	1,420	14,620	91,760	462	3,003
1975	6,409	1,014	5,651	1,539	14,968	90,804	467	3,109
1976	6,615	885	4,343	1,411	13,583	89,675	436	3,040
1977	6,888	894	4,950	1,691	14,722	94,929	459	3,311
1978	7,086	921	5,302	1,902	15,501	94,677	467	3,490
1979	6,903	870	5,268	2,017	15,341	93,341	472	3,548
1980	6,873	844	5,090	2,100	14,981	90,630	462	3,663
1981	6,700	800	5,200	2,300	15,200	88,500	474	3,836
			Indexes:	1956-60 = 100				
1961-65	125	115	117	119	119	113	114	124
1966-70	186	108	134	135	147	141	126	152
1971-75	215	106	167	212	178	153	139	218
1976-80	245	96	181	289	189	162	145	246
1973	211	104	157	170	172	154	137	212
1974	229	106	170	187	186	160	146	235
1975	230	111	175	244	191	159	147	243
1976	237	97	134	224	173	159	137	238
1977	247	98	153	268	187	166	145	259
1978	254	101	164	301	197	166	147	273
1979	247	92	163	320	195	163	149	278
1980	246	92	157	333	191	158	145	287
1981	240	87	161	364	194	155	150	300

Sources: U.S. Department of Agriculture, Agricultural Statistics of Eastern Europe and the Soviet Union, 1950-70, June 1973, and USSR: Review of Agriculture in 1981 and Outlook for 1982, Supplement 1 to WAS-27, May 1982.

[a]Includes other meat, such as horse and rabbit.

capita level of gross national product achieved in the USSR. In 1980 per capita consumption of meat and fat was 57 kilograms. If fats that are almost universally excluded in such estimates for other countries are deducted, per capita consumption of meat was 49 kilograms. This consumption level is approximately half that of the United States and significantly below the levels achieved in Hungary, Poland, and the G.D.R. In fact, it may be the lowest of any of the Eastern European centrally planned economies or, at best, tied for last place with Romania and Yugoslavia.

MILK PRODUCTION
AND LIVESTOCK NUMBERS

In 1980 milk production per cow in the socialized sector was less than in 1970, when 2,312 kilograms was nearly the lowest in Eastern Europe and substantially below the Finnish average. Only Yugoslavia and Romania had lower milk outputs per cow in 1970 than did the Soviet Union.

A factor that could explain the low Soviet milk output per cow, at least in part, is that the majority of the cattle are dual purpose. The breeds are designed for both milk and beef production, instead of specialization with dairy breeds for milk and beef breeds for meat. Even this explanation does not help much. Finland borders on the Soviet Union and endures even more difficult climatic conditions than the Soviet Union. In the late 1970s, milk output per cow in Finland was nearly 4,300 kilograms, compared to 2,200 in the Soviet Union. In Finland cows accounted for 42 percent of the cattle numbers, compared to 38 percent in the Soviet Union. Did Finland sacrifice beef output to achieve higher milk output? The answer is no: Beef production per head of cattle in the inventory was the same in the two countries in 1978.[2] Thus, for each animal in the inventory Finland obtained almost twice as much milk and the same amount of beef as did the USSR. The German Democratic Republic had milk output per cow of 3,840 kilograms in 1979, some 80 percent higher than in the Soviet Union.

Another reason for low milk yields may be the use of inappropriate planning and success indicators. For reasons difficult to understand, planning goals and success indicators have long emphasized the size of the livestock inventory at the end of the year.

Perhaps the reason is that the number of animals can be counted; perhaps the reason is some odd faith that output is proportional to inventory numbers. Perhaps the emphasis on numbers is simply a further indication of how poorly Soviet planners and bureaucrats understand agriculture.

A 1981 Soviet article on feed use in the Baltic Republics helps explain why the use of livestock fodder (feed including concentrates) increased more than livestock output during the last five-year period throughout the Soviet Union. In other words, the amount of feed used per unit of livestock output increased during the period, in part because "assignments regarding the number of livestock to be kept and the mix of crops to be planted are imposed on farms. And sometimes, too many livestock are kept, animals are severely underfed and fodder goes for nought."[3]

It is hard to imagine a stronger condemnation of a system of agricultural management than this brief quotation. The emphasis upon the number of livestock often leads to severe limitations upon the amount of feed available for each animal, which is not only wasteful of feed but may amount to cruelty to the animals. An article in the *Moscow News* contained another appropriate quotation from *Pravda*:

> Today we have 0.53 conventional head of cattle per capita— i.e., about the same as the USA and slightly more than the Common Market countries. But we are behind them as far as the productivity of the animals is concerned. The priority given to the extensive factor—the growth of the herd—has resulted in a situation where, despite the stronger material-technical base and increased fodder production, the expenditure of fodder per head of cattle has practically not increased. It would be best to use the strengthening of the fodder base to increase the productivity of livestock and poultry.[4]

If a *Pravda* reporter or editor understands the reasons for the low productivity of the livestock sector and the slow or nil growth of livestock output, why do not the officials in Gosplan and the Ministry of Agriculture?

In 1970 there were significant increases in the procurement prices for livestock products through payment of a premium of 50 percent over the base procurement price for all livestock products sold in excess of the annual plans by collective and state farms. As

I noted more than a decade ago: "It is of more than passing interest that the receipt of the premium for sales in excess of the annual plan requires 'that there has been an increase in the number of animals the farm had on hand at the beginning of the year.'"[5] Apparently the same practice still prevails; pressure has been put upon farms continuously to increase their livestock numbers so that they can receive the premium for above plan deliveries.

FOOD PRICE SUBSIDIES AND THE
LIVESTOCK SECTOR

The failure of Soviet meat, milk, and egg production to meet demand at the officially established prices in the state and cooperative stores made it necessary for the government to promulgate a new food program in May 1982. The ordinary Soviet citizen cannot obtain meat, milk, and eggs in the regular retail stores, and various forms of food rationing have emerged in most parts of the Soviet Union. Because of the shortage of animal and poultry products at official prices, it has become necessary to institute alternative distribution systems for meat and other livestock products. The second important fact is that growth of output of livestock products has fallen to a shockingly low rate since the mid-1970s, in part because adverse weather conditions have reduced feed supplies, especially of pastures and forage crops.

The third reason is that the present performance level is being achieved at enormous costs, high rates of investment, high costs of production of livestock products, and the growing burden of food price subsidies that in 1982 had reached approximately 35 billion rubles.

This is an appropriate point to present information concerning consumption levels and the retail prices of livestock products that have prevailed since 1962. It may be noted that in 1976, 47 percent of all consumption expenditures in the USSR was for food, beverages, and tobacco, compared to 20 percent in the United States.[6] If only food is considered, a third of consumer expenditures were for food in the USSR and 16 percent for the United States. On a per capita basis total consumption in the USSR has been estimated at a little less than 35 percent of the U.S. level. Food consumption per capita in the USSR was approximately half the U.S. level in 1976. While such estimates are subject to error, and it makes considerable difference whether consumption is valued in dollars or rubles, there can be no doubt per capita consumption of both food and non-food is at a much lower level in the USSR than in the U.S. Comparisons of total consumption, which includes housing, medical care, education and transportation, show quite clearly that the relatively large share of consumption expenditures required for food is not largely offset by low prices for such items as housing, health care, and public transportation.

Table 5.2 presents a sampling of meat, milk, oils and fats, and egg prices. The average ruble-dollar ratios are given at the bottom of the table for three livestock product groups and for bread and cereals. For the livestock groups and the fats and oils groups in 1976 the ruble had a purchasing power of about $1.15 when the USSR weights are used and a little less than $1.00 when U.S. weights are used. In effect, in 1976 for the meat, milk, egg, and oils and fats consumer goods the average prices were approximately the same in rubles and dollars. Since 1976 food prices in the United States have increased by approximately 50 percent. Since the state store prices in the USSR have remained unchanged, the 1981–82 price relationships would be about 65 to 70 kopeks per dollar or very nearly the official rate of exchange of 75 kopeks per dollar.

The food prices in the USSR may be considered in the context of per capita disposable income of 920 rubles in 1976 and an estimated 1,100 in 1981. The state store prices have remained unchanged since 1962, when per capita disposable income was approximately 400 rubles. For the period from 1965 to the late 1970s, per capita disposable income increased at an annual rate of 5.6 percent, while the per capita output of livestock products increased by 1.7 percent annually.[7] It is thus hardly surprising that retail demand has significantly outstripped the supply of livestock products in the retail markets.

The statement that not all meat passes through retail stores is obvious from comments in the press and personal observations: hardly any fresh or cured meat passes through the retail stores. An important official in the Soviet Academy of Sciences explained how he obtained meat. At his office each Tuesday he placed an order for the amount of meat permitted him for his family; on the following Tuesday, the meat was on his desk.

TABLE 5.2

Prices of Selected Food Products, USSR and U.S. in 1976

(Per kilogram)

	USSR (Rubles)	U.S. (Dollars)		USSR (Rubles)	U.S. (Dollars)
Beef, round roast	1.98	2.63	Butter	2.41	2.85
Pork, leg roast	1.88	2.67	Margarine	1.80	0.96
Chicken, whole fresh	3.40	1.27	Vegetable Oil	1.79	1.57
Turkey, whole fresh	3.56	1.64	Lard	1.72	0.86
Ground beef	1.88	1.52	Whole milk (liter)	0.48	0.52
Bacon	2.70	1.95	Canned milk	0.94	1.01
Pork sausage, fresh	2.20	1.96	Cottage cheese	1.00	1.44
Frankfurters	2.48	1.87	Processed cheese	3.00	3.59
Boiled ham, whole	3.66	1.84	Eggs, large dozen	1.54	0.88
Corned beef, canned	2.60	3.21	Eggs, medium dozen	1.06	0.59
Lunch meat	2.91	3.12	Bread, white	0.30	0.68

Average ruble-dollar rates	USSR Weights[a]	U.S. Weights[b]
Meat	1.063	1.040
Milk, eggs and cheese	0.850	1.012
Oils and fats	0.938	1.203
Breads and cereals	0.519	0.612

Source: Consumption in the USSR: An International Comparison, Joint Economic Committee, 1981, pp. 20 and 40-42.

[a]The average ruble price compared to the average dollar price when consumption patterns of the USSR are used to weight the various items in each category.

[b]The average ruble price compared to the average dollar price when consumption patterns of the U.S. are used to weight the various items in each category. For all food the ruble-dollar rate is 0.789 when USSR weights are used and 1.036 when U.S. weights are used.

A story published in *Trud* described how enterprises in the city of Klaipeda on the coast of Lithuania distribute scarce goods.[8] "The system of supplying enterprises on the basis of advance orders from workers, which has been organized by the Klaipeda City Trade Administration, not only saves consumers' free time but also guarantees the fair distribution of scarce foodstuffs and manufactured goods." Orders are taken at places of employment for a wide variety of foods—packaged meat, plum jam, condensed milk, butter, canned peas, catsup, lemon juice, raisins and pickles. Meat is apparently limited to 1.5 to 2 kilograms of pork and beef per week per family. This system supplies 100,000 out of the 185,000 living in the city. It was not stated how the other 85,000 living in Klaipeda were provided access to "scarce goods." "To tell the truth, it takes a lot of time and energy," was the comment of the chairman of a plant trade union involved in the distribution scheme. In short, a dual state distribution system has risen, with state and cooperative stores on the one hand and the trade union distribution system in the plants on the other.

While the increase in milk prices that would equate demand to the existing supply might not be shockingly large, it appears that the meat supply per capita is significantly below what consumers would demand even at prices that prevail in Western Europe. One could imagine a solution to the milk problem through acceptable price increases, especially if the marketed supply were increased by providing feeds to substitute for milk for young calves and if there were improvements in marketing and processing milk to increase the amount available for human consumption. However, the meat situation will become one in which consumers are satisfied with available supplies and prices only if there is a significant increase in meat production. The USSR may find itself in the same situation with respect to meat supplies and prices that produced the Polish crisis. Surely the ever growing gap between the demand and supply for meat and other foods must be a source of continuing political concern.

EFFORTS TO FIND A SOLUTION

During the past quarter century a number of efforts have been made to bring about a significant increase in the production of livestock products, especially meat. The data and indices in Table

5.1 indicate that the efforts have met with some degree of success but have not eliminated the imbalance or kept the imbalance from growing. A fairly rapid output growth has resulted in no significant reduction in the shortfall of demand relative to supply.

The efforts made over the past fifteen years to find a solution to this imbalance in supply and demand for livestock products can be classified under five categories: (1) Increased incentives, (2) Increased feed supplies, (3) Expansion of the mixed feed industry, (4) Creation of industrial livestock enterprises, and (5) Encouragement of the private sector. These have involved very large expenditures, especially the increase in incentives. If nothing else, Soviet officials must be given credit for trying to find solutions even though the outcomes have been less than expected or required.

INCREASED INCENTIVES

The prices of livestock products were increased significantly in 1965 and again in 1970. For example, 1970 state procurement prices for meat were almost 50 percent greater than in 1965; the prices of milk and eggs increased by 30 and 15 percent, respectively. Starting in 1970 a premium of 50 percent was paid for deliveries in excess of the quantities specified in the procurement plan for each farm.

While the price of milk was increased in 1979 to a level nearly 40 percent above the 1970 level, there was no change in the base procurement prices for other livestock products, except for minor adjustments in some republics in 1981. Yet, during the 1970s, when there was no change in prices paid to farms for meat animals, the cost of production on collective farms increased by more than 50 percent for hogs and cattle and on state farms by 65 percent for cattle and 43 percent for hogs (see Table 4.3). By the end of the 1970s all the positive incentive effects of the substantial price increase in 1970 had fully eroded on the majority of the state and collective farms.

One of the important costs of the stable retail prices and the huge food subsidy is that changes in prices paid to the farms become a major political decision, involving questions of significant modifications in the allocation of the national governmental budget. There is clear evidence that such involvement leads to significant delays in making reasonable and appropriate adjustments in the prices paid to the farms.

INCREASED FEED SUPPLIES

All the plans and decrees for two decades have emphasized the expansion of feed supplies. From 1965 through 1973/74 there was significant success in expanding feed supplies. In terms of oat equivalents, concentrates fed increased by 65 million tons or by 57 percent, while total feed increased by almost 100 million tons or by 36 percent. However, growth slowed significantly thereafter. In 1978/79 total feed supplies were estimated just 12 percent greater than in 1973/74; it may be noted that both 1978 and 1973 were outstanding crop production years. Since 1978/79 the estimated amount of grain fed has stagnated or actually declined. The U.S. Department of Agriculture projects the amount of grain fed in 1982/83 at 121 million tons or 4 million tons less than in 1978/79.

EXPANSION OF THE MIXED
FEED INDUSTRY

In 1980 the output of the mixed feed industry was 65 million tons, and further increases in the output of mixed feed are planned for the years ahead. In 1980 the total amount of concentrates fed to livestock was approximately 140 to 145 million tons. Consequently, nearly half of the total concentrates fed was channeled through the mixed feed industry. Producing mixed feeds permits combining various feeds in the appropriate proportions to create balanced rations for particular kinds of livestock. By proper preparation a wide range of feeding materials can be combined into appropriate livestock rations.

However, there can be significant disadvantages as well. The mixed feed industry imposes high costs upon the farms. In addition, a large percentage of the total concentrates fed comes from procuring most of the feed, which consists of grain, from the farms and then returning a large share to the farms. The transportation costs involved in this process are substantial. It is true that a large part of the output of the mixed feed industry goes to the industrial livestock enterprises, especially the poultry enterprises. But if any significant amount of the mixed feeds is returned to the ordinary state and collective farms, some of the presumed advantages of the farms' large scale have been lost. The scale of the farms and the skills and capacitites of the managers and other personnel are more than adequate to permit each farm to process its own mixed feed from its supplies of grain and purchased oilmeals, vitamins, mineral supplements, and disease prevention materials. The equipment required for preparation and mixing of concentrate feeds is both simple and easy to operate; so far as servicing the normal state and collective farms, all the mixed feed industry should have to do is to supply the supplementary materials needed to transform the locally available supplies of grain into an appropriate ration for each major type of livestock.

Why is such a simple approach not adopted? Some of the reasons may reflect the lack of confidence that planners and bureaucrats have in farm people. It may be that the Ministry of Procurements, which controls much of the mixed feed industry, sees its control of the industry as a means of increasing its power and importance. It is not beyond the realm of possibilities that control over critical feed materials is used to enforce procurement goals.

INDUSTRIAL LIVESTOCK ENTERPRISES

In 1971 two decrees were issued that emphasize the creation of large-scale industrial livestock enterprises similar to ones that exist in Western Europe and North America, as part of the movement to gain the advantages of specialization. While some of the complexes were to be developed on existing collective and state farms, many were new undertakings. The complexes were to be highly capital intensive and were to provide for significant savings in feed and substantial increases in labor productivity.

While nearly half of all poultry is produced in the complexes, they produce no more than 15 percent of all meat output. Somewhat more than half the eggs are produced on the complexes, which are relatively unimportant in producing milk (no more than 4 percent of total production).

While the complexes have produced some savings of feed and significant savings of labor, the capital per head of livestock is very high, double to treble that on ordinary farms. Available evidence indicates that production costs are lower on the complexes than on normal livestock enterprises. However, the Soviet method of estimating costs seriously underestimates capital costs. If costs were calculated as they would be on farms in the United States, the cost advantages of the complexes would be quite small.

ENCOURAGEMENT OF THE
PRIVATE SECTOR

There is little evidence that the private sector has responded to a significant degree to opportunities for producing more livestock products under the terms established at the beginning of 1981. To summarize briefly, the farms may provide their members or workers with the feed required for the private sector to expand production, provided the output is sold to the collective or state farms at the state procurement prices.

It is not surprising that private livestock production failed to increase significantly in 1981. During a year of tight feed supplies the farms were naturally reluctant to turn part of their feed supplies over to the private sector. And without more feed from the socialized sector the private sector cannot expand its livestock production.

Many expect that expanding livestock production in the private sector will reduce feed requirements. There is little evidence to support this view. It is probably true that the livestock output now produced in the private sector requires less traditional feeds, especially concentrates, than the socialized sector uses. But this result, which is due to the availability of food wastes from the household and scavenging of feed, cannot be extended as livestock output expands. Thus, the expectation that total livestock production can be achieved from a given feed supply by expanding livestock production in the private sector will not be realized.

SUMMARY COMMENTS

The expansion of livestock production, meat, milk, eggs, and wool, will depend upon increasing total feed supplies, improving the quality of those feed supplies through increasing the protein availability, and reducing the amount of feed required for a given amount of livestock output. Experience has indicated that none of the three components will be easily and promptly met.

Researchers in the Soviet Union recognize that livestock rations are deficient in protein. The domestic sources of protein materials to supplement the grains and fodder materials are relatively limited, consisting primarily of meal from cotton production, sunflowers, and the limited production of pulses. There is no significant production of soybeans, which provide much of the protein supplementation for livestock feeds in North America and Western Europe.

Since 1975, the USSR has imported significant amounts of oilseeds. However, the quantities involved have been rather limited—peak imports were 1.8 million tons in 1979—and have been required at least in part to offset the disappointing harvests of sunflowers. During the 1970s sunflower production averaged a sixth below the 1966–70 average, and production in 1980 and 1981 was at an annual average level of 4,625 thousand tons, some 1,650 thousand tons or more than a quarter below the level of the late 1960s. Consequently, the recent imports of oilseeds did very little to improve the protein content of livestock rations. In fact, given the increased quantities of concentrates and other feeds, there could have been a slight decline in the percentage of protein in the rations.

During the 1960s the output of livestock products increased at an annual rate of 3.7 percent; during the 1970s the annual rate of increase declined to 2.0 percent. All the increase during the 1970s occurred during the first half of the decade, and no increase in aggregate livestock output has occurred since 1975. A stagnant level of livestock output could not be considered a desirable option for the 1980s. Measures were required to achieve a positive rate of growth. However, the policy changes associated with the Eleventh Plan were not sufficient to meet the livestock output goals of that plan. Consequently, it was not surprising when Brezhnev announced late in 1981 a new Food Program would be put forward in 1982. In Chapter 7 we will review the program and indicate its probable effectiveness in increasing livestock output.

CHAPTER SIX

Crop Production:
The Role of Climate

Climatic factors significantly influence agricultural production. The effects are of two sorts. One is the long-run average impact on crop yields and the second, the annual variability of climatic factors that affect yields. In the Soviet Union both aspects of climate have been the subject of discussion, and numerous efforts have been made to evaluate their effects upon crop production. Large parts of the Soviet agricultural area fall into one of two categorizations: where there is adequate heat, moisture is a limiting factor, and where there is adequate moisture, heat is inadequate. There are, of course, substantial agricultural areas in the Soviet Union that have both quite satisfactory moisture and heat.

Many observers attribute a significant part of the shortcomings of Soviet agriculture to adverse climatic factors. Climatic factors can influence the potential for crop production in a given territory and the rate at which agricultural output increases over time. Karen Brooks, in Part II, addresses the issue of differences in productivity between the USSR and climatically similar areas. In this chapter, I use yields and yield trends to compare recent and current performance of the crop production sector in the USSR, with much emphasis upon grains.

CLIMATIC ANALOGIES

One approach for analyzing both the past performance and the prospects for grain and feed production is to compare the performance, both actual and potential, for areas that have similar climatic conditions. Data on crop production and yields for the analogous areas can be used to evaluate recent and current level of performance of Soviet agriculture by comparing rates of growth over a period of approximately a quarter century and by comparing yield trends of important crops for the USSR and the analogous areas.

One view holds that output performance of Soviet agriculture has been very poor and lags significantly behind the agricultures of climatically similar areas in terms of rates of growth of output or in terms of the productivity of particular resources, such as the yield per hectare of land. In some regards, Soviet agriculture seems to be performing quite well, while in other ways its performance is inadequate. There is little likelihood that current shortcomings of Soviet agriculture can be significantly reduced during the 1980s either to achieve a much higher rate of growth of crop or livestock products or to reduce the enormous costs imposed upon the Soviet economy.

Table 6.1 presents an updated study of climatic analogies for relatively small and homogenous areas of the Soviet Union. Due to the limited availability of data for oblasts, I have had to estimate the distribution of grain for the small areas given in Table 6.1, and it has not been possible to compare average yields for comparable areas in the USSR and North America for recent years. An earlier study has been updated by an analysis of yield trends for each of the small geographic areas, states, and provinces in North America. It seems a reasonable assumption that there have not been significant climatic shifts that would affect the comparability of the areas today relative to the early 1950s.

The yield trends given in Table 6.1 are based on data for 1955 through 1979 for the analogous areas, and are in terms of centners (100 kilograms) per hectare per year. The final result is a weighted annual increase in grain yield per hectare of 0.3 centners for the grain areas analogous to the USSR. The annual yield change in the USSR for 1956 to 1980 was 0.31 centners per hectare, almost identical to that obtained as the weighted sum of the yield increases for the analogous areas.

The yield data used for the analogous areas exclude corn, while the Soviet yields include the small area of corn, approximately 2.3 percent of the total grain area. In the Soviet Union the corn yield increased at a rate of 0.7 centners per hectare; if corn were excluded from the Soviet data, the yield increase would have been 0.3 centners per hectare.

A second approach was to analyze the long-term trends in and absolute level of grain yields for five states and the Prairie Provinces of North America. The five states are North Dakota, South Dakota, Nebraska, Montana, and Wyoming; the three provinces are Manitoba, Saskatchewan, and Alberta. This region does not

TABLE 6.1

Yield Increases in Climatically Analogous Areas, 1955–80

USSR Region	Weight of Region in USSR Grain Area (percent)	Yield Increase in Analogous Area (centners per hectare per year)	Analogous Area
Ukraine and Moldavia			
Spring grains	6.9	0.30	S.D.
Winter wheat			
Area I	0.8	0.44	Neb., S.E.
II	0.3	0.22	Neb., N.W.
III	1.5	0.37	Neb., S.W.
IV	0.2	0.45	Neb., Cen.
V	1.1	0.22	Neb., N.W.
VI	1.4	0.25	Mont., E.C. or N.C.; Colo., N.W.
Winter rye	1.2	0.28	U.S., Canada
Central Black Earth	8.4	0.25	Man.
Middle Volga	4.9	0.30	N.D.
Belorussia	2.0	0.35	Minn.
Baltic Republics and Kaliningrad	2.0	0.35	Minn.
European West	2.2	0.35	Minn., E.C., W.C.
European Northwest	0.8	0.35	Minn., E.C., W.C.
Central Industrial	2.9	0.35	Minn., N.W.
Upper Volga	2.6	0.30	N.D.
Krasnodar	1.9	0.50	Neb., N.E., East
Stavropol	2.3	0.45	S.D. (spring); Neb. (fall)
Kamensk	3.3	0.35	Wyo., S.E.
Remainder, North Caucasus	0.8	0.50	Neb.
Lower Volga	5.4	0.15	N.M.
Molotov and Sverdlovsk	1.7	0.30	Alberta, E.C.
Bashkir and Udmurt	3.2	0.25	Mont.
Chkalov and Cheliabinsk	4.8	0.30	S.D., West

Table 6.1
(continued)

USSR Region	Weight of Region in USSR Grain Area (percent)	Yield Increase in Analogous Area (centners per hectare per year)	Analogous Area
Western Siberia	9.8	0.30	Man., Sask.
Eastern Siberia	4.1	0.30	Sask.
Far East	0.8	0.30	N.D.
Kazakh, except Alma Ata	0.3	0.30	Wyo., Mont., S.D., Sask.
Alma Ata	0.3	0.30	
Central Asia	1.7	0.30	
Transcaucasus	0.9	0.30	
Total or average	99.5	0.30	

Sources: See Table 4.1.

fully duplicate the conditions of grain and feed production in the Soviet Union, but it is a relatively close match. Table 6.2 presents data on yield levels and changes since 1910–1919. The top part of the data includes the major grains other than corn; the bottom part includes corn in addition to the other major grains. The addition of corn significantly increases the mean yield, even though the corn area is only a little more than 10 percent of the grain area of the region. The yield data for USSR include all grains and pulses, including corn. It should also be noted that the yield data for the USSR for the years since 1950 are in terms of bunker weight and exceed the amount of clean, dry grain by an average of about 10–15 percent. Thus, the yield data for the USSR are not comparable over the whole period, and the data for the years before 1930 are presented only for rough comparisons.

For the comparisons that exclude corn in the North American area, grain yields in the Soviet Union have increased in relative terms from 74 percent in the 1955–64 decade to 84 percent for 1975–79. This is a significant improvement. However, if corn is included in the North American data there has been no trend in

TABLE 6.2

Grain Area, Production and Yields, Five States and Prairie
Provinces and USSR, 1910-79[a]

| | North American Areas | | | USSR[b] | Relative Yield (percent) |
	Area (million hectare)	Production (million tons)	Yield (centners/ hectare)	Yield (centners/ hectare	
	A. Wheat, Oats and Barley				
1910-19	19.3	19.5	10.1	6.3	62[c]
1920-29	25.9	26.8	10.3	7.9	77[d]
1945-54	30.2	33.8	11.2	7.7	69[e]
1955-64	27.2	37.1	13.6	10.0	74
1965-74	26.9	47.0	17.5	14.0	80
1975-79	28.1	50.9	18.1	15.2	84
	B. Wheat, Oats, Barley and Corn				
1910-19	23.8	26.2	11.0	6.3	57[c]
1920-29	31.8	35.8	11.3	7.9	70[d]
1945-54	35.1	42.9	12.2	7.7	63[e]
1955-64	31.0	46.4	14.9	10.0	67
1965-74	29.9	65.3	21.8	14.0	64
1975-79	31.7	70.9	22.4	15.2	68
	C. Wheat, Oats and Barley, Including Summer Fallow				
1945-54	42.2	33.8	8.0	6.5	0.81
1955-64	40.2	37.1	9.2	8.9	0.97
1965-74	40.7	47.0	11.5	12.2	1.06
1975-79	41.7	50.9	12.2	13.9	1.14
	D. Wheat, Oats, Barley and Corn, Including Summer Fallow				
1945-54	47.3	42.9	9.1	6.5	0.71
1955-64	44.0	46.4	10.5	8.9	0.85
1965-74	43.7	65.3	14.9	12.2	0.82
1975-79	45.3	70.9	15.7	13.9	0.88

Sources: See Table 4.1.

[a]North Dakota, South Dakota, Nebraska, Montana, Wyoming.

[b]All grains and pulses in USSR. To be comparable the USSR yields should be reduced by 10 to 15 percent to convert bunker yield to clean, dry grain.

[c]1909-13 average.   [d]1925-29 average.   [e]1950-54 average.

the relative yields for the periods from 1955 to date, or for that matter, for the period from the 1920s. But the absence of trend in the relative yields of the two areas including corn should not be permitted to overshadow the substantial increase in the absolute level of yields. Between 1950–54 and 1975–79 the grain yield in the USSR doubled. This is an annual growth rate of 2.76 percent and of 0.3 centers per hectare per year for the USSR.

If adjustment is made for the differences in method of calculation, Soviet grain yields appear about 75 percent those in the North American area if corn is not considered and about three-fifths as much if corn is included in the North American yield calculation. Do these data indicate that there is room for substantial increase in Soviet grain yields in terms of a catching up process? The answer is that there may be some room for catching up, but that these comparisons exaggerate it. The yield data referred to are in terms of output per unit of area devoted to the particular grains, either in terms of planted or harvested area. The yield data exclude the amount of fallow area as a part of the base for calculating the yields. The relative amount of fallow land is much higher in the North American area than in the USSR. If the fallow land is included for 1975–79 (Parts C and D of Table 6.2), the average yield for the North American area, excluding corn, was 12.2 centers and, including corn, 15.7 centers per hectare. Because of the much smaller relative amount of fallow in the USSR, the inclusion of summer fallow in calculating grain yield reduces the average yield by rather little, from 15.2 centers to 13.85 centers per hectare.

The two approaches for comparing the trend and level of Soviet grain yields gave very similar results. For the past quarter century, grain yields have increased in the analogous areas by 0.3 centers per hectare and in the five states plus the Prairie Provinces by 0.26 centers per hectare (if corn is not included) and by 0.44 (if corn is included). When the fallow area is included the annual yield increase was 0.18 centers if corn is excluded and 0.31 centers if corn is included.

The comparisons indicate that grain yields in the USSR have been increasing at essentially the same rate as in the climatically similar areas. The comparisons of the levels of grain yields indicate that yields in the USSR, when corn is excluded in the comparison areas, are at a reasonable level.

While grain yields will probably increase in the future in the USSR, as in North America, there does not seem to be a major potential for "catching up." One possible avenue for increasing yields in the USSR is to increase the area devoted to corn, which the Eleventh Plan includes: corn production is assumed to double between 1980 and 1985. In the USSR corn yields have been double the yields for all grains. However, in recent years the corn area harvested as grain has been about 3 million hectares. The area devoted to corn for grain in 1985 may be about 6 million hectares. This assumes that there will be an upward trend in corn yields, but this small shift in the relative importance of corn may increase grain production by about 4.5 million tons and increase the national average yield by no more than 3.5 centners per hectare.

FEED SUPPLIES

While grain production can be increased in the future, there is no reason to expect revolutionary increases in yields. Yield increases of 0.3 centners per hectare per year may be anticipated, but more than a decade of such increases would be needed to substitute for grain imports of approximately 40 million tons.

For the recent levels of livestock production, concentrates based on grains have not been the major limiting element in the feed supply. Significant increases in livestock production during the 1980s and beyond will be critically dependent upon increasing the output of forage crops and pasture. Relying primarily upon increasing grain production to provide a large share of the additional feed is not a viable option. Even if it were possible to expand grain production at a rate sufficient to meet livestock production goals for 1990, it is most unlikely that doing so would be the lowest cost means. The potential for increasing the production of forage is very great. This is indicated by the yield comparisons in Table 4.1 and the discussion that follows on specific forage crops.

Whether measured in rubles or dollars, the output of livestock products in the USSR in the late 1970s has been approximately 75 to 80 percent of the U.S. output. The amount of concentrates fed, which includes grains, plus millfeeds, oilmeals, grass and clover meals, and animal byproducts, in the USSR in recent years has been about 145 million tons if the feed value of milk is excluded and somewhat more than 150 million tons if milk is included. In the United States for the same years the concentrates fed have averaged about 155 million tons.

It is true that the amount of feed required per unit of value of livestock output depends upon the composition of the livestock output. But the composition of livestock output is a policy variable: it can be influenced by prices and the types of feed that are available. Policy makers in the USSR could modify the composition of output by increasing the production of products that have relatively low feed requirements (poultry) and reducing the output of products that have relatively high requirements (beef) per ruble of output.

HAY YIELDS

Hay yields in the USSR range from a little more than half to as low as a third of yields in climatically comparable areas. (See Table 4.1) Data available from the USSR indicate that hay yields comparable to those obtained in the Canadian Prairie Provinces or the U.S. Northern Plains States can be achieved in the USSR. Table 6.3 presents data for the Russian Republic (RSFSR), which

TABLE 6.3

Hay Yields in USSR and Finland

Period	RSFSR		Latvia		Estonia		Belorussia		Finland
	A^a	P^b	A	P	A	P	A	P	All Hay
(Centners per hectare)									
1961–65	11.0	14.3	22.9	19.4	26.9	21.6	11.1	18.7	34.5[c]
1966–70	15.7	15.7	27.8	22.9	30.3	28.3	14.2	24.9	35.0
1971–75	13.4	17.0	--	--	--	--	20.6	34.3	38.4
1976–78	16.3	18.3	42.7	28.3	36.0	39.7	21.3	31.0	38.7

Sources: Narodnoye khozyaystvo, republics of RSFSR, Latvia, Estonia, Belorussia, various years, and Statistical Yearbook of Finland (Suomen Tilastollinen Vuosikirja), various years.

[a]Yield is for annual hay.

[b]Yield is for perennial hay.

[c]Average of 1960 and 1965.

has nearly 60 percent of the annual plus perennial hay in the USSR, and for Latvia, Estonia, and Belorussia, as well as Finland. Hay yields in the RSFSR are some 10 to 15 percent below the USSR average. Latvia almost doubled the yield of annual hay from 1961–65 to 1976–78 and reached a yield in excess of 4 tons per hectare or double the national average. The yield of perennial hay in Latvia, while substantially above the national average, is lower than one might expect. The Estonian yield of perennial hay is double the average for the RSFSR, and the annual hay yield is almost double. Yield increases in Belorussia have been significantly greater than in the RSFSR over the past two decades. In 1961–65 the yields of annual hay were the same in the two republics, but by 1976–78 the yield in Belorussia was nearly a third higher. For perennial hay the yield difference was 30 percent during 1961–65 and 70 percent during 1976–78.

The hay yield for Finland in the early 1960s was much higher than the average for the USSR or RSFSR and higher than for any of the other three republics included in the table. Over the two decades the yield increased relatively little, and by 1976–78 the yield of annual hay in Latvia and perennial hay in Estonia exceeded the average yield for Finland. The Finnish yields indicate that yields in the northern and western parts of the USSR, where a large percentage of the wheat is grown, can be more than one ton in excess of the recent average yield for the USSR. In fact, the data for Finland and the three republics indicate that yields of 150 percent of the USSR average are probably attainable.

Because of the importance attached to the yields of hay and other forage crops, a third approach was used to throw light on the role of climate and soils upon such yields. The assumption underlying the analysis was that there should be approximately the same relationship between the yield of hay and of a major grain in the United States and the USSR. In other words, if Soviet climatic and soil resources permit a grain yield the same as that in the United States, these resources should permit the same hay yield. The grains used in the analysis were wheat and corn.

The two regression equations are:

$$\text{Hay yield} = 0.642 + 1.80 \ (\text{wheat yield})$$
$$\text{Hay yield} = 0.953 + 0.77 \ (\text{corn yield}).$$

The average wheat yield in the USSR for 1976–80 was 1.64 tons; the hay yield in the United States for this wheat yield would be 3.6 tons per hectare. This yield may be compared to an average hay yield for the USSR, 2.04 for annual and perennial hay. The yield based on the U.S. hay-wheat yield relationship for the USSR average wheat yield is 75 percent higher than the actual yield. In recent years the average wheat yield in the Ukraine has been about 3 tons per hectare, and the yield of annual and perennial hay has also been 3 tons per hectare. The U.S. hay-wheat yield relationship would indicate a hay yield of 6 tons per hectare or double the actual Ukraine hay yield.

If the hay-corn yield regression is used with the average USSR corn yield of 3.24 tons per hectare, the predicted hay yield is 3.45 tons per hectare. This is very nearly the same as the yield derived from the hay-wheat regression. The results from these regressions support the view that policy factors rather than climate and soil are important in determining hay yields.

If the hay-wheat regression equation is used with the grain yields for Estonia and Latvia, the predicted hay yields are reasonably close to the actual yields. The recent hay yield in Estonia was 38 centners per hectare and the grain yield was 25 centners; the predicted hay yield was 51 centners, about a third higher than the actual yield. For Latvia the predicted hay yield was 50 centners, compared to the actual yield of 35 centners. For the RSFSR the predicted hay yield was 35 centners, more than double the actual yield of 16 centners.

SILAGE YIELDS

Silage can be prepared from a variety of crops: annual hays, perennial hays, and corn are commonly used, with the latter the most important source in both the USSR and the United States. Soviet silage yields, including green chop, are low, averaging about 15 tons per hectare in recent years. In the three Lake States corn silage yields average 30 to 35 tons per hectare; in the three Northern Plains States the yields are lower, a little less than 20 tons per hectare. However, in both North and South Dakota part of the low silage yields reflects harvesting much of the corn crop as silage during years of low grain yields. It is also during these years that silage yields are low. The corn silage harvested area in the USSR does not seem to vary enough from year to year to influence silage yields in the same way.

Silage corn, including green chop, is grown on about 17 million hectares. Thus, increasing yields has a significant potential for increasing the feed supply and reducing the demand for grain. But it is not obvious what measures can be taken to increase silage yields. Apparently a significant part of the silage and green chop area represents corn planted late, after another seeding failed. Late planted corn will have low yields, in terms of quantity and quality. After a significant positive yield trend for corn silage from the late 1950s to the early 1970s—from 9.9 to 13.0 tons per hectare—there was no significant increase during the 1970s. For 1975–78 corn silage yields averaged a little less than 14 tons per hectare. These yields may be compared to averages of about 14 tons for North and South Dakota and 28 tons in Michigan and Minnesota. Thus, there appears to be room for a significant increase in USSR silage yields, since much of the silage is grown in areas similar to Michigan and Minnesota.

TECHNICAL CROPS

From the 1930s until the present, three crops—cotton, sugar beets, and sunflowers—have had a high priority in the Soviet allocation of resources, including research, and in the prices paid to farms. Until 1960 more than half of the money income of collective farms derived from these three crops and flax. The areas of these four crops have been approximately one-tenth of the grain area.

For some time Soviet officials and agricultural scientists could point with considerable pride to their achievements in the production of cotton, sunflowers, and sugar beets. But during the 1970s the yields of sunflowers and sugar beets stagnated or actually declined. However, this was not the case with cotton, where yields are relatively high and increasing.

All cotton produced in the USSR is irrigated. The cotton is relatively long staple, at least compared to most cotton produced in the United States. Pima cotton produced in the southwestern part of the United States is irrigated and has a relatively long staple length. Table 6.4 compares the average yields of cotton, in terms of

TABLE 6.4

Yields of All Cotton in the USSR and American
Pima Cotton in Three States, 1961–1980

(Kilograms of Lint Cotton per Hectare)

	Arizona	New Mexico	Texas	USSR
1961–65	646	534	592	673
1966–70	601	426	494	781
1971–75	714	384	427	892
1976–80	868	485	580	957

Sources: U.S. Department of Agriculture, Agricultural Statistics,
various issues; USSR: Review of Agriculture in 1981 and
Outlook for 1982, Supplement 1 to WAS-27, May 1982; and
Agricultural Statistics of Eastern Europe and the Soviet
Union, 1950–70, June 1973.

kilograms of lint cotton per hectare, for three states and the USSR, 1961–1980. The USSR average yields are above the yields in any one of the three states for each of the five-year periods. Further, the yield increase of 42 percent in the USSR was twice as great as the yield increase in Arizona. The other two states actually registered yield declines for the two decades. In the case of cotton, high and increasing yields have been achieved even though climatic conditions are not optimal.

TABLE 6.5

Sunflower Seed Yields in the United States and the
USSR, 1966–80

(Centners per Hectare)

Period	United States	USSR
1966–70	10.7	13.2
1971–75	9.2	13.2
1976–80	13.6	11.8

Sources: See Table 6.4

Table 6.5 compares the average yields of sunflowers in the United States and the USSR. Production in the United States was at a low level until the mid-1970s, when new hybrid varieties were rapidly introduced. Production of sunflower seeds increased sixfold between 1976 and 1979. The new varieties yielded substantially more than the older varieties and in addition had a much higher oil content. The oil content was comparable to that of the Soviet varieties. During the decade from 1966–75 the average yield of sunflower seeds in the USSR was nearly 30 percent higher than in the United States. But for 1976–80 the yield advantage was reversed because of a sharp increase in yields in the United States and a decline in yields in the USSR.

Adverse climatic conditions have been responsible for part of the decline in Soviet sunflower seed yields, but other factors have been important as well. In recent years the open pollinated sunflower varieties have become susceptible to a wide variety of diseases. Many diseases are soil-borne, and their impact is aggravated by farms' following relatively short rotations of 3 to 4 years rather than the recommended 8 to 10 year rotations. A 1980 review of the sunflower difficulties by the U.S. Department of Agriculture concluded: "The Soviets have cited other problems in raising the output of sunflower seed, including deteriorating seed quality, inadequate supplies of fertilizers, herbicides, and defoliants. Also the Soviets claim that many farms are not allocating the best land to sunflowers. . . . Should the Soviets switch to a hybrid program over the next ten years, some of the disease problems could be mitigated, but many other difficulties could remain."[1] It is difficult to understand why hybrids were not first developed there rather than in the United States, given the great importance of sunflowers in the USSR.

Yield comparisons for sugar beets are presented in Table 6.6. The states included are climatically similar to the areas in which sugar beets are grown in the USSR, though the analogies are rather less close than those we have used for grains. While some problems arise in comparing absolute yield levels, the differences in recent yield trends are striking. Sugar beet yields in the USSR have hardly increased since 1966–70, while there have been significant yield increases in each of the three states. For the quarter century included in the table, the yield increase for the USSR

TABLE 6.6

Sugar Beet Yields in Three States and the USSR, 1956–80

(Tons per Hectare)

Period	Minnesota	North Dakota	Michigan	USSR
1956–70	27.8	19.3	32.3	18.4
1961–65	26.0	26.4	35.4	16.5
1966–70	28.7	27.8	38.9	22.8
1971–75	32.7	31.8	40.3	21.7
1976–80	35.8	36.8	42.4	23.6

Sources: See Table 6.4.

was 28 percent, while the yield increases in the states ranged from a low of 28 percent for Minnesota to a high of 191 percent for North Dakota. Yields during the latter half of the 1970s were significantly higher than for the latter half of the 1960s for each of the three states.

The evidence from the yield comparisons for the technical crops gives some support to the conclusion that when the Soviets have given a crop high priority the yields are comparable to those in climatically similar areas. This is clearly the case for cotton and was true for sunflowers until recently. Even the example of the sunflowers indicates that for a time performance can be at a high level. The sunflowers may indicate that the failure of the nonfarm economy to provide adequate support has a high cost in terms of low and perhaps declining yields and production. Sunflowers may also indicate that monopoly in plant breeding and seed production is bad, and that some of the recent difficulties might not have occurred if there had been more competition in these two areas.

SHORT TERM CLIMATIC EFFECTS

The discussion of the effects of climate on crop production has been concerned primarily with determining the role of climate in affecting the average or long run level of crop yields and production. This discussion supports the conclusion that policy factors are responsible for much of the relatively poor performance of

Soviet agriculture. Comparisons of yields of various crops with climatically similar areas indicate numerous instances where the yield differences are far larger than unrecognized climatic factors could explain. However, where crops have received high priority, especially for grains and cotton, yield differences are relatively small or do not exist. In the case of the grains, the lower Soviet yield is due primarily to the limited amount of summer fallow, and the lower yield has little adverse effect upon production, though yield variability is much greater than it need be.[2]

The Central Intelligence Agency has made an important study of the effects of climate on grain yields, projecting yield levels for spring and winter wheat for four different climatic patterns, represented by the weather conditions that prevailed in four different time periods, 1970–73, 1962–75, pre-1960, and 1962–65. The pre-1960 period describes the long-term average of climatic conditions.[3]

Based on these different climatic scenarios the range in the projected 1980 yield of winter wheat was from 25 to 29.5 centners per hectare; for spring wheat the range was from 9.6 to 14 centners. While the absolute differences in yields from the poorest to the most favorable weather were approximately the same at about 4.5 centners per hectare, the relative variability of spring wheat yields attributed to climate was more than twice as large as for winter wheat. Spring wheat is generally grown in less favored areas, due either to limited rainfall or warmth, than is winter wheat and is thus more susceptible to climatic variations.

The report presented three projections of total grain production for the average of the years 1976–80. The highest output level, based on the assumption of the weather of 1970–73, was 242 million tons. The intermediate level, based on the climate for 1962–75, was 223 million tons. The low projected output level was based on what was described as the "worst four consecutive years of the past 15 years"; the projected level for this scenario was 200 million tons. The actual average annual production during 1976–80 was 205 millions tons, slightly above the worst case scenario. The difference between the high and low projection was 42 million tons or about 20 percent of the low projection.

As a supplement to this analysis, two tables provide further indication of the role of climatic variability upon short run output

TABLE 6.7

Yield Trends for Grains for Varying Periods, USSR

	Centners/Hectare, Annual Change
1950 to	
1976	0.336
1977	0.328
1978	0.343
1979	0.325
1980	0.313
1981	0.296
1956 to	
1974	0.397
1975	0.321
1978	0.355
1979	0.326
1980	0.308
1981	0.282
1962 to	
1975	0.404
1978	0.433
1981	0.289
1966 to	
1981	0.124[a]
1970 to	
1981	−0.042[a]

Sources: U.S. Department of Agriculture,
           Agricultural Statistics of Eastern
           Europe and the Soviet Union, 1950–70,
           ERS–Foreign 349, p. 30, June 1973, and
           USSR: Review of Agriculture in 1981
           and Outlook for 1982, Supplement 1 to
           WAS–27, May 1982, p. 20.

[a]Not significant.

performance. Table 6.7 presents a series of yield trends, which reveal substantial differences in annual yield growth rates for the grains depending upon the choice of the beginning and end dates. For example, a yield trend from 1950 to 1978, estimated from a regression, indicates an average yield increase of 0.343 centners per hectare. However, if the last year is 1981 instead of 1978 the annual rate of increase declines to 0.296 centners. An even more striking result is obtained if the beginning year is 1962; note the annual increases when the period ends in 1978 or 1981.

Table 6.8 organizes yield data in a somewhat different way through the use of successive five-year moving averages, starting with 1966. The differences between successive averages are often quite striking. For example, the average grain yield for 1970–74 was 15.6 centners, compared to 14.7 centners for 1971–75. On a harvested area of 128 million hectares the difference in average total production was nearly 12 million tons. Some of the other differences were nearly as large.

It is clear that climatic variability can and does significantly affect crop output, not only from one year to the next but for periods as long as five years. This variability makes it difficult for Soviet officials to make concrete plans and for those who study Soviet agriculture to put great confidence in short run projections. I would add, however, that some of the output variability is avoidable and partly due to policy choices.

TABLE 6.8

USSR: Five-Year Average Grain Yields, 1966–81

(Centners per Hectare)

Period	Yield
1966–70	13.7
1967–71	14.0
1968–72	14.4
1969–73	15.1
1970–74	15.6
1971–75	14.7
1972–76	15.1
1973–77	15.3
1974–78	15.4
1975–79	15.2
1976–80	16.0
1977–81	15.2

Source: See Table 6.7.

CLIMATE AS A LIMITING FACTOR

There is a sense in which the Soviet climate imposes a potential restraint upon agricultural performance. In many parts of the Soviet Union nature extracts a great penalty if farm operations are not carried out in a timely fashion. Where the climate is more benign, as in the American Corn Belt and much of Western Europe, the loss from delays in planting or seeding and in harvesting is much less punishing than in the Soviet regions, where growing seasons are quite short and/or moisture is severely limited. Timeliness is also important where rain may fall at time of harvest. Consequently, shortcomings in the stock, supply, and maintenance of farm machinery can and do impose heavy costs upon agricultural output.

An analysis of the yield increases obtained by planting on time has been made for the Canadian Province of Nova Scotia.[4] This province has climatic characteristics substantially similar to those in the more humid areas of the European part of the Soviet Union. In 1976–79 the mean yields were 1.9 tons per hectare for oats, 2.5 tons for barley, and 2.4 tons for mixed grain. A significant percentage of the grain in the province now is planted on time, but the province's yield is adversely affected by farmers who do not plant on time. The yield increases estimated for always planting on time over never planting on time (tons per hectare) were 0.8 for oats, 1.4 for barley and 1.7 for mixed grains. A somewhat more realistic estimate of the gains that might be achieved is to consider the yield gains that would be realized from an increase from 50 percent to 80 percent of the area planted on time. This increase in timeliness of planting would result in mean annual yield increases of 0.3 to 0.5 tons per hectare. Compared to the actual mean yields, a modest increase in timeliness of planting could increase yields by 15 to 20 percent.

This particular study referred only to the benefits of timeliness of planting. Other significant gains can be achieved by timeliness in harvesting, a subject Soviet agricultural scientists frequently refer to in their studies.

CLIMATIC EFFECTS

There can be no doubt that climatic factors affect both the level of agricultural output and its variability in the USSR. But I believe that it has been shown that policy choices have influenced a significant proportion of these two effects. Different policy choices could increase total agricultural production significantly and could reduce annual variability. The policy choices obviously are not simple ones in the framework within which Soviet agriculture functions. Even a casual review of agricultural policy since the death of Stalin indicates how extremely resistant to change the administration and planning of Soviet agriculture is.

CHAPTER SEVEN

The 1982 New Food Program

At the beginning of the 1970s, the USSR was almost self-sufficient in agricultural products, with the value of agricultural imports and agricultural exports in rough balance. In 1982, the net deficit in agricultural trade was approximately $18 billion. In the first year of the 1970s the USSR had net grain exports of 7 million tons; when Brezhnev presented his new food program in May 1982, net grain imports for the year were 45 million tons. In the late 1960s, the USSR was a small net exporter of meat; in 1981 it was the world's largest meat importer, with imports of 1 million tons.

These statistics reflect a significant deterioration in the performance of Soviet agriculture. The substantial shift of resources to agriculture that occurred after 1964 and the modest improvement in per capita food consumption that has been realized explain why Brezhnev said in Novermber 1981: "The problem of food is, on the economic and political level, the central problem of the whole 5-year plan." At that meeting of the CPSU Party Plenum, he announced that a new food program was being prepared and that the program would be discussed at a regular plenary session of the CPSU Central Committee in 1982.

MAJOR FEATURES OF THE FOOD PROGRAM

The food program Brezhnev presented on May 24, 1982, included no significant new initiatives. The marginal changes are likely to have little or no effect on the output performance of the food economy. One can only express surprise that a program to address such an important problem and given such advance notice was so unimaginative. The basic planning, administrative, and organizational features of Soviet agriculture remain unchanged. As has happened several times over the past two decades, the bureaucratic structure was rearranged, and more money was thrown at agriculture in the form of higher procurement prices, forgiveness of debts, and substantial funds allocated for cultural facilities (camps, clubs), consumer services, roads, and housing for low profitability farms. For 1983 the increased expenditures upon agriculture, including writing off debts, amount to 30 billion rubles. The food price subsidy bill on meat, milk, bread, and potatoes will increase to at least 51 billion rubles and will exceed the value of their retail sales. In other words, what the Soviet citizen pays at the retail store or place of employment for these products will be less than half of what it costs the state to bring the products to the consumer. Of course the Soviet citizen pays for the rest, but as a taxpayer rather than as a consumer.

Some who follow Soviet agricultural policy thought that Brezhnev in his November 1981 speech was indicating that the food program would include a major change to give the individual farms substantial independence from bureaucratic control. At least such a thought seemed a reasonable interpretation of his speech:

> In drawing up the food program, an important place should be assigned to such major problems as the improvement of the economic mechanism and the system of management—the management of agriculture and of the agro-industrial complex as a whole. And, of course, local management. The collective farms and state farms themselves should have the final say in deciding what should be sown on each hectare and when one job or another should begin. The district level of management should also be strengthened in every way.[1]

Did the food program give the collective farms and state farms the final decision? Hardly. What Brezhnev said in May 1982 was:

> It's necessary resolutely to get rid of administrative fiat and petty tutelage with respect to collective and state farms, which can rightfully be called the foundation of all agricultural production. No one should be permitted to demand that the farms fulfill any assignments not envisaged by the state plan or to ask them for any information except as established by state reporting requirements. This rule should be observed strictly at all levels and with no exceptions. I hope, comrades, that we are unanimous on how important and how necessary this is.[2]

Earlier in the speech he noted the wide differences in natural conditions and said: "There is no place here for stereotypes, for trying to make everyone fit the same pattern. What is especially needed here is managerial initiative, independence in making decisions and enterprise." He then stated that the Central Committee recognizes the "need to strengthen the collective and state farms in every way and to enhance their independence, both organizationally and from the standpoint of economic management." But he never stated the farms should decide what to produce, how to produce it, and when to carry out specific operations so long as they meet the state procurement plans.

In fact, in the few paragraphs before these references to independence and initiative, he described two new layers of bureaucracy, one being agro-industrial associations at the district, territory, province, and autonomous republic level and the other agro-industrial commissions at the republic and union level. The agro-industrial associations at the first level are to have special significance, namely to be "a really full-fledged and democratic management agency. . . . that will be fully capable of influencing production with consideration for the interests of the collective farms and state farms." The role of the associations would appear to be inconsistent, at least to some degree, with putting responsibility for the functioning of collective and state farms upon their members and management.

Both Khrushchev and Brezhnev recognized, more than once, the desirability of giving greater initiative to individual farms. In 1955, under Khrushchev's urging, a decree gave managers of collective and state farms more authority to make their own decisions and to have some influence even in determining their procurement obligations. While the procurement plans were finally to be set by the government, the farms were to decide the most appropriate crop patterns and livestock production to meet the procurement obligations. But nothing happened, except that in March 1964 another decree "emphasized the 1955 decree and threatened punishment to all state officials infringing on the still restricted planning autonomy of farms."[3] The 1964 decree actually resolved "To condemn as harmful and a hindrance to the development of agriculture the unnecessary imposition from above on the collective and state farms of assignments for the size of sown areas, their structure, the number of livestock and other production indices. To prohibit local Party, Soviet and agricultural agencies from establishing production assignments for the collective and state farms for any indices except those approved by the state plan."[4]

In March 1965, presumably at the direction of Brezhnev, the Central Committee of the Communist Party resolved: "It is necessary to put a resolute end to the practice of administration by fiat and command and of replacing leaders and specialists on collective and state farms and to eradicate instances of ostentation and ballyhoo."[5] At the 1965 meeting, Brezhnev said: "We must put an end to the practice of command and administration by fiat, to petty tutelage, to the usurping of the functions of the leaders and specialists of the collective and state farms, [we] must eradicate any manifestations of ostentation and ballyhoo."[6]

In preparation for his May 1982 speech, Brezhnev or his speech writer must have cribbed from the March 1964 resolution and his speech in 1965: The words are almost identical.

Will farms be permitted greater initiative under the new Food Program than they have had in the past? The historical record of broken promises does not hold out much hope for significant change. The introduction of two new bureaucratic layers is especially ominous.

The problem of directing agriculture through "administrative fiat and petty tutelage" has been recognized as a barrier to production and efficiency in Soviet agriculture for more than a quarter century. Both Khrushchev and Brezhnev were apparently unable to take authority from the bureaucracies and give it to the farms where it belonged. Thus, each effort to achieve decentralization of authority has ended in reshuffling existing bureaucracies, creation of new bureaucracies, or both. But in no instance does there appear to have been a significant transfer of authority or initiative to the farms.

GOALS AND RESOURCES

The Food Program is a plan for the development of food and agriculture for the 1980s. Thus, it included some modifications of the Eleventh Plan and of the broad outlines of the Twelfth Plan for 1986–90. Table 7.1 compares the goals for the Eleventh and Twelfth plan periods with actual performance for 1976–80. Its last column shows the annual rate of growth from the 1976–80 output level required to achieve the goals for the Twelfth Plan. The largest growth rate is 3.3 percent for sunflower seeds, against the very poor performance of 1976–80. If 1971–75 were used in the comparison, the annual growth rate would be reduced to 1.4 per-

cent. Meat output is planned to grow at an annual rate of 3.1 percent for the 1980s, but this rate of growth is unlikely to be attained. Grain output is to grow at 2.1 percent annually, a rather
modest goal. Milk production is to grow slowly at 1.2 percent, but
the primary shortcoming with the milk sector is utilization of the
available supply and not aggregate output. Egg production is to
grow at a rather modest rate of 2.2 percent, probably below what
could be achieved.

Only brief note will be taken of the planned resources for the
1980s and for 1986–90. Tractor deliveries for the decade are to be
from 3.74 to 3.78 million; deliveries for the latter half of the decade are identical to those planned for 1981–85. The same is true of

TABLE 7.1

Plan Goals for Eleventh and Twelfth Five-Year Plans and
Actual Production for 1976–80, USSR

	1976–80 Actual	1981–85 Plan	1986–90 Plan[a]	Annual Growth Rate to Achieve 1986–90 Goals (%/yr.)[b]
	(million tons)			
Grain	205	239	252.5	2.1
Meat	14.9	17.25	20.25	3.1
Milk	93.2	98	105	1.2
Sugar Beets	88.4	100	102.5	1.5
Sunflower Seeds	5.3	6.7	7.35	3.3
Potatoes	82.4	88	91	1.0
Eggs (billions)	63	72	78.5	2.2

Sources: "The USSR Food Program for the Period Up to 1990" (Pravda and
Izvestiya, May 27, 1982, pp. 1–4).   Translated in The Current
Digest of the Soviet Press, XXXIV, No. 21 (June 23, 1982),
pp. 9–13, 23; and XXIV, No. 22 (June 30, 1982), pp. 7–15;
and "In the CPSU Central Committee and the USSR Council of
Ministers" (Pravda and Izvestiya, May 28, 1982, pp. 1–2).
Translated in The Current Digest of the Soviet Press,
XXXIV, No. 23 (July 7, 1982), pp. 11–13, 19, 21; and The USSR
in Figures for 1980 (Russian edition), pp. 108–09.

[a]Midpoints of a range.

[b]Growth rate from 1976–80.

combines: the decades planned deliveries of 1.17 million are double the goal for the Eleventh Plan. Fertilizer deliveries to agriculture in 1990 are to increase by 57 percent over actual deliveries in 1980, but only a quarter more than the original plan for 1980. Truck deliveries for 1986-90 are planned to be about 7 percent greater than for the current plan period.

Investment in agriculture is to remain at high levels for the Twelfth Plan. The percentage of the national investment allocated to agriculture is to be 27 to 28 percent, while for the total agro-industrial complex the percentage is to be 33 to 35. Each is marginally higher than the percentages for 1981–85.

These resource goals, as well as the many others included in the Food Program, do not imply any significant shift in resources to agriculture as the decade comes to its end. True, an enormous quantity of resources will be made available. But unless these resources are of higher quality, better maintained, and much more effectively utilized, past experience indicates that the modest increase will have an equally modest impact upon agricultural output.

Given the enormous costs of the Food Program, the output goals are remarkably modest. Even if met, meat consumption will be generally below the levels prevailing in Eastern Europe. Perhaps more important, even if the 1990 goals for meat and milk are met, demand for these products will continue to exceed supply at current prices in the state stores. In other words, the new Food Program will not result in the ready availability of meat and milk products in state stores unless their prices are increased substantially. If one of the objectives of the Food Program was to eliminate the need for price adjustments and at the same time return meat and milk products to the shelves of the state retail stores, that objective will not be met. In fact, instead of narrowing, the gap between demand and supply for meat could actually widen during the decade, since the growth of nominal or money incomes will result in a faster growth of demand for meat than the planned growth in supply.

Furthermore, if the policy of fixed nominal retail prices is retained throughout the 1980s, the heavy financial drain of subsidies will grow. The output of meat and other subsidized products will increase and at the same rate of subsidy per unit of output, the subsidy bill will increase. If the past is any guide, it will be necessary to increase the prices paid to the farms for most farm products as their costs increase. Thus, the gap between prices paid to farms and what consumers pay is likely to widen and the subsidy bill to grow. If the subsidy bill is held in check by delaying farm price increases, output growth will be adversely affected.

One can speculate that the new leadership that seems to be emerging in the USSR may come forward with a more imaginative reform of food and agricultural policies than is embodied in the Food Program and the other current policies. Such reform should encompass several major modifications of current policies. One would be to abandon the policy of fixed nominal prices for food as well as for other major consumer items. Until food prices are at a level that will approximately equate supply and demand, the Soviet economy will continue to impose enormous costs upon its citizens. This is especially true for the women who are forced to spend an inordinate amount of their time shopping or, perhaps more accurately, searching often fruitlessly for ordinary goods made difficult to obtain by inappropriate pricing policies.

Another would be to really give the farms the authority to make decisions with a minimum of intervention from planning and other officials, an objective long supported by the top leadership but circumvented by the bureaucracy. But if the farms are to be given initiative and freed from "petty tutelage and administrative fiat," the prices paid to the farms and the prices of equipment and purchased inputs must serve as appropriate guides for the allocation of resources on each farm. The price system serves this function reasonably well in most economies, including now at least the socialist economies of Hungary and Yugoslavia. With the price system as distorted as it is in the USSR, giving farms full discretion in all production decisions would result in an inappropriate mix of food output. With existing prices, the differences in profitability among farm products are simply too great for these prices to serve as appropriate guides to production. Price reform is essential for decentralization of decisions.

Nor could the reforms ignore the need to devise incentives and penalties that would induce the enterprises providing goods and services for agriculture, including inputs to agricultural production and the transportation, marketing, and processing of farm output, to carry out their function in an efficient and timely manner. Currently enterprises suffer few if any adverse consequences from the annual loss of a tenth of total fertilizer output or from the enormous losses of a fifth or more of food during transportation, processing, and marketing.

But there can be no certainty that the new leadership will undertake significant agricultural reforms. To do so would mean risking adverse public reaction to sharp price increases for food; if meat and other livestock products are to be readily available in the stores, prices might well have to be doubled. Nor can it be assumed that the bureaucracy that now administers agriculture with such disastrous results could be turned to more productive activities. The bureaucracy that now controls agriculture and rural life wields enormous power; this power is not likely to be readily relinquished. Three decades of efforts to reform that bureaucracy have been without positive results.

There was no radical break with the past when the current leadership consolidated its position in the mid-1960s. While the present agricultural and food situation leaves much to be desired and the financial and resource costs continue to grow, these costs can probably be managed for at least the 1980s. Thus, there can be no certainty that the new leadership will behave differently in the 1980s than did the previous leadership in the 1960s. This may well be the case even though Soviet agriculture is in greater disarray now than it was two decades earlier.

CHAPTER EIGHT

Agricultural Performance in the 1980s

Even if the 1990 output objectives of the Food Program are met, important policy problems will still face the Soviet economy. Continuing to adhere to the policy of fixed nominal prices for most food products will result in empty shelves in the state stores, rising prices in the collective farm markets, further expansion of alternative distribution schemes for many food products, and an increasing financial burden from the growing food price subsidies.

The plan goals for agriculture for 1986–90 (or for 1990 as well) are modest in terms of growth rates and absolute levels of output. Moreover, the output goals for neither the Eleventh Plan nor the Twelfth Plan are likely to be met.

FEED REQUIREMENTS

The critical restraint on the growth of livestock output is the availability of feed. While there can be some improvement in the productivity of feed, most of any increase in output of livestock products must derive from additional feed availability. Domestic feed output from all sources was so limited during 1976–80 that the USSR had to import more than 100 million tons of grain. During the first two years of the Eleventh Plan, grain imports have increased to a total of nearly 90 million tons. But livestock output has increased very little since 1975, even with this very large increase in imported grain. From 1960–62 to 1978–80 livestock output increased by 68 percent. Feed use increased by approximately 62 percent, according to estimates made by Zahn.[1] The small increase in livestock output per unit of feed was due primarily to the significant relative increase in the production of poultry and eggs, which produce more output per unit of feed than do cattle or hogs.

The shifts in the composition of the feed output have serious implications for the future unless a significant improvement occurs in the output of feed crops other than grains and concentrates.

During the 1960s and 1970s the share of concentrates (grain, grain by-products, milk, and oilseeds) in the estimated total feed supply increased from 25 to 42 percent of the total. The share of forage crops declined from 51.5 percent to 42 percent, while the share of pasture declined from 23 to 17 percent. In absolute terms the amount of concentrates fed increased by 168 percent and the amount of all other harvested feeds by just 31 percent. The estimated feed supplied by pasture increased by less than 20 percent, and most of that increase occurred before 1971/72.[2]

The comparisons in the previous paragraph are for the 1960s and 1970s; data for 1971/72 to the end of the 1970s indicate some slowing down in the growth of the share of concentrates and grain in total feed supply. But even for this period, livestock output increased 2.4 percent, grain used as feed by 4.4 percent, and coarse and succulent feeds plus pasture by 1.9 percent, all in annual rates.

There is no reliable method for estimating the amount of grain and other concentrates required to produce a given planned or actual level of livestock output. The sum of all feed required is subject to some uncertainty, but the greatest difficulty is projecting the percentage of total feed that will be provided by concentrates, including grain. It is safe to assume that all other feed supplies will be used before concentrates are used, especially if part of the concentrates are imported, but to use this assumption we must know how much the output of other feeds will increase over a period of time.

If the trends in available feed supplies and feed requirements evident for the 1970s are extended until 1985, we obtain total feed requirements of approximately 500 million oat feed units with approximately 39 percent of the feed units projected to be supplied by grains (46.5 percent by all concentrates). The grain required for feed in 1985 amounts to 162 million tons. If one assumed that the share of grain remained constant at the 1978–80 level, grain required for feed in 1985 would be 150 million tons and total concentrates 176 million tons. I believe that the better projection is the 162 million tons of grain used as feed. This assumes that grain use as feed would increase by 30 percent while livestock output increased by 17 percent.[3]

If the 1985 livestock goals are met and the feed use of grain is 162 million tons, would such feed use be possible with the 1985 grain production goal of 245 million tons? Assuming a waste factor of 13 percent of gross grain production and industrial, food, and seed use of 79 million tons (actual usage in 1980/81), and no grain imports or exports, grain production would need to be 277 million tons. If these extrapolations are taken seriously, the shortfall in grain production in 1985 if the grain goal were met would be 32 million tons.

The 1981–85 plan calls for an increase of 22 percent in the procurement of coarse and succulent feeds in the socialized sector, compared to 1976–80; such an increase would amount to 25 million tons of oat feed units or the equivalent of 21 million tons of actual grain. The projection of grain used as feed for 1985 implied an increase in feed units from coarse, succulent, and pasture feed of 15 percent for both the private and socialized sector.[4] If one assumes no increase in feed derived from pasture, the increase in coarse and succulent feeds for both the socialized and private sectors is 20 percent, which is close to the 22 percent increase in procurements in the socialized sector.

The projection of total feed used in 1985 assumes a small increase in feed requirements per ruble of livestock output. The increase of 3 percent is somewhat counter to the trend for the two decades ending in 1980. However, during the 1970s feed usage increased by 22 percent while livestock output increased by 18 percent. Assuming that there will be some increase in livestock inventories by 1985, a factor not considered in the feed requirements, a small increase in feed used per ruble of livestock output does not seem unreasonable.

This speculative approach to future feed requirements indicates the importance of increasing the output of forage crops, such as hay, silage, and green chop, if the Soviet Union is to have any chance of gradually reducing its dependence upon imported grain. However, the calculations presented above underestimate the problems faced by Soviet agriculture in reducing dependence upon imported grain and other feeds. In making these calculations, it was assumed that the 1985 grain production goal would be met. We shall now consider the strong probability that the goal is too optimistic.

GRAIN AND OTHER FEED
PRODUCTION POTENTIALS

Concentrates, primarily grains or grain by-products, are the largest single component of the feed supply and have been the most rapidly growing one. But together succulent and coarse feeds are approximately equal to concentrates as a source of feed units, while pasture has provided about a sixth of total feed. However, the relative importance of pasture as a feed source has declined over the past quarter century.[5]

In terms of the use of the cultivated land, tame hay utilizes approximately 44 million hectares of a total cultivated area of 217 million. The grain area is about 127 million hectares, while corn silage is harvested from about 17 million hectares and potatoes from 7 million.[6]

The grain production goal for 1981–86 is 238 million tons and for 1986–90 from 250 million to 255 million tons. Neither of these goals nor the 1985 goal of 245 million tons is likely to be met.[7] Based on the trends of grain yields presented in Table 6.7 and climate or weather for either 1950 to 1980 or 1960 to 1980 for 1981–86, I would predict average grain production of 218 million tons and 237 million tons for 1986–90, assuming 127.5 million hectares of grain for both periods.[8] For 1985 the projected grain production is 226 million tons and 245 million tons for 1990.

As the data on grain yields given in Table 6.3 indicate, yields can vary substantially from one five-year period to another even when the only difference between such periods is dropping one year and adding another. Climatic differences for any five-year period could result in outputs that deviate from the projections based on long-term climate by plus or minus 7.5 percent and with either very favorable or very unfavorable climatic conditions by as much as plus or minus 10 percent. Thus, grain production in 1981–86 might range from a high of 234 million tons to a low of 202 million tons without causing too much surprise.[9] For 1986–90 a reasonable output range would be from 255 million tons at the upper end to 220 million at the lower end.

The projections for 1981–86 take no account of actual grain production in 1981 and 1982. If 1981 grain production were 175 million tons (no official production figure has been given by the

Soviets) and the 1982 grain production were 170 million tons, it would take average grain production for 1983–85 of 222 million tons to give annual output for the plan period of 202 million tons. There have only been three years in Soviet history in which grain output has exceeded 222 million tons. A plan period output of 10 percent less than the projected output based on average weather, or 196 million tons cannot be ruled out. Nor, for that matter, is some figure below 196 million unimaginable.

What are the possibilities for expanding the production of coarse and succulent feeds during the 1980s? Earlier it has been noted that yield levels for hay and other forage crops are very low. While tame hay yields have been improving in recent years, the yields of other forage crops have changed very little.

The potential for increasing all forage crop yields, including hay yields, is substantial. Furthermore, there is no great mystery concerning what is required to increase such yields: improved seeds, weed control, lime, fertilizer, and harvesting at appropriate times are among the most important means. None of the measures required is beyond the technical capacities of the Soviet agricultural system. As I believe that the climatic analogies have shown, the low yields cannot be explained by unfavorable conditions. And the data on hay yields for Estonia and Latvia show that hay yields can approach those in the analogous North American areas where appropriate measures are taken.

As noted above, cultivated hay is grown on 44 million hectares and corn silage on 17 million hectares. These two forage crops offer the primary potential for significant expansion in non-concentrate feeds. The goals for the Eleventh Plan and 1985 already call for output increases not likely to be attained. Based on the trend in the production of coarse and succulent feeds for the 1970s ending with 1978, a very good year in yields, the production of these forage crops would increase by no more than 16 percent between 1978–80 and 1985. This is well below the increase of 20 percent assumed in the projection of grain used as feed for 1985. Consequently, the estimate of 162 million tons of grain fed to livestock might be on the low side for meeting the 1985 goal for livestock output.

PROBABLE LIVESTOCK PRODUCTION

The 1985 plan calls for 18.2 million tons of meat (slaughter weight), 102 million tons of milk, and 75 billion eggs. The plan goals for the Twelfth Plan are 20 million to 20.5 million tons of meat, 104 million to 106 million tons of milk, and 78.5 billion eggs. Except for the meat goal, the Twelfth Plan goals call for very modest increases over 1985. The milk and egg goals for the 1980s could be met, though to increase milk production by the amount required means to achieve a sharp reversal of the recent decline in milk output per cow. Presumably if and when feed availability improves, milk production per cow could increase to 2,350 kilograms by 1985.

Earlier 1985 grain production was projected to be 226 million tons; the plan goal is 245 million tons. As noted, if the 1985 livestock goals are to be met, feed use of grain would have to be a minimum of 162 million tons in 1985, requiring a total availability of 277 million tons. If the output of coarse and succulent feeds falls below plan levels, even more grain would be required. To achieve the livestock goals for 1985 would require grain imports of from 50 to 60 million tons.

However, seen from the situation in mid-1982, even if feed supplies were freely available, neither the Eleventh Plan nor the 1985 goal is achievable. For 1981 and 1982 both meat and milk production have been well below the levels required to meet the 1981-85 goals. To meet the 1981–85 goal of 17.25 million tons of meat would require production of more than 18.5 million tons for each of the last three years of the plan. With production 15.2 million tons in 1981 and approximately the same amount in 1982, expanding output so rapidly is not possible. The probable meat production for 1981–85 is of the order of 16 million to 16.5 million tons, with the lower figure more likely. Milk output will probably miss the Eleventh Plan goal by almost 10 percent; in fact, milk production for 1981–85 may be no more than for 1976–80. Egg production should meet all the goals set for the 1980s.

Even with favorable climatic conditions the Twelfth Plan goal for meat production will not be met, nor is it likely that the milk production goal will be met, though that may be a result of a revision of the goal that takes into account fuller utilization as food of the available supplies of milk. Meat production of 18 million tons, plus or minus a half million tons, could be achieved for 1986–90. This would permit about a 10 percent increase in per capita meat consumption relative to 1980.

GRAIN AND FEED IMPORTS

If the grain production projections for average weather are accepted for the remainder of the 1980s, as well as the rough projections of livestock output, feed grain imports in substantial quantities will be required throughout the 1980s. Precise estimates of grain imports are not possible, and a considerable amount of judgment and speculation is required. For 1983–85 it seems reasonable that grain imports would average 30 million to 35 million tons. For the remainder of the decade, for the livestock production that I have projected, grain imports could be somewhat less, perhaps 25 million to 30 million tons. However, if Soviet officials attempt to increase meat production to the 20 million ton level, grain imports could average as much as 40 million tons for 1986–90. It should be noted that increasing grain availability for feed by 15 million tons would add only 4 percent to the feed supply each year during the late 1980s.

THE CENTRAL NONBLACK SOIL
ZONE PROGRAM

Soviet agricultural scientists and the leadership both believe that the region classified as the Central Nonblack Soil Zone offers substantial potential for expansion of agricultural production, especially for meat and milk products. Khrushchev gave emphasis to the region, and the 1965 agricultural policy measures gave considerable weight to the potential of the area. In 1974 the current leadership announced a major program for the region, though limited to the part of the Central Nonblack Soil Zone in the Russian Republic and extending into Belorussia and the Baltic Republics.

The zone is enormous in size, amounting to 2.8 million square kilometers, an area the size of the United States east of the Mississippi River. As our climatic analogies indicate, much of the region is similar in terms of climate to Michigan, Wisconsin, Minnesota, and Manitoba. While the soils are of rather poor quality, moisture is generally adequate for production of feed crops, potatoes, and vegetables. The performance of agriculture in Belorussia and the Baltic Republics during the past two decades indicates that the output potential is significant, if proper farming practices are followed and adequate levels of inputs such as lime and fertilizer are applied. Substantial investments in land improvements are required to realize the potential, and the RNGZ plan, (for the Central Nonblack Soil Zone in the Russian Republic) appears to provide sufficient funds for these purposes. The program, inaugurated in 1974, was reemphasized and strengthened in 1981.

However great the promise and the potential of the program may be, its agricultural performance during 1976–80 can only be described in pessimistic terms. Substantial investments were made during those years, though there is some question about the quality of the work. If 1976–80 average production levels are compared to 1971–75, the following percentages emerge:

Grain	110
Meat	107.5
Milk	101.1
Eggs	131
Potatoes	81.5
Flax	75
Gross Agricultural Output	103.4

The increase in gross agricultural output was only a little more than a third of the 9 percent increase for the USSR for the same period.

Whatever may be the potential for improvement of agricultural performance in the zone, one must conclude that the region will not make any significant contribution to Soviet agricultural output during the remainder of the 1980s. In fact, there is some evidence that the region will continue to lag behind the rest of the USSR in output growth, due at least in part to the rapid loss of the younger members of the farm labor force that is likely to continue.

The potential of the zone probably cannot be realized with the current organizational structure of agriculture. Some form of highly decentralized farming, perhaps even private farming, may be required, as well as major investments in roads, drainage, irrigation, land leveling, rock removal, and other forms of land improvements. Machinery especially adapted to the region would be highly desirable; field sizes are small, and the large machinery common in Soviet agriculture is ill adapted to the conditions of the zone.

I do not suggest that the Soviet state give up ownership of the land, but that it devise a form of tenure that will result in better relationships between machine, land, nature, and man than prevails. Successful farming under the conditions of the nonblack soil zone requires painstaking and intelligent attention to detail, hard work, initiative, and appropriate combinations of inputs. Productive effort must be differentially rewarded, compared to the mere putting in of time, which now seems the pattern.

ROADS, THE CORNER GROCER, AND
THE PRICE SYSTEM

Careful reading of the numerous provisions of the USSR Food Program helps explain the serious state of Soviet agriculture and rural life. Most points relate to particular disadvantages of rural life, though the reason for one quite remarkable policy development in an economy with a per capita income at the USSR level prevails throughout the economy. At one point Brezhnev noted the significant social and cultural difference between the city and the countryside and the large investment required to reduce the difference:

> Measures for the social restructuring of the countryside are an organic part of the Food Program. This means the construction of well-appointed housing, mainly of the farmstead type, with outbuildings for personal auxiliary farming. The construction of schools, children's preschool institutions, and clubs will be expanded. Medical, trade, and consumer services to the rural population are being improved.
>
> There is no need to prove that the more energetically and thoroughly we engage in the construction of housing, cultural and consumer-service facilities, and roads in the countryside, the more productive peasant labor will become. Therefore, we plan to channel roughly 160 billion rubles into these purposes in the 1980s. This is a large number, even on our scale. But it's not only a large number. It's a major policy aimed at effacing the social differences between city and countryside—and, hence, at

implementing one of our programmatic demands, scientifically substantiated by Marxism-Leninism. (Prolonged applause.)[10]

There may be many more low and unprofitable farms than outsiders might have imagined. The Program includes forgiveness of 9.7 billion rubles of bank loans, postponement of repayment of 11.1 billion rubles until 1990, and waiving interest on the deferred loans. The magnitude of the loans—almost 21 billion rubles—is very great indeed.

The new program recognized the lack of commercial facilities to serve rural people. One element in a program to improve social and living conditions in the countryside was "To ensure a 100% increase in the sales volume of consumer services in rural localities over the decade." Reference was also made to the need to increase the number of self-service laundries, repair shops, outpatient clinics, pharmacies and "to strengthen the instructional facilities of rural schools."

The problems of rural roads and transportation were also addressed in the following resolutions: "To organize reliable transportation connections between collective farms and state farms and district centers. During the decade, to build in rural localities approximately 130,000 kilometers of general-use motor roads and 150,000 kilometers of intrafarm roads."[11] This is an enormous program, with a cost of billions of rubles. But an economist in the Ministry of Agriculture in 1978 noted that this program would do little more than make a good start in providing adequate roads for rural areas. Yu A. Mezhberg concluded that it was necessary to build 900,000 to 1,000,000 kilometers of paved roads at a cost of 120 billion rubles in a fifteen-year program.[12] At the rate of construction envisaged in the Food Program, it will be well into the next century before the task of providing paved roads through the rural areas will have been completed.

The Program further stated as its objective: "To systematically increase the total length of rural bus lines, so that by 1990 almost all central settlements of collective farms and state farms will have bus connections with district centers."[13] This commitment is not so strong or complete as it may seem. "Central settlements" may refer to the headquarters of the farms. There are less than 50,000 farms, but there are more than 400,000 rural settlements. Conse-

quently, even at the end of the decade the majority of rural settlements may not be served by a bus line.

The last point is perhaps the most remarkable of all. One systematic relationship observed in rural areas all over the world as
economic development (increasing real incomes) occurs is that the
importance of payment "in kind" declines and eventually nearly
disappears. At very low levels of real income a large fraction of the
income of farm workers is in food products produced on the farm
where the service is performed. But as real incomes increase and
the economy becomes more monetized, payment in kind becomes
less efficient and desirable and gradually diminishes. But not so in
modern Russia. Why? Brezhnev approached the topic in this way:

> Many letters received by the CPSU Central Committee note
> that in recent years the significance of payment in kind has been
> clearly underestimated. This has a negative effect on the inter-
> ests of collective farmers and state farm workers, weakens the
> basis for the development of personal auxiliary farming, and nar-
> rows the possibilities of collective farm markets.
>
> Therefore, provision has been made to expand the practice of
> payment in kind. Thus, workers in brigades and teams that grow
> grain crops will receive, free of charge, up to 15 percent of the
> grain that is grown over and above the plan. It is suggested that
> all permanent employees, as well as citizens recruited for the
> harvest, be issued grain as part of their earnings. Authorization
> has been given to issue to state farm personnel, as well as to
> other citizens who take part in the growing and harvesting of
> potatoes, vegetables, fruit, berries, grapes, melons, and feed
> crops, up to 15 percent of the output obtained under the plan
> and, for output above the plan, a figure to be set by the farms. It
> is recommended that collective farms use the same procedure.[14]

The Food Program covered the topic very briefly: "To increase
the amounts of payments in kind to collective farmers and state
farm workers, above all grain, fruits, vegetables and feed."[15]

In-kind payments can provide a positive incentive for work only
when money has lost a good part of its value, either because goods
and services are not readily available or because there is a dual
price system with the prices in one part of the system significantly
higher than in the other. The dual system has the characteristic
that a wide range of goods is readily available in the system with
the higher prices, and few goods can be found in the one with the

lower stated prices. The real value of in-kind payments compared to money is an indicator of the degree of suppressed inflation existing in the USSR. Brezhnev apparently recognized, perhaps inadvertently, that in-kind payments are desired because such payments are worth more than the money that the farmers would otherwise receive. One argument that Brezhnev gave for the negative consequences of having reduced in-kind payments was that to have done so "narrows the possibilities of collective farm markets." What Brezhnev did not mention is that he had a major role in increasing the importance of money wages to collective farm members and reducing the importance of in-kind payments, all in the name of social and economic progress.

THE FUTURE OF RURAL COMMUNITIES

Over the years various schemes for the restructuring of the countryside have appeared. Khrushchev set out to build agrogorods—urban type settlements. However, the enormous investment required and peasant resistance defeated him. In recent years nearly 350,000 small rural communities have been designated "futureless."[16] Their population numbers more than 15 million; of these almost 14 million were in communities where the bulk of the population engages in agriculture. Almost a sixth of the rural population lives in communities so designated. Apparently all settlements with less than 200 residents are futureless communities, and some with a larger population may also be cast into limbo. Once a community is designated futureless, steps are apparently taken to ensure there is no future. *Pravda* on March 5, 1982 carried a story about a futureless town of 300 people just 40 kilometers from Alma-Ata. It lacks a kindergarten; its children have to walk 3 kilometers to school. It is a half hour's walk to a water pump. A canal that earlier permitted the spring rains to run off is now silted, and spring floods are a frequent occurrence. "There's no denying that the future looks gloomy now for many futureless villages. Nearly 40% of Alma-Ata Province's 300 communities—with a total of 62,000 inhabitants—have been assigned to this category. But here is an interesting fact: In the past 10 years not a single one of these villages has disappeared from the province map. This indicates that the resettlement of the inhabitants of small villages is not a rapid process and must not be artificially rushed. . . ." But since this village, named Kuldzhin-skoye, "is futureless and its population is subject to resettlement," it finds itself in a state of limbo. As a futureless village "capital outlays will not be spent for constructing buildings and other facilities there. . . ."

How much loyalty, dedication, and hard work can a society expect when it washes its hands of 350,000 communities and 15 million people? An additional quotation from Boris Mozhayev, the author of rural prose cited earlier, emphasizes the fragility of rural life:

> It is time to make it clear that the rural way of life that has been conceived and established over the ages (I am referring to the good villages) has never tolerated and will not tolerate absurd and careless treatment. Every element in it—including the type of house and the place where it is built—is important to rural life, including rural culture. The social life of the old village and its spiritual climate were very stable and served to unify the peasants and give them a strong sense of communal identity. Everything played its role, from traditional children's games, which taught skills, comradeship and healthy rivalry, to the well-orchestrated sequence of Russian holidays, whose rituals, developed over the course of centuries, served to reinforce people's sense of common ties. Of course, the old rural way of life and the type of social intercourse associated with it either are ending or already have ended. But the people who plan life in the countryside must think about how all this can be replaced in order to prevent the spiritual ties among rural people from being broken. We must seek forms of intercourse among rural residents that are based on actual labor relations. It is important to develop and legally sanction a whole system of measures for affecting rural culture, everyday life, and upbringing. We need more specially trained rural cultural workers, of which there are presently very few. The place where the distinctions between city and countryside should be eliminated is not in the fields but on the collective farm street. Rural residences should be on a par with urban residences, and the Palaces of Culture on remote collective farms should not be inferior in terms of either facilities or program to those of urban factories. There must be a uniform system of rural construction for the entire land. Activities must be planned to take the place of the old holidays, rituals and public performances—to serve, as they once did, to bring people together and alternate work with interludes of recreation and celebration. What is needed is a system, and not just spontaneous amateur cultural activities.[17]

Farm people, whether living in futureless settlements or normal villages and towns, would find much greater satisfaction with their lives and circumstances if Soviet officials understood the lessons so well stated and acted in response to the lessons. If such had been the case for the past several decades, Soviet agriculture would today be performing much closer to its potential than it is.

IS SOCIALIST AGRICULTURE
THE PROBLEM?

I argued earlier that the agricultural potential of the nonblack soil zone could not be realized with the current organizational structure of agriculture. This does not mean that the Soviet state must give up the ownership of the land. In other words, the primary means of production could remain the property of the people as a whole.

Many potential improvements in the performance of agriculture could be realized in a socialist framework. But Soviet officials have shown a remarkable narrowness of vision in considering ways of making socialist agriculture more productive. They have talked of giving farms greater initiative for a quarter of a century; nothing happens. Prices are reformed, but livestock production remains the least profitable. Yet it is livestock output shortfalls that present the greatest social and economic problems to the economy.

As yet no solution has risen to the problem of relating effort and reward within the structure of socialist agriculture. For this reason peasants show much greater interest in private plot activities than in participation in either the collective or state farms. However, there is no reason people cannot be rewarded on the basis of their contribution to production, even within the structure of collective or state farms. The Chinese have been far more imaginative than the Soviets. Until such relationships are created, Soviet agriculture is going to be short of labor, inefficient, and high cost. Much more is required before Soviet agriculture can overcome its major shortcomings, but until labor is adequately rewarded most other changes will have little effect.

The Food Program provides a glimmer of hope, though one must hasten to add that the proposal to relate reward to the contribution of work is still in the stage of formulation and has a familiar ring of ideas that have been around for at least two decades, and even since Marx.

Immediately following the admonition to increase payments in kind, the Food Program specified that various governmental agencies "are to work out and implement, in branches of the agro-industrial complex, measures for the wide-scale introduction of methods of the organization of labor and incentives that will ensure a close connection between the earnings of personnel and the final results of the agricultural year. To disseminate the experience of work according to brigade contracts, as well as of the work of teams paid according to a job rate-plus-bonus system for output." It would appear that there will now be an effort to introduce something similar to the link or *zveno* system that was so widely heralded as a panacea nearly two decades ago. Under this system a small group of workers were allocated land, machinery, and other inputs and received their incomes on the basis of the outcome of the resources they controlled.

What organizations were changed with working out these matters? If it were not such a serious matter, one could imagine a satirist had drawn up the following list: the Union-Republic Councils of Ministers, the USSR Ministry of Agriculture, the USSR Ministry of Fruit and Vegetable Farming, the USSR State Committee for the Supply of Production Equipment to Agriculture, the USSR Ministry of Procurements, the USSR State Committee on Labor and Social Questions, and the All-Union Central Council of Trade Unions. Would it not have been simpler to tell the farms they could introduce the team system and let them work it out? Apparently, the farms cannot be trusted in this matter, as in so many, many others.

While it is true that a socialist agriculture could be made into an efficient agriculture, there is little prospect that this will be the outcome in the USSR in the reasonably near future. The Food Program did nothing to eliminate or soften the major sources of inefficiency in the organizational structure of agriculture. Only time will tell if the increased attention to the agricultural input and marketing sectors will make these sectors more responsive to the needs of the farms. Past experience indicates that improvement will be modest, at best.

PART II

PRODUCTIVITY IN SOVIET AGRICULTURE

KAREN McCONNELL BROOKS

Introduction

In Part I, D. Gale Johnson has presented an overview of the organization of Soviet agriculture and an evaluation of past performance and future prospects. A conclusion of his discussion is that yields in the livestock sector, both of animal products per animal and forage feeds per hectare, lag considerably behind those of Europe and North America. Soviet grain yields, however, do not lag appreciably behind those in climatically comparable areas of North America, particularly if the differential use of fallow land is included in the comparative calculations.

A fuller view of Soviet agricultural performance can be seen when not only yields but also resources used to achieve the yields are compared for climatically comparable areas within and outside the USSR. Yields result from the application of labor and purchased inputs to land, and optimal yields depend on the costs of inputs relative to each other, and to output prices. Where land is plentiful and cheap and labor and purchased inputs relatively expensive, the economically optimal yield per hectare may be far from the maximum achievable under the best known technology.

The observed yield depends on both the choice of technology and the efficiency with which the chosen technology is applied. Economic efficiency in production can be achieved if opportunities for world trade are taken into account in determining the level of domestic production, if input proportions are chosen to

I would like to thank D. Gale Johnson, Yair Mundlak, and T.W. Schultz for research direction and helpful comments on the manuscript. Arcadius Kahan helped and encouraged me throughout most of this project, and I am sorry that I could not share the results with him. Participants in the agricultural economics workshop at the University of Chicago commented on the work at several stages. John Antle generously shared his computer program with me. Vaclav Laska in Regenstein Library at the University of Chicago and the Slavic bibliographers at the University of Illinois in Champaign-Urbana helped me find materials.

117

minimize the cost of production of that level of output, and if production is technically efficient.

In the following sections, the technical efficiency of Soviet agriculture is compared to that of climatically similar areas outside the country, in an effort better to understand how resources are used in Soviet agriculture. That Soviet agriculture has over the past fifteen years absorbed large quantities of labor and capital with disappointing results is common knowledge both within and outside the Soviet Union. The comparison of output per unit input in the Soviet Union with that of agriculture in climatically similar areas of North America indicates that total factor productivity in the non-Soviet areas is between one and a half and twice that of the USSR. In other words, if factors used in Soviet agricultural production have the same opportunity costs as do comparable factors in the non-Soviet areas of the sample, Soviet agricultural output is about one and a half times or twice as expensive as that produced in climatically similar parts of North America.

In two important respects this is a conservative estimate of the productivity difference. The data used in the study cover the years from 1960 through 1979. Thus, only one of the four most recent consecutive bad years that have served to focus so much attention on Soviet agriculture is included in the comparison. The agricultural inputs included in the productivity comparison are land, labor, machinery, fertilizer, and animals. Much of the capital invested in Soviet agriculture in the past fifteen years has been used for construction, particularly of livestock facilities. Soviet accounting and reporting practices make it very difficult to derive a measure of the value of agricultural structures that can be used in cross-country comparisons. For this reason, the investment in construction that has yielded the low returns frequently noted in Soviet commentaries is excluded from the comparison. These exclusions should be kept in mind in evaluating the productivity comparisons, as should the ordinary difficulties that make cross-country comparisons approximate, at best.

D. Gale Johnson has outlined some of the probable explanations for the observed difference in total factor productivity in the first part of this volume. Reasons discussed include bureaucratic interference in farm decision making, poor quality inputs, lack of a smoothly functioning system of supply of off-farm inputs, and distorted price incentives. In this section, the system by which farm laborers are assigned to work and are paid is examined as an impediment to technical efficiency. A well functioning agricultural labor market, or an equivalent substitute, is necessary for efficient allocation of labor when agricultural technology is changing relatively little, but it becomes even more important when large numbers of agricultural workers are leaving agriculture and rural areas for nonagricultural jobs. The extent to which the Soviet agricultural labor market has been able to cope with the demands of industrialization and demographic change is the subject of the final section.

CHAPTER NINE

The Technical Efficiency
of Soviet Agriculture

A production process that is technically efficient allows maximum output from a set of inputs, given the current state of knowledge of how inputs are transformed into outputs. Alternatively, in a technically efficient enterprise, a given output cannot be produced with a smaller quantity of one or all inputs. In the vocabulary of production functions, technically efficient production takes place on the efficiency frontier. The production function expresses output as a function of inputs, and the efficiency frontier is represented by the function situated in output space farthest from the input axes. It shows the maximum output that can be produced from any given bundle of inputs with the current knowledge of production processes.

Technical efficiency is thus defined in such a way that we need never worry about how to recognize it. We do not know the maximum output that can be produced from given inputs: we know only what we see. Thus, if we estimate aggregate production functions for two economies and find that one function lies everywhere above the other, we cannot conclude that the more productive economy is operating on the efficiency frontier. We can conclude, however, that the less productive economy is not, providing that the functions are properly specified and estimated.

Measurement of relative technical efficiency is not an exercise that economists often undertake, because under competitive conditions bankruptcy acts as a disciplinary sanction against gross technical inefficiency. The more interesting economic questions are those that relate to economic optimality, such as the choice of factor proportions and the allocation of domestic consumption between imports and domestic production. In evaluating Soviet agriculture, however, a rough quantitative understanding of technical efficiency relative to comparable non-Soviet areas is useful. Underlying the specific goals stated in each of the recent five-year plans are two more fundamental objectives of Soviet agricultural policy: increased output and reduced costs of production. A better understanding of the technical efficiency of Soviet agriculture helps in evaluating the likelihood that either or both of these objectives can be achieved.

Leonid Brezhnev stated in his presentation of the new Food Program in May 1982 that domestic self-sufficiency in food is a goal to which the Soviet government attaches great importance. The grain imports of recent years remind Soviet citizens that this goal has not yet been met, in spite of its professed high priority. The domestic political sensitivity of grain imports is largely of the government's own making, but it is very real, nonetheless. Vodka is affectionately referred to by some Moscow punsters as "kolos Ameriki" (grain of America), a pun on "golos Ameriki" (Voice of America). The grain boycott and the upsurge of popular protest in Poland further stimulate official concern.

Output can be increased either by allocating more resources to agriculture or by increasing the productivity of inputs already in use. In practice, any growth strategy combines the two sources of output increase, but the two can be separated conceptually as movements along the production function (allocating more variable inputs) or shifts in the function (greater productivity from the same inputs.) If all inputs, including land, can be increased so that the production process is replicated, then output is increased, but neither the location of the production function in output space nor the position of the economy on the production function is affected as long as aggregate returns to scale are equal to unity. Large-scale settlement of new lands was a major component of agricultural output growth in the USSR during the 1950s and early 1960s, when the new lands in Kazakhstan and the southern part of the Russian Republic were settled. However, it is not considered an option for future growth.

The strategy of increased application of variable inputs to a fixed input (land) is discussed in the Soviet literature as "intensification" of production. This strategy, in a static economy without technological progress, is characterized by diminishing returns to the variable inputs and increasing costs of output. Thus, the marked increase in costs of production in recent years, when adjusted for increased prices of purchased inputs, is a predictable accompaniment to output growth resulting from increased application of variable inputs to relatively fixed inputs, in the absence of cost-reducing technological progress. It is a cost of domestic self-sufficiency and slow technological change, and not by itself a sign that farm managers and workers are not doing their jobs.

Increasing costs can be mediated by technological change that shifts the production function, and it is here that technical efficiency is of interest. As marginal costs of output rise with greater use of variable factors, anything that results in greater output from the same inputs, in particular from the inputs in shortest supply, has a high payoff. Success in research and experimentation in new varieties, new inputs, and new cultivation practices shift the production function outward and make possible achievement of increased output per unit input.

An economy known to be operating on the efficiency frontier has no option other than the discovery of new techniques to achieve reduced costs of production. An economy known not to be operating on the efficiency frontier can also invest in research that pushes the frontier out, but it is likely to realize higher returns by undertaking research and economic reform that would close the gap separating it from the efficiency frontier. It can "catch up and overtake," as Khrushchev put it. "Catching up" is not much talked about these days, but "mobilizing internal reserves" is.

The complementarity between agronomical research and economic reform is recognized in Soviet literature and is well expressed in a recent work on agricultural economics published by Moscow State University:

> Of the varied factors [affecting] increased efficiency of agricultural production, of special significance are, first, faster paced scientific-technological progress and the all-around industrialization of production; and, second, improvements in the mechanism of economic management. The first direction encompasses the so-called production-technical factors of increased efficiency in agricultural production, and the second,— the social-economic. The increased provision of equipment to agriculture, its all-around industrialization, and the use of the accomplishments of scientific-technical progress open wide possibilities for growth in efficiency of production. But these are simply potential possibilities. Their realization depends on the management mechanism.[1]

The finding that total factor productivity in Soviet agriculture is about a half or two-thirds that in comparable areas of North America should be both good and bad news for Soviet policy makers, if it is news at all. It indicates potential, at least, for significant improvement in performance, if the needed mix of applied research and policy change are implemented. This improvement could take the form of increased output from inputs currently used in agriculture, a saving of inputs used to produce the current level of output, or a combination of both. The productivity comparison also indicates that returns to greater investment in agricultural production and research will probably continue to be low if reforms are not undertaken.

Productivity is measured in this study as total factor productivity through the estimation of production functions. For the purpose of comparing efficiency, total factor productivity is preferable to partial measures, such as yields or labor productivity, because factors are substitutable in production. In the productivity comparison, a function for the Soviet and non-Soviet samples is jointly estimated. The coefficients of the inputs must equal in the two samples, but the intercepts, or levels, of the functions are allowed to vary.

CLIMATE AND SOVIET AGRICULTURE

The comparison of productivity is valid only if data on outputs and inputs for the Soviet and non-Soviet areas can be converted into comparable units, and if the areas that comprise the Soviet and non-Soviet samples are well matched in terms of natural conditions. Annual time series of published agricultural data are available for the fifteen Soviet republics from 1960 to the present, and this study uses the twenty years between 1960 and 1979. The Soviet sample consists of pooled time series and cross section observations for the fifteen Soviet republics. The non-Soviet sample includes the ten American states of Minnesota, North Dakota, South Dakota, Nebraska, Montana, Colorado, New Mexico, Arizona, Utah, and Nevada; the Canadian provinces of Ontario, Manitoba, Saskatchewan, and Alberta; and Finland.

No place in the non-Soviet sample is intended as a direct analogue to a particular Soviet republic. However, the non-Soviet sample as a whole includes the wheat belt of North America to correspond to the Soviet wheatlands and steppes; the moist dairy and mixed farming regions of Minnesota, Ontario, and Finland to correspond to the Baltic republics, Belorussia, and the northwestern provinces of the Russian Republic; and the rangelands, fruit and vegetable areas, and irrigated agriculture of Colorado, New Mexico, Arizona, Utah, and Nevada to correspond to the Soviet Caucasus and Central Asia. The non-Soviet sample was chosen on the basis of work on climatic analogues done by D. Gale Johnson in the 1950s, and discussed in Part I of this volume.[2] The objective of that study was to find non-Soviet areas similar climatically to regions of the USSR for which yield data on specific grain crops were available, so that Soviet and non-Soviet yields could be compared while holding climatic conditions constant. Most of the analogues chosen were crop reporting districts in the United States that correspond climatically to oblasts in the USSR. Climate analogues can be chosen on this small geographic scale with some confidence, but it is very unlikely that geographic units as large as states, provinces, or republics would be similar enough to serve as direct analogues. Yet it is for states, provinces, and republics, and not for smaller geographic units, that the input and output data are available. Forming the samples from the larger geographic units that encompass the direct climatic analogues thus only partially accounts for the different natural conditions in the Soviet and non-Soviet areas. A variable representing climatic conditions directly is included in the estimations to compensate for the deficiencies in sample selection.

There is little controversial in the proposition that the states, provinces, and one country in the non-Soviet sample have natural environments similar to those of the Soviet republics. A writer reporting on grain production in North America in the Soviet journal *Zernovoe khoziaistvo* (Grain Farming) in 1980 chose almost identical climatic analogues.[3]

The Soviet sample includes the entire USSR. The non-Soviet sample excludes almost all of the American Corn Belt, plus the good agricultural land in the southeast and in California. The absence of a corn belt is clearly a handicap for Soviet agriculture, but one that should not be exaggerated. Many of the areas comparable climatically to regions in the USSR are traditionally strong agricul-

tural producers. In addition, the high latitude of much Soviet agricultural land is not an unmitigated penalty against crop production. Under proper management, the long day length can compensate to a degree for a short growing season. In a discussion of
potential photosynthetic activity in different parts of the world,
J.H. Chang writes:

> Therefore the climatic resources in these high latitude areas of
> high potential photosynthesis can be best utilized by crops with
> a short growing season, a low minimum threshold temperature, a
> moderate saturation light intensity, and a moderate leaf area in-
> dex. The latitudinal belt between 50 degrees and 60 degrees N
> in Western Europe leads the world in wheat yield per unit area
> and many vegetables grow to huge proportions in the north-
> lands.[4]

Yields depend on cultural practices, as well as climate, but it appears that northern location confers benefits as well as problems
for agricultural production.

A measure of the total photosynthetic potential of each sample
area is included in the estimations in order explicitly to capture
climatic diversity within the sample. Agroclimatologists have not
had much success in describing empirically the relationship between climate or weather and agricultural production, even for
specific crops.[5] This is in part because plant growth responds not
only to the quantities of heat, sunlight, and moisture available, but
also to their timing. Because different crops thrive under different
conditions and can be grown with varying agricultural techniques,
it becomes even more difficult to rank climatic regimes according
to their potential for agricultural production. Nevertheless, few
would argue with the assertion that the Ukraine is more favorably
endowed for agriculture than is Kazakhstan. Proper specification
of production functions requires recognition of this difference in
endowment. Since we cannot define specifically the climatic
difference between the Ukraine and Kazakhstan that we wish to
capture, the measure derived is bound to be crude. However, if
the measure allows a relative ranking of the natural conditions in
the thirty Soviet and non-Soviet sample areas of the joint sample,
and if the ranking is consistent with common sense and performs
acceptably statistically, its crudeness will be excusable.

One such composite measure of the natural environment has been developed by Buringh, van Heemst, and Staring in their study of the potential food production of the world.[6] They divide the world into broad soil zones. For each soil zone, they calculate the potential production of dry matter in kilograms per hectare per year in roots, stems, leaves, flowers, and fruits in a cereal crop, assuming that all other conditions are optimal and that plant growth is limited only by the amount of solar energy available in that location. They then introduce a number of reduction factors to account for suboptimal conditions specific to that location. The re-duction factors of principal importance for this study are those for soil quality and moisture availability.

The potential dry matter, when multiplied by the relevant re-duction factors, serves as a composite measure of the agro-climatological potential of a region. For example, the potential dry matter (PDM) of the wheatlands in North Dakota is 34. In the good black soil of this region, the factor of soil condition is high (0.9), but there is little moisture, so the factor of water reduction is low (0.6). The factor of water reduction is the limiting factor, and the modified PDM for this part of North Dakota is 20.4. Buringh, van Heemst, and Staring assume that on irrigated lands, the factor of soil condition is uniformly 0.8, since poor quality soils will not generally be worth irrigating.

The Buringh, van Heemst, and Staring data for soil zones were transferred to the political units that make up the Soviet and non-Soviet sample by weighting the PDM of each soil zone in, for example, a state, by the cultivated area in that zone. For reasons explained in the appendix, the Buringh, van Heemst, and Staring data for the Soviet Union presented an unrealistically high mea-sure of the agroclimatological potential of several Soviet republics and would have burdened the Soviet sample with a spurious handicap. An alternative to the Buringh, van Heemst, and Staring data for the USSR is provided in a study by V. V. Egorov, who ranks the Soviet republics using a methodology similar to that of Buringh, van Heemst, and Staring, but in different units.[7] Buringh, van Heemst, and Staring's PDM and Egorov's index were merged to derive the climate variable shown in Table 9.1. Details on the derivation of the climate variable are contained in the appendix.

The climate variable is constructed to capture differences in av-

TABLE 9.1

Climate Variable

Soviet Republics[a]		Non-Soviet Areas	
RSFSR	19.14	Finland	12.77
Ukraine	20.90	Minnesota	25.95
Lithuania	20.37	North Dakota	17.95
Latvia	18.27	South Dakota	14.29
Estonia	17.39	Nebraska	25.48
Georgia	20.37	Montana	14.67
Azerbaidzhan	21.95	Colorado	20.68
Armenia	18.97	New Mexico	20.11
Uzbekistan	28.28	Arizona	33.07
Kirghizia	20.37	Utah	24.60
Tadzhikstan	20.90	Nevada	37.48
Turkmenia	44.08	Ontario	26.26
Kazakhstan	15.28	Manitoba	19.56
Belorussia	21.25	Saskatchewan	16.60
Moldavia	25.12	Alberta	16.75
Unweighted Average	22.18		21.75

Sources: See text and appendix.

[a]There is no order in the listing of Soviet and non-Soviet areas, and no two areas are intended as direct climatic analogues.

erage agroclimatological conditions in cross section, and is constant in time series. Since the climate variable has a rather tortuous derivation, it cannot really claim to be much more than common sense with two decimal places. Perhaps the problem with such a variable is that only those estimating production functions really need it, and such a limited market discourages those who could produce a higher quality measure.

The purpose of the climate variable is to capture climatic differences within and between the Soviet and non-Soviet samples, to compensate for imperfect matching of the two samples, and to separate, to some degree at least, the measure of the quantity of land from its quality. Even if it cannot be justified scientifically, the climate variable probably does its job fairly well. Kazakhstan is ranked lower than the Ukraine and a bit lower than Saskatchewan. This is appropriate because northern Kazakhstan receives on the average between 50 and 100 mm less precipitation annually than does Saskatchewan. About 15 percent of Kazakh cultivated area is in the mountains and the southern part of the republic, and 30 percent of this is irrigated. Arizona ranks higher than New Mexico because more of Arizona is irrigated. Nebraska and Moldavia are ranked almost equally, and each is above the Ukraine. South Dakota is ranked slightly lower than Kazakhstan.

The climate variable constructed for this study and shown in Table 9.1 is an attempt to represent long-term climatic conditions. An important component of climate not captured by this variable is the annual fluctuation in weather conditions around long term trends. It has been argued that Soviet agricultural practices, in particular the lesser use of clean fallow in grain production, make agricultural output more vulnerable to annual fluctuations in weather than would be the case if alternative techniques were used. In an interesting study of climate and grain yields in the United States, Canada, the USSR, and Western Europe, Iu. L. Rauner presents the following data on the probability that grain yields will deviate from trend by the given percent for one, two, three, and four years in a row in the USSR, Canada, and the United States.

Rauner's probabilities are based on 175 years of data for the USSR, and about 100 years for the United States and Canada. According to these data, the probability that grain yields in Canada will be 20 percent below trend in a given year is 18 percent and the probability that yields will be that low for two years in a row is 3.7 percent. For the Asian territory of the USSR, the probabilities of yields 20 percent below trend for one and two years are twice as high as for Canada; 36 percent and 9 percent, respectively. The probabilities of bumper yields in the Asian part of the USSR are also about twice as high as for Canada. Thus, there is little doubt that yields are more variable in the Asian territory of the USSR than they are in Canada. Documentation of the difference in variability, however, tells little about causation.

Rauner's data do not include the bad years of the late 1970s and early 1980s. It is interesting to note that, according to his data, the probability that grain production would be 10 percent below trend for four years in a row is less than 1 percent. Yet, this apparently happened in 1979–1982. The low likelihood of this event based

TABLE 9.2

Variability in Grain Yields: USSR, U.S., and Canada

	% Deviation from Trend	Probability of Deviation Enduring t Years in a Row: t=			
		1	2	3	4
European USSR	+10	.25	.04	.01	.00
	−10	.30	.05	.01	.00
	+20	.04	.01	.00	.00
	−20	.08	.02	.007	.00
	+30	.00	.00	.00	.00
	−30	.03	.00	.00	.00
Asian USSR	+20	.32	.07	.02	.00
	−20	.36	.09	.03	.01
	+50	.04	.00	.00	.00
	−50	.05	.00	.00	.00
Simultaneously in both Asian and European USSR	−10	.15	.03	.005	.00
	+10	.06	.01	.00	.00
U.S.	+10 or more	.185	.028	.00	.00
	−10 or less	.210	.038	.00	.00
Canada	+10 or more	.290	.075	.012	.00
	−10 or less	.365	.10	.025	.00
	+20 or more	.145	.025	.00	.00
	−20 or less	.180	.037	.00	.00
U.S. and Canada simultaneously	[+10,+20]	.073	.000	.00	.00
	[−10,−20]	.085	.012	.00	.00

Source: Iu. L. Rauner, Klimat i urozhainost' zernovykh kul'tur (Moscow: Nauka, 1981), pp. 54,71.

on past experience adds to the puzzle of what has gone wrong besides the weather since the mid-1970s.

OUTPUT MIX AND INPUT USE IN SOVIET AGRICULTURE

A recurrent problem that inhibits inclusion of the USSR in comparative economic studies is that of converting Soviet data to units commensurate with those used in other parts of the world. Since the ruble is not convertible, it is unclear what exchange rate should be used in the valuation of output. In addition, domestic relative agricultural prices in the United States, Canada, Finland, and the USSR differ. Aggregation of agricultural output by domestic prices in the four countries and conversion of the aggregates according to exchange rates would invite distortion at two stages. This problem is not unique to studies involving the USSR or Eastern European countries; most studies based on aggregate data from many countries must solve the problem. Hayami and Ruttan, in their study of agricultural productivity, use an output index based on wheat relative prices, and a similar approach is used in the present study.[8] The price of a ton of wheat serves as the numeraire in each country, and the domestic prices of other commodities in the United States and the USSR relative to wheat in 1970 are the wheat relative prices for the non-Soviet and Soviet samples. The wheat relative prices are shown in Table 9.3.

The high price for corn relative to wheat in the non-Soviet sample is explained by the corn blight of 1970. This introduces a distortion, but not a large one, since there is relatively little corn in the sample. The normal Soviet relative purchase price for corn is even higher than the unusual U.S. 1970 price.

It is apparent from Table 9.3 that purchase prices for fiber are high in the USSR relative to the United States. Soviet prices for meat in 1970 were high, especially for poultry. Milk in the USSR in 1970 was priced lower relative to wheat than it was in the United States, but Soviet milk prices have been increased in recent years.

Gross output of the commodities listed in Table 9.3 in each of the thirty geographic units for each of the twenty years was aggregated first using Soviet wheat relative prices, then using U.S. wheat relative prices. The geometric mean of the two output aggregates was used as the measure of output. Thus, any peculiarities in domestic relative prices in the United States and the USSR are reflected in the output measure used for both parts of the sample.

Data on the production of each of the commodities are from official published sources. The Soviet data include official figures on private sector output. Soviet official output data are for "bunker weight" of the crop, and this is the weight in the truck as it comes off the field, before drying and cleaning. Soviet data on production of wheat, rye, corn, barley, oats, and millet were discounted 11

TABLE 9.3

Wheat Relative Prices, U.S. and USSR, 1970[a]

	USSR	U.S.		USSR	U.S.
		(Per Metric Ton)			
Wheat	1.00	1.00	Mixed Grains	.--	.85
Rye	1.07	.79			(Canada)
Corn	1.26	1.07	Swedes and Roots	.--	.78
					(Canada)
Barley	.77	.90	Rapeseed	.--	2.16
Oats	.69	.88			(Canada)
Millet	.87	.--	Buckwheat	.--	1.50
Rice	3.17	2.33			(Canada)
Potatoes	1.13	1.00	Dry Beans	.--	3.31
Fruits	3.08	2.90			(Canada)
Raw Cotton	5.50	3.10	Mustard Seed	.--	1.69
Sugar Beets	.31	.38			(Canada)
Sunflowers	2.04	2.60	Peanuts	.--	5.19
Vegetables	1.64	1.79	Beef,		
Soybeans	2.52	2.14	slaughter weight	26.55	21.79
Tea	9.13	.--	Pork,		
Flax Fiber	1.96	.--	slaughter weight	27.06	17.68
Peas	2.06	1.97	Lamb,		
Flax Seed	4.15	1.93	slaughter weight	19.92	15.95
Castor Beans	7.77	4.16	Poultry	24.61	9.46
Sorghum	.--	.92	Milk	1.86	2.58
			Eggs (per 1000)	.98	.67
			Wool,		
			greasy basis	47.93	16.01

Source: Wheat relative prices adapted from data in Gregor Lazarcik, Comparative Levels of Agricultural Output and Purchasing Powers of Currencies for Agricultural Products of Eastern European Countries, USSR, and USA, 1959, 1966, and 1970, Occasional Papers of the Research Project on National Income in East Central Europe (New York: L.W. International Financial Research, Inc., 1975), pp. 47-50.

[a] U.S. price per metric ton of wheat, 1970: $48.87 (received by farmers). USSR price per metric ton of wheat, 1970: 103 rubles (paid to farms).

percent to account for different allowance for moisture and trash.[9]

In this measure of aggregate output, all commodities are assumed to be of the same quality in all sample units. No adjustment is made, for example, for different grades of wheat grown in different areas. For commodities that are themselves aggregates, such as fruits and vegetables, no adjustment is made for the different commodity mixes—apples and oranges are added by weight. Nor is adjustment made for varying quality of the same commodity; e.g., the sugar content of sugar beets or the oil content of sunflower seeds. The exclusion of quality considerations probably on balance benefits the Soviet Union. A possible exception is cotton.

In the first stage of analysis, gross agricultural output is used, with no subtraction for intermediate inputs, such as feed and seed consumed in the production process.

When output of the Soviet republics is aggregated first by Soviet domestic relative prices and then by U.S. domestic relative prices, the comparison of the two indices gives a view of which republics gain most from the Soviet agricultural price structure. Table 9.4 shows the ratio of average output over the twenty years aggregated in Soviet prices to that aggregated in American prices for each of the republics. Output in Soviet prices is higher than in American prices for each of the republics, but the real gainers from Soviet prices are the Central Asian republics of Uzbekistan, Kirghizia, Tadzhikstan, and Turkmenia.

TABLE 9.4

Relative Gains from the Soviet Agricultural Price Structure

(Ratio of Average Output in Soviet Domestic Prices
to American Domestic Prices)

RSFSR	1.07	Uzbekistan	1.45
Ukraine	1.05	Kirghizia	1.22
Lithuania	1.08	Tadzhikstan	1.37
Latvia	1.06	Turkmenia	1.53
Estonia	1.07	Kazakhstan	1.12
Georgia	1.07	Belorussia	1.08
Azerbaidzhan	1.21	Moldavia	1.07
Armenia	1.07		

Source: See text.

Standardization of output in wheat relative units allows an overview of the commodity mix produced in each of the thirty geographic units and suggests similarities and differences in the types of farming practiced. The proportions of the value of output in wheat units derived from the different commodities on average over the twenty sample years are shown in Table 9.5.

TABLE 9.5

Commodity Composition of Output

	Wht	Crn	OG	Sor	Bts	Sun	Pot	Cot	Soy	FV	Tea	Mt	Mlk[a]	Total
	(Twenty-Year Average Value in Wheat Units, in Percent)													
FIN	3	0	10	0	1	0	6	0	0	2	0	27	45	94
MIN	3	22	4	0	1	0	1	0	10	2	0	32	19	94
ND	29	2	15	0	2	2	5	0	1	0	0	31	7	94
SD	6	14	6	1	0	0	0	0	2	0	0	58	7	94
NEB	5	28	1	6	1	0	0	0	3	0	0	49	4	97
MONT	26	0	9	0	3	0	1	0	0	0	0	56	3	98
COL	8	6	2	1	5	0	4	0	0	4	0	60	6	96
NMEX	3	2	0	7	0	0	1	0	0	5	0	70	7	95
ARIZ	3	0	2	4	1	0	2	0	0	29	0	47	9	97
UTAH	5	1	4	0	3	0	2	0	0	5	0	48	22	90
NEV	2	0	1	0	0	0	0	0	0	0	0	83	11	97
ONT	2	8	7	0	0	0	2	0	0	0	0	43	25	87
MAN	18	0	16	0	1	0	1	0	0	0	0	39	8	83
SASK	56	0	17	0	0	0	0	0	0	0	0	11	5	89
ALB	19	0	23	0	1	0	1	0	0	0	0	40	8	92
RUS	10	1	7	0	2	1	12	0	0	5	0	31	22	91
UKR	7	3	4	0	7	3	11	0	0	9	0	30	19	93
LIT	1	0	5	0	1	0	14	0	0	5	0	41	27	94
LAT	1	0	5	0	1	0	15	0	0	5	0	38	31	96
EST	1	0	6	0	0	0	18	0	0	4	0	39	29	97
GRU	2	4	1	0	0	0	3	0	0	28	23	23	11	95
AZE	6	0	1	0	0	0	2	20	0	23	1	25	14	92
ARM	4	0	1	0	1	0	5	1	0	29	0	29	22	92
UZB	1	1	1	0	0	0	1	58	0	10	0	14	9	95
KIR	6	2	2	0	7	0	3	10	0	9	0	34	15	88
TAD	2	0	1	0	0	0	1	44	0	15	0	21	10	94
TUR	1	0	0	0	0	0	0	53	0	7	0	21	7	89
KAZ	25	0	6	0	1	0	3	1	0	3	0	36	15	90
BEL	1	0	6	0	1	0	29	0	0	5	0	31	23	96
MOL	4	9	1	0	5	5	2	0	0	33	0	25	11	95

Source: See text.

[a]Wht=Wheat, Crn=Corn, OG=Other Grains, Sor=Sorghum, Bts=Beets, Sun=Sunflower, Pot=Potatoes, Soy-Soybeans, FV=Fruits and Vegetables, Tea=Tea, Mt=Meat, Mlk=Milk, Cot=Cotton.

The commodities that are not grown in both the Soviet and non-Soviet samples stand out clearly. Cotton is the major crop in Soviet Central Asia, but it was virtually absent from the American southwest prior to the 1970s. Tea is important in Georgia, and nowhere else in the Soviet or non-Soviet sample. Soy and sorghum are grown in quantity only in the U.S., and sorghum is an important grain in the dry states of Nebraska, New Mexico, and Arizona. Rice is grown only in Soviet Central Asia. It is most important in Uzbekistan, where it constituted 2 percent of total output over the twenty-year period. Most of the North American Corn Belt has been excluded, but corn is still relatively more important in Minnesota, South Dakota, and Nebraska than it is in Moldavia, the Ukraine, and Georgia. One change announced in the recent Soviet Food Program for the 1980s is an increase in the corn area in these republics. Potatoes are more important in the Soviet than in the non-Soviet areas. The degree of specialization in livestock or crop production in the Soviet republics is lower than in the non-Soviet areas. Meat and milk production are closely tied in the USSR.

The agricultural inputs of interest in this study are land, labor, machinery, fertilizer, and animals. Inputs are defined in physical units, and so the problems of valuation are not so severe as is the case with output. However, the units of reporting of the inputs must be reconciled among the four systems of national accounts. A brief discussion of the definition and derivation of the input data follows. More detailed information and sources are included in the appendix.

Land is measured in thousands of hectares and includes cultivated land but excludes perennial pastures and grazing land. For the USSR, the variable includes cultivated land, including summer fallow, plus land devoted to perennial fruits. For North America, land is area planted to crops plus summer fallow. Because the use of summer fallow in the USSR differs from that in the northern United States and Canada, it is important that summer fallow be included in the land measure. Natural pastures and grazing lands are excluded because of the difficulty of determining what weights should be used in aggregating this poorer quality land with the higher quality, more intensively used land. Exclusion of grazing lands affects Montana, Colorado, New Mexico,

Arizona, Utah, Nevada, Uzbekistan, Kirgizia, Tadzhikstan, Turkmenia, and Kazakhstan. Thus, it is not a decision that has obvious implications for only the Soviet or the non-Soviet part of the sample.

The different national accounts are most difficult to reconcile for the labor data. According to the 1970 census, 50 percent of those employed in agriculture in the USSR are women, and so the labor variable must include workers of both sexes. In the USSR during much of the period from 1960 to 1979, many people included in the agricultural work force were fully employed only at peak seasons. At these times, the regular agricultural work force is supplemented by nonagricultural laborers assigned to agricultural work. In the United States, one of the characteristics of changing agriculture during this period has been the increase in part-time farming, which makes the agricultural labor statistics difficult to interpret. In this study I attempt to define the labor input in terms of days worked in agriculture. No adjustment is made for the differential quality of the labor force in different places, or for its change over time. The days worked may be of differing length, but the data do not permit adjustment for this over the sample period.

Soviet agricultural laborers work in collective and state farms and in the private sector. Employment figures for the collective and state farms are reported differently, and no meaningful labor data for the private sector are reported. Aggregate data show a consistent decline in the number of people employed in agriculture in the USSR. Between 1965 and 1979 agricultural employment declined from 25.8 million to 23.1 million people.[10] This is a relatively small decline. When days worked in agriculture are calculated, the aggregate decline in labor input is seen to have been modest over the twenty-year period. The data on days worked are derived from published indices of total output and output per day. Only agricultural labor on the farms is included. The data and details of their derivation are included in the appendix.

On the national level, days worked in agriculture on collective and state farms declined about 10 percent between 1960 and 1970, then roughly stabilized between 1970 and 1979. The data at five-year intervals for the republics and the national total are shown in Table 9.6.

The relative stability in the national totals of labor input in

TABLE 9.6

Days Worked in Socialized Agriculture (Millions)

	1960	1965	1970	1975	1979
RSFSR	2947	2755	2534	·2496	2347
Ukraine	1544	1471	1343	1279	1245 ·
Lithuania	94	94	77	68	70
Latvia	68	61	50	48	47
Estonia	33	30	25	25	24
Georgia	99	99	90	95	96
Azerbaidzhan	105	105	106	122	121
Armenia	48	49	44	46	49
Uzbekistan	330	343	379	423	406
Kirghizia	67	75	78	82	84
Tadzhikstan	77	75	79	87	· 83
Turkmenia	56	60	65	78	88
Kazakhstan	322	340	319	351	364
Belorussia	327	327	291	271	250
Moldavia	130	141	146	148	135
USSR	6247	6025	5626	5619	5409

Sources: See appendix and text.

socialized agriculture, particularly for the 1970s, is seen in Table 9.6 to reflect quite differing trends in the European and non-European republics. In the Baltic and Slavic republics, the decline in labor input has been on the order of 20 to 25 percent over the twenty years. In the Central Asian and Caucasian republics, the increase has been of approximately the same relative magnitude as the decline in the European republics.

The forces behind the divergent regional trends in agricultural labor use are both economic and demographic and are likely to persist into the future. As discussed more fully below, low birth rates and rapid increase in demand for nonagricultural labor in the European republics have resulted in an outflow of labor from agriculture quite consistent with that observed historically and currently in industrializing economies. High birth rates and slow creation of nonagricultural jobs in Central Asia and parts of the Caucasus, coupled with language barriers to interregional migration, have resulted in a buildup of the rural population in these areas. In addition, collective farms, rather than state farms, are more common in Central Asia than in the European republics, and collective farms have fewer defenses against absorption of excess labor.

The data on days worked shown in Table 9.6 include but do not explicitly show the significant increase in temporary agricultural labor over the period. In 1965 temporary workers worked about 2 percent of the total reported person-years in agriculture, and in 1979 the figure had risen to between 5 percent and 10 percent.[11] The temporary workers are students, nonagricultural state employees, and rural people not otherwise employed. The figure also includes full-time employees of collective farms who are not farm members, however, and this makes its interpretation more difficult. There is little dispute that the use of temporary workers has increased, particularly, but not only, in the areas where outmigration has been greatest. An interesting statement on the use of nonfarm workers for agricultural work is contained in an article in *Voprosy ekonomiki* (Problems of Economics) in 1981 by Ye. I. Manevich, and reproduced in *The Current Digest of the Soviet Press*:

> Enterprises tend to keep a certain amount of surplus manpower on hand so they will be able to send people to do seasonal agricultural work without jeopardizing plan fulfillment. The number of workers and office employees who are sent from nonagricultural branches of the economy to help out on farms during the harvest season has actually increased in recent years: In 1970 this figure was 40% higher than it was in 1960, and in 1978 it was 140% higher than in 1970. In 1979 15.6 million people (assuming each person did one month's work), including 7.8 million workers in material production, were diverted from their regular jobs to work on farms. In general, the agricultural output produced by these personnel is twice as costly as that produced by regular agricultural workers. Calculations show that the efficiency of the agricultural work done by industrial workers is only one-fourth of their efficiency at their normal workplaces. Furthermore, in 1979 the time lost by industrial workers traveling to and from temporary farm jobs totaled 7.8 million working days, assuming that only two days were spent on such travel—the total would be 15.6 million working days if the trip took four days, as is often the case. This is equivalent to the annual working time of 55,000 to 110,000 workers.[12]

The total average annual regular work force in agricultural enterprises in 1979 was 26.2 million people. About 10 percent of these were employed in nonagricultural activities. Thus, the supplementary seasonal work force of 15.6 million person-months probably represents between 5 percent and 10 percent of the total agricultural labor input. I assume in calculating total days worked from the official data that the temporary workers are included in the productivity and wage data.

The private sector must be included in Soviet aggregate labor input data, and private sector data are more difficult to acquire than are data on the socialized sector. The importance of the private sector varies considerably across republics, however, and exclusion of private sector labor input would seriously bias cross section study of Soviet agricultural productivity. I create a measure of days worked in the private sector by aggregating labor input per unit output over reported output of products in private agriculture in each of the republics. The derivation of the measure is discussed more fully in the appendix. The data at five-year intervals are shown in Table 9.7.

The data on days worked in the private sector show declines in the Russian Republic and the Baltic republics and increases or stability in the other republics. The national totals are roughly constant over the twenty-year period, with a slight rise between 1960 and 1970, and a slight decline in the 1970s. According to official data, the proportion of total output produced in the private sector declined over the period. This trend is not inconsistent with rough stability in the labor input in the private sector, because the private sector did not have equal access to the more productive inputs allocated to the socialized sector. According to the data shown in Table 9.6 and Table 9.7, in the early 1960s about one quarter of the total labor used in agriculture was in the private sector. The proportion was essentially the same in the late 1970s.

The little corroborative evidence about the relative proportions of labor expended in the socialized and private sectors suggests that this figure is about right. According to a recent report of a sample of 905 agricultural workers on state and collective farms in different regions of the country, the average worker spends 12.8 hours per week on his or her private plot.[13] This is equivalent to 95 standard work days per year. A worker who put in a standard work year of 260 to 270 days on a state farm and 95 additional days in private agriculture spent 73 percent of the total work time in the

TABLE 9.7

Days Worked in Private Agriculture (Millions)

	1960	1965	1970	1975	1979
RSFSR	1101	1112	1064	956	827
Ukraine	539	563	574	572	561
Lithuania	55	60	59	53	44
Latvia	29	29	26	22	18
Estonia	12	11	10	8	7
Georgia	39	40	45	51	59
Azerbaidzhan	22	28	35	42	48
Armenia	10	11	12	13	14
Uzbekistan	37	48	62	78	93
Kirghizia	12	17	20	22	22
Tadzhikstan	8	12	16	21	24
Turkmenia	6	8	9	10	11
Kazakhstan	72	90	101	104	102
Belorussia	153	169	172	163	147
Moldavia	22	24	26	28	30
USSR	2117	2222	2231	2143	2007

Sources: See appendix and text.

socialized sector. Much of the work in private agriculture is done by adolescents and retired family members not employed in the socialized sector. Thus, it is unlikely that in 1979 less than 25 percent of the total labor was spent in the private sector.

An alternative estimate of days worked at the national level has been made by Stephen Rapawy, whose estimates are larger than those in Table 9.6 by about 15 percent.[14] Rapawy includes non-agricultural farm employment, and so the two estimates are quite consistent. His estimates of private sector labor are higher by about a third than those used in this study. The differences in the two estimates of private sector employment result from choice of different base years and use of slightly different methodology. The secular trends in both estimates are quite similar.

Finnish agricultural labor data are reported in days worked and include both men and women. The data were used without adjustment.

U.S. and Canadian agricultural labor data are reported in numbers of people employed. The United States Department of Agriculture publishes separately data on the regional breakdown of labor input per unit output for different crops. For several sample years the juxtaposition of the two sets of data implied a work year of 200 days per person in the Lake States, 208 days in the Mountain States, and 212 days per person in the Northern Plains. I used these factors to convert employment figures to total days worked in the separate U.S. states. The Northern Plains figure was used for Canadian provinces.

The machinery variable is the sum of tractors, trucks, and combines weighted by horsepower. Important other farm equipment, such as milking machines and cotton pickers, are not included because the data required for full representation of machinery used on farms are not available for the USSR. The exclusion of auxiliary machinery affects parts of the sample more than others and weakens the performance of the machinery variable.

Fertilizer is measured in tons of active ingredients. Animals are measured as an aggregate of cattle, hogs, sheep and goats, and poultry. The weights for aggregation are those used by Hayami and Ruttan; 0.8, 0.2, 0.1, and .01, respectively.

Summary data on input use per unit output in the thirty cross-sectional units of the sample are shown in Table 9.8

As can be seen in Table 9.8, gross output of crop and livestock products per hectare in the Soviet and non-Soviet areas on average over the twenty-year period was quite comparable. Output per hectare in the Ukraine is similar to that in Nebraska and higher than South Dakota. Lithuania, Latvia, and Estonia are comparable in this respect with Finland, Minnesota, and Ontario. Output per hectare in the Caucasian and Central Asian republics compared favorably on average over the twenty years with that of Colorado, New Mexico, Utah, and Nevada, although land productivity in none of the Soviet republics matched that of Arizona. Output per hectare in Kazakhstan was on average a bit lower than that of North Dakota, Montana, Manitoba, Saskatchewan, and Alberta. Gross output of crop and livestock products per hectare of cultivated land is on the same order of magnitude in the Soviet and non-Soviet sample areas, according to these data.

The differences between the Soviet and non-Soviet areas are most striking in the use of labor. Labor productivity is lower by a factor of ten or more in the Soviet republics than in the non-Soviet. The only exception is the comparison of Finland with Es-

TABLE 9.8

Means of Summary Data on Input Use and Productivity

	Output/ Land[a]	Output/ Labor[b]	HP/ Land[c]	Ft/ Land[d]	HP/ Labor[e]	An Out/ Animal[f]
Soviet						
RSFSR	3.25	122	1.25	.03	47	4.62
Ukraine	5.93	109	1.57	.06	29	4.79
Lithuania	7.49	145	2.07	.13	40	7.34
Latvia	7.15	155	2.20	.15	49	7.01
Estonia	8.70	219	2.44	.17	63	7.80
Georgia	8.98	73	2.67	.10	22	2.46
Azerbaidzhan	5.25	58	2.54	.07	28	2.18
Armenia	7.12	69	3.30	.08	32	2.86
Uzbekistan	8.50	73	2.94	.18	25	2.79
Kirghizia	6.03	82	2.67	.09	36	2.88
Tadzhikstan	7.42	66	3.45	.15	30	2.19
Turkmenia	9.28	78	4.37	.20	37	2.67
Kazakhstan	1.58	124	1.09	.01	85	3.22
Belorussia	7.49	105	2.02	.14	28	5.16
Moldavia	7.25	99	1.89	.05	26	5.09
Non-Soviet						
Finland	6.41	187	6.96	.15	216	7.20
Minnesota	6.29	1297	4.39	.08	906	7.02
North Dakota	1.60	1302	1.93	.02	1569	3.79
South Dakota	3.19	1608	2.23	.01	1119	4.34
Nebraska	5.04	1776	3.11	.06	1086	4.24
Montana	1.80	1358	2.06	.01	1552	2.87
Colorado	3.82	1374	3.01	.03	1074	4.12
New Mexico	6.29	926	5.48	.05	782	3.26
Arizona	12.08	1028	5.26	.18	438	4.00
Utah	4.94	719	5.65	.04	824	3.90
Nevada	4.47	1378	3.57	.02	1103	2.58
Ontario	9.44	1007	7.22	.10	770	7.05
Manitoba	2.29	1151	2.55	.02	1268	5.20
Saskatchewan	1.25	1012	1.70	.01	1368	3.56
Alberta	2.26	1076	2.40	.02	1138	4.15

Source: See text.

[a] Wheat units per cultivated hectare (1 wheat unit = 1 metric ton).

[b] Wheat units per thousand days worked.

[c] Horsepower of tractors, combines, and farm trucks per cultivated hectare.

[d] Tons active ingredients fertilizer per cultivated hectare.

[e] Horsepower of tractors, combines, and farm trucks per thousand days worked.

[f] Output of meat, milk, eggs, and wool expressed in wheat units per animal unit.

tonia. Finland has the lowest labor productivity of any of the non-Soviet areas and is within the range of that of the Soviet republics. Estonia has the highest labor productivity of the Soviet republics, and on average over the period labor productivity in Estonia was greater than in Finland.

Machinery per man-day is a bit lower in the Soviet than in the non-Soviet areas. Usable horsepower is in fact lower still, because it is readily acknowledged that many Soviet agricultural machines stand idle for lack of repairs and spare parts. Horsepower per man-day is very low in the Soviet areas, reflecting the high labor intensity of Soviet agriculture. Horsepower per thousand person-days is shown as HP/Labor in Table 9.8.

Fertilizer use per hectare of cultivated land in the Soviet republics was, on average over the period, equal to or greater than that in the non-Soviet areas. In all Soviet republics except Kazakhstan, the Ukraine, and parts of the RSFSR, fertilizer use has been increasing faster than in comparable non-Soviet areas and is now greater in the USSR. Fertilizer use per hectare in the Ukraine now equals that in Nebraska. The Russian Republic is so large that its aggregate figure cannot meaningfully be compared with that of particular non-Soviet areas, but its fertilizer use per hectare roughly quadrupled over the twenty-year period.

The importance of restricting international comparisons to climatically similar areas is particularly evident with respect to data on fertilizer use. From national averages of fertilizer use per hectare, it appears that the USSR lags behind the United States in fertilizer use. According to FAO data on fertilizer consumption, 106 kilograms of active fertilizer ingredients were applied per hectare of arable land in the United States in 1978, and the corresponding figure for the USSR was 79 kilograms.[15] A conclusion that is sometimes drawn from these national data is that the USSR can achieve significant increases in yields at relatively low cost by increasing fertilizer use until it approaches that in the United States. However, the data in Table 9.8 show that the USSR did not lag behind climatically comparable areas in North America in fertilizer use over the twenty-year period. Now Soviet fertilizer use exceeds that in climatically similar parts of the United States. The high national average figures for the United States are due to the high fertilizer responsiveness of corn. Higher yields can be obtained in the USSR with greater fertilizer use, but the current levels of fertilizer use suggest that most areas of the USSR are already on quite a flat portion of the fertilizer response curve and that increased yields can be obtained in this way only at high cost.

Regional differences in fertilizer use in the USSR are quite marked, and the data indicate that responsiveness to additional fertilizer use would probably be greater in some areas than in others. In table 9.9, 1980 data on fertilizer use for different crops in the fifteen republics are presented.

TABLE 9.9

Fertilizer Use by Crop and Republic, 1980

(Kilograms Active Ingredients per Seeded Hectare)

	Cotton	Sugar Beets	Grain (No Corn)	Corn	Potatoes
USSR	417	438	51	215	274
RSFSR	---	413	45	161	275
Ukraine	---	462	77	196	234
Belorussia	---	377	225	---	306
Uzbekistan	447	---	143	360	393
Kazakhstan	353	465	9	296	162
Georgia	---	381	156	234	339
Azerbaidzhan	277	---	141	204	151
Lithuania	---	538	168	---	357
Moldavia	---	365	157	247	136
Latvia	---	719	237	---	390
Kirgizia	561	455	121	341	256
Tadzhikstan	442	516	66	412	482
Armenia	---	516	155	355	391
Turkmenia	353	---	117	267	270
Estonia	---	---	238	---	339

Source: Vestnik statistiki, 1981, no. 3, p. 78.

In Kazakhstan in 1980, only 23 percent of the grain lands received any fertilizer at all.[16] With the lesser use of fallow in Kazakhstan relative to the North American wheatlands, the need for supplementary fertilizer is correspondingly greater in Kazakhstan. From Table 9.8 it appears that on average fertilizer use in Kazakhstan is about equal to that in the Prairie provinces and the Northern Plains States, but from Table 9.9 it is clear that little of the fertilizer used in Kazakhstan is applied to wheat.

Productivity per animal unit (An Out/Animal) is the output of meat, milk, eggs, and wool expressed in wheat equivalent units per animal unit. This data item is puzzling because it does not indicate that Soviet animal productivity is significantly lower than that in Europe and North America, even though official Soviet data on meat and milk yields per animal show the yields to be quite low. In the late 1970s, annual milk yields per cow in Finland were about 5000 kilograms, and in Minnesota about 4500. Soviet milk yields were highest in Estonia (3500 kilograms) and lower in the Russian Republic, the Ukraine, and Belorussia (2200, 2400, and 2300, respectively). Yet from the data in Table 9.8, Estonia appears to have higher animal output per animal unit than does Finland or Minnesota. The figure for the Russian Republic is quite low, considering the fact that dairying accounts for about the same proportion of the value of gross output there as in Minnesota. The data on animal productivity in Table 9.8 do not show the sharp difference in animal productivity between the Soviet and non-Soviet areas that other evidence leads us to expect. This could be either because the aggregation of animal output and animal units has obscured some of the productivity difference, or because Soviet gross output data on livestock products are inflated. If the animal productivity data are biased in favor of the Soviet sample, then the productivity differentials are correspondingly understated.

The data presented in Table 9.8 suggest that the main difference in input use and factor productivity between Soviet and non-Soviet samples is in use of agricultural labor. Availability of machinery, and especially machinery in good repair, is a bit lower in the Soviet areas. Soviet fertilizer use is quite comparable to that in the non-Soviet sample, although its application to particular crops appears to differ considerably between the Soviet and non-Soviet samples and among the Soviet republics.

The detailed empirical results of the relative productivity comparisons are presented in the following section, together with a brief discussion of statistical methodology. A broader interpretation of the results and their implications for Soviet agricultural policy and prospects continues in the next section.

ESTIMATION OF THE PRODUCTIVITY DIFFERENTIALS

The data described in Table 9.8 were used to estimate log linear production functions. In the first set of estimations, data for the

Soviet and non-Soviet areas were pooled. Independent variables were land, labor, machinery, fertilizer, animals, climate, a time trend, and separate dummies for the Soviet and non-Soviet intercepts.[17]

Table 9.10 shows the gross productivity comparison for the whole Soviet and non-Soviet sample and for separate regions within the joint sample. In equation 1, the thirty Soviet and non-Soviet sample areas are pooled, and the difference in the Soviet and non-Soviet dummies, or intercepts, corresponds to a productivity difference of 35 percent. In equations 2, 3, and 4, the samples are divided somewhat arbitrarily into northern and southern regions. The division was made in an attempt to separate the primarily grain and livestock regions from the regions that combine high value intensive irrigated and non-irrigated farming with grazing. The northern areas included the Soviet republics of the RSFSR, the Ukraine, Latvia, Lithuania, Estonia, Kazakhstan (for grain), Belorussia, and Moldavia, and the non-Soviet areas of Finland, Minnesota, North Dakota, South Dakota, Nebraska, Montana, Ontario, Manitoba, Saskatchewan, and Alberta. The southern Soviet republics included Georgia, Azerbaidzhan, Armenia, Uzbekistan, Kirghizia, Turkmenia, and Tadzhikstan. The non-Soviet southern areas were the American states of Colorado, New Mexico, Arizona, Utah, and Nevada.

The division of the joint sample into northern and southern regions shows that the estimated gross productivity difference in the northern areas is relatively small—17 percent (equation 2). However, when Finland is deleted from the northern sample, so that the comparison is between the Soviet northern republics and the U.S. states of Minnesota, North Dakota, South Dakota, Nebraska, and Montana, and the Canadian provinces of Ontario, Manitoba, Saskatchewan, and Alberta, the estimated productivity gap widens considerably, from 17 percent to about 100 percent (equation 3). The coefficients of land and animals decline, and that of labor increases.

If Finland makes so much difference, does it belong in or out of the northern sample? Since Finland is contiguous with the USSR and has a long history of close association with Russia, it seems to provide a natural comparison with the northern dairy regions of the USSR. However, the Finnish organization of agriculture is for

TABLE 9.10

Gross Productivity, Joint Estimation

Equation	1 Joint	2 Joint North	3 2, No Fin	4 Joint South	5 1, No Climate	6 3, No Climate
Land	.34 $(13.08)^a$	.18 (7.20)	.08 (2.86)	.20 (18.18)	.29 (11.60)	.02 (.84)
Labor	.12 (5.74)	.15 (9.05)	.35 (11.51)	.30 (7.06)	.10 (4.64)	.42 (17.59)
Machinery	−.04 (−.98)	.06 (1.41)	.05 (1.15)	−.06 (−1.61)	−.004 (−.10)	.06 (1.56)
Fertilizer	.30 (22.23)	.14 (9.57)	.15 (11.09)	.22 (9.85)	.31 (22.15)	.16 (12.07)
Animals	.30 (13.56)	.41 (17.40)	.32 (13.09)	.43 (8.59)	.33 (14.91)	.29 (12.32)
Climate	.008 (5.68)	.03 (17.28)	.01 (3.77)	.007 (5.74)		
Trend	−.005 (−.23)	.005 (2.57)	.008 (4.05)	.014 (5.32)	−.003 (−1.23)	.008 (3.96)
Soviet dummy	2.88 (25.95)	3.29 (34.77)	3.73 (34.69)	2.29 (9.85)	2.86 (25.13)	3.87 (37.61)
Non−Soviet dummy	3.18 (19.18)	3.45 (23.64)	4.44 (23.30)	3.17 (10.37)	3.09 (18.26)	4.78 (27.80)
PC deleted	0	0	0	1	0	0
R^2	.988	.993	.993	.997	.988	.993
% Gap	35	17	103	141	26	148

Source: See text and appendix.

[a]Numbers in parentheses are t−statistics.

several reasons inappropriate for even the geographically similar areas of the USSR. Finland has chosen to maintain small family farms at considerable cost for both cultural and economic reasons. The population of Finland is small, and workers who cannot be absorbed by industry tend to leave the country. There is fear that

TABLE 9.11

Separate Estimation of Soviet and Non-Soviet Equations

Equation	7 Soviet Whole	8 Soviet North	9 Soviet South	10 Non Whole	11 Non North	12 Non South
Land	.65 (13.27)[a]	-.06 (-1.30)	-.04 (-.47)	.22 (7.86)	.19 (4.87)	-.01 (-.32)
Labor	.37 (10.96)	.02 (.30)	.62 (10.28)	.19 (6.96)	.23 (6.26)	.19 (3.12)
Machinery	-.30 (-3.87)	.37 (27.56)	-.19 (-2.46)	.18 (3.70)	.17 (2.23)	.31 (11.25)
Fertilizer	.34 (20.91)	.18 (7.67)	.23 (7.53)	.13 (7.14)	.03 (1.16)	.17 (4.58)
Animals	-.14 (-2.49)	.47 (6.59)	.42 (4.92)	.47 (18.80)	.47 (18.13)	.69 (16.76)
Climate	.02 (6.75)	.053 (5.09)	.004 (2.77)	.02 (11.24)	.03 (9.25)	.03 (11.31)
Trend	.0002 (.105)	-.016 (-3.97)	.02 (5.03)	.005 (2.24)	.01 (3.80)	.007 (1.95)
Intercept	4.26 (30.60)	2.70 (13.75)	3.51 (11.58)	1.27 (6.34)	1.88 (4.67)	.21 (27.25)
PC deleted	1	1	0	0	1	2
R^2	.993	.997	.891	.956	.991	.997

Source: See text and appendix.

[a]Numbers in parentheses are t-statistics.

if more people leave farming than can find work in Finnish industry, the migration out of the country will accelerate.

Some Soviet nationalities probably share fears similar to those of the Finns about the effects on national identity and cultural traditions of sizeable migrations out of the linguistic and cultural borders of the republic, but there is little reason for agricultural policy set in Moscow to assuage these fears with economic measures designed to keep people in agriculture. Especially in the northern

TABLE 9.12

Productivity Comparison of Joint Sample, Net Output

Equation	13 Net Joint All	14 Gross North U.S. and Sov	15 Net North U.S. and Sov	16 Net South All
Land	.39 $(13.45)^a$	−.10 (−2.70)	−.08 (−2.08)	.18 (3.82)
Labor	.30 (10.40)	.40 (11.81)	.42 (11.98)	.33 (7.14)
Machinery	−.16 (−3.70)	.18 (3.85)	.16 (3.35)	−.04 (−.97)
Fertilizer	.30 (21.70)	.13 (8.69)	.12 (7.91)	.19 (7.87)
Animals	.17 (5.79)	.35 (11.16)	.31 (9.36)	.48 (8.81)
Climate	.005 (3.63)	.007 (2.11)	.007 (1.86)	.01 (8.22)
Trend	.007 (3.05)	.006 (2.95)	.01 (6.14)	.01 (4.21)
Soviet dummy	3.45 (28.51)	3.68 (34.16)	3.67 (32.71)	1.83 (7.23)
Non−Soviet dummy	4.31 (22.18)	4.49 (23.04)	4.61 (22.70)	2.74 (8.25)
PC deleted	0	0	1	1
R^2	.989	.995	.993	.996
% Gap	136	125	156	148

Source: See text and appendix.

[a]Numbers in parentheses are t−statistics.

republics, demand for nonagricultural labor is increasing fast enough so that those who leave agriculture can usually find work within their own linguistic boundary, if they so choose. In addition, a major effort is underway to settle sparsely inhabited areas of the Russian far east. State-supported, labor intensive agriculture may make sense in the case of Finland, but there is little rationale for it in the northern parts of the USSR. The North American model, in which few people work large areas of land, corresponds more closely to the natural endowment of Soviet agriculture and to the high demand for labor in the nonagricultural economy. The data suggest that factor use and productivity in Soviet northern agriculture correspond relatively closely to Finnish levels, although it should be remembered that according to official Soviet data, milk yields per cow in most of the Soviet north are half of the average Finnish level. Soviet factor proportions and productivity should correspond more closely to North American levels, if resources in the USSR are to be used optimally. The comparison of Soviet northern and North American agriculture is thus probably more appropriate. By this comparison, American and Canadian productivity is about double that of comparable areas in the USSR.

In the southern region the productivity difference is more than 100 percent (equation 4). The gap appears to be greater than in the northern region, although both are large.

No particular conclusions are drawn in this study from the magnitudes of the estimated coefficients of the inputs, but the credibility accorded the estimated productivity differences depends on the reasonableness of the other coefficients, and for this reason they deserve comment. In general the coefficients of the conventional inputs in the joint equations add up approximately to unity. The machinery variable performs poorly in several of the equations, serving as a reminder that tractor, combine, and truck horsepower is not an adequate proxy for total machine power used in agriculture. The problem becomes most troublesome when areas are included in which machines other than tractors and combines are important, as is the case in the Soviet cotton belt. The coefficient of animals is quite high in all but one of the equations. This is to be expected, because the output measure includes the gross value of livestock products, with no deduction for feed at this stage. Animals thus make a large contribution to gross output. In later estimations, an attempt is made to subtract concentrates fed.

The coefficient of the climate variable is significantly different from zero in each of the equations, and favorable climate contributes positively to output. Climate, as measured by the variable used here, makes a larger difference in northern areas than in southern. The climate variable is included in the estimation in levels, not logs, as the deviation from the sample mean. Thus, average climate contributes neither positively nor negatively to output. In equation 1, an improvement in climate of one point on the scale above the sample mean is associated with an output increase of 0.8 percent.

One function that the climate variable should serve is to separate, to some extent, the quality of land from the quantity. When output from small quantities of highly productive land is compared to that of large quantities of poor land, the correlation between output and the number of hectares will not be very meaningful and may be small or negative. Therefore, it is reassuring that the effect of including a measure of climate in the regressions is to increase the coefficient of the quantity of land. This can be seen by comparing equations 1 and 5 and 3 and 6 in Table 9.10.

Comparison of equations 1 and 5 shows that the total Soviet and non-Soviet samples appear well matched climatically. Dropping the climate variable in equation 5 makes little difference. However, when the northern samples are compared without Finland (equations 3 and 6), the climate variable matters. Explicit inclusion of climate reduces the measured productivity gap considerably.

The time trend shows the pace of residual technical change, or the change in productivity not accounted for by the physical quantities of the included factors. In equation 1, the time trend is essentially zero. In equation 2, productivity not accounted for by the included inputs is shown to have improved in the joint northern sample areas at an annual rate of about .5 percent.

The estimated coefficients shown in Table 9.10 appear in general reasonable, although the limitations of the data underlying them should be kept in mind. The R2 are high. Multicollinearity does not appear a major problem with the data set, since most or all of the principal components are retained in the equations.

Further disaggregation of the sample into its component Soviet and non-Soviet parts unfortunately reduces some of the spread in the data, but provides a different view of the relationships underlying the joint estimations. When the data from the fifteen Soviet republics are pooled, the estimated coefficients are bizarre enough to suggest that the northern and southern parts of the Soviet sample should be treated separately. In equation 7 in Table 9.11, the estimated coefficient of land is very high (.65). Coefficients of both machinery and animals are negative. When the Soviet sample is split into northern and southern regions (equations 8 and 9), the large land coefficient disappears. The labor coefficient is very small for the Soviet north (.02), and very large for the south (.62). The magnitudes of these coefficients are undoubtedly exaggerated, but they do express the very different use of labor in the two regions. Machinery, fertilizer, and animals have all the explanatory power in the Soviet northern equation. Fertilizer and animals, as well as labor, appear important in the Soviet south. Equation 9 contains so many anomalies that either the reported data or the underlying production process must be quite distorted.

The three Soviet equations are not very attractive by the standards usually used to judge estimated production functions. However, they are consistent with some known characteristics of Soviet agriculture. Labor is important in the south and less so in the north. Machinery is important in the north, and the variable used here does not capture the mix of machinery most important in the south. Fertilizer is highly correlated with increased output in both the north and the south and is more important in the irrigated agriculture of the south. Higher output is correlated in cross section with better natural conditions.

According to these estimates, factor productivity not accounted for by the included inputs fell in the northern Soviet republics at a rate of about 1.6 percent per year and grew in the southern republics at 2 percent annually. There is little corroborative evidence for these trends in technical change, but they may not be far wrong. The poor rate of return to investments in agricultural inputs is a frequent official complaint, and many such comments are made in specific reference to the campaign to improve agriculture in the nonblack soil zone of the northern republics. Many of the southern republics began the period with very low productivity and have improved since then, even though the joint southern estimation indicates that on average over the period, the republics were quite backward.

Diamond and Davis estimate a corresponding rate of growth in total factor productivity for the whole USSR of 1.0 percent per year for 1961–70, and 0.4 percent annually for 1971–77.[18]

Estimations for the non-Soviet sample areas separately are shown as equations 10, 11, and 12 in Table 9.11. When the non-Soviet areas are disaggregated into northern and southern regions, the coefficients do not change as dramatically as they do for the Soviet equations. The coefficient of land in the non-Soviet southern equation is essentially zero, suggesting that inclusion of irrigation in the climate variable is not very effective in capturing differences in land quality. The coefficient of animals in the same equation is very high.

It is well known that seeding rates in the Soviet Union are very high and that feed is used quite inefficiently. Evidence and details on seeding rates are presented in the next section. At this point, it is useful to examine how much difference the Soviet use of seed and feed makes in the productivity comparisons. The effect of differential seeding rates and feed use can be seen by comparing the relative productivity measures, first when gross output is used as the dependent variable and, second, when a concept of net output that excludes grain and potato seed and grain concentrates fed is used as the dependent variable.

Seed is a significant proportion of the total crop only for the small grains and potatoes, and subtraction of the seed used for these crops takes care of most of the output used for seed. Data on seed use are available only for the United States and the USSR, and, for comparisons of productivity with seed and feed subtracted from gross output, the Canadian provinces and Finland were dropped from the sample.

Since 1971, imported feed has been used in the production of a portion of Soviet animal products. I assume that official data on grain concentrates fed in the fifteen republics include imported grains used as feed, as well as domestically produced grains freed for feeding purposes by the importation of food grain. The subtraction of grain used for feed thus corrects not only for agricultural inputs supplied by agriculture to itself, but also for imported inputs not explicitly recognized in the production functions. For the United States, data on feed grain used for feed are published by the Department of Agriculture, and wheat and rye fed can be derived from the disposition data for these crops. The concept of net product used here excludes only grain and potatoes used as seed, and grain concentrates fed. No subtraction is made for sunflower, soy meal, or byproduct feeds.

Table 9.13 shows that seed and feed when calculated as described above constitute between 15 percent and 20 percent of the gross output of the Soviet northern republics, and about 10 percent of that of the American northern plains states. In the southern growing regions, where pasture provides much of the animal feed, gross and net output are quite close.

The removal of seed and concentrate feed from the measure of output has virtually no effect on the estimated productivity gap for the southern region. This is as expected, because many animals in these areas are grazed, and because small grains are not a significant proportion of total output. In the northern region, re-

TABLE 9.13

Net Output Indicators

	Net/Gross[a]	Net/Land[b]	Net/Labor[c]
Arizona	.85[d]	10.32	876.75
Armenia	.88	6.23	59.88
Azerbaidzhan	.89	4.69	51.82
Belorussia	.81	6.10	85.59
Estonia	.83	7.25	179.92
Georgia	.91	8.16	66.66
Kazakhstan	.82	1.31	102.91
Kirgizia	.86	5.18	70.81
Latvia	.86	6.16	133.55
Lithuania	.85	6.39	121.24
Minnesota	.88	5.56	1367.08
Moldavia	.87	6.33	84.89
Montana	.93	1.68	1266.30
N Dakota	.93	1.48	1211.44
Nebraska	.87	4.38	1547.84
Nevada	.90	4.02	1211.01
New Mexico	.89	5.60	816.79
RSFSR	.81	2.62	97.43
S Dakota	.88	2.80	1412.20
Tadzhikistan	.87	6.49	58.00
Turkmenia	.93	8.66	73.26
Ukraine	.84	4.97	90.52
Utah	.87	4.28	621.29
Uzbekistan	.98	8.31	72.09

Source: See text and appendix.

[a] Net output as a proportion of gross output.

[b] Net output per hectare.

[c] Net output per thousand days worked.

[d] All figures are averages over the sample period.

moval of seed and feed adds about 25 percent to the estimated productivity gap. Because Canada and Finland have been dropped from the non-Soviet sample in the net output estimation, the net equation should be compared to an estimation of relative gross productivity containing only American and Soviet observations. Equations 14 and 15 in Table 9.12 show the relevant comparison.

The gross and net equations for the northern region are quite similar. The main difference between the two is in the dummy variables that measure the productivity gap. Each equation is marred by the negative coefficient of land. The coefficient of animals falls as expected in the net equation, but not by much. The effect of removing seed and feed on the estimated productivity gap for the northern area is in the expected direction and of a reasonable magnitude (25 percent), although a bit on the high side.

SOVIET USE OF SEED AND FEED

The empirical results presented in the last section can be summarized. Gross output includes double counting of seed and feed consumed in the production process. The northern and southern areas of the samples differ enough that they should be compared separately. Factor use and gross factor productivity in the Soviet northern republics appears to differ relatively little from that in Finland. When Finland is deleted from the non-Soviet sample, so that the comparison is between the northern USSR and comparable areas in North America, the North American areas produce about twice as much per unit input as do the Soviet areas. When the southern Soviet republics are compared to the states of the American southwest, the productivity gap is even larger, between 100 and 150 percent.

Seeding rates and feeding efficiency differ significantly between the Soviet and North American areas in the sample. Seed and grain concentrates fed account for about 10 percent of gross output in the northern parts of the North American sample, and from 15 percent to 20 percent of gross output in the Soviet northern republics. When seed and concentrates fed are subtracted from gross output, so that a concept of net output is compared across samples, the productivity gap widens by about 25 percent. Thus, poor use of seed and grain for feed reduces Soviet efficiency relative to

American, but the loss at that stage does not appear as great as the loss caused by the factors that bring down gross productivity.

Even though poor use of seed and feed is not the major component of inefficiency in Soviet agriculture, remedial measures in this area, particularly with regard to seeding rates, would appear quite straightforward. For this reason, it is interesting to investigate further the evidence on Soviet seeding rates.

When the U.S. and Soviet seeding rates are compared, it is apparent that seeding rates are much higher in the USSR. Aggregate data on the proportion of the crop used for seed are not available for the USSR. In the breakdown of the costs of production (*sebestoimost'*), however, it is reported that home produced seed is valued at the cost of production and purchased seed at the purchase price. If it is assumed that most seed is produced on farms, aggregate data on the proportion of the crop used for seed can be derived. The information, for example, that the cost of production of a ton of wheat was 50 rubles in the RSFSR in 1970 and that seed when valued at the cost of production accounted for 10 rubles of the total implies that approximately one fifth of the total crop was used for seed. Data for potatoes suggest that in Belorussia, where potatoes are a major crop, about 30 percent of total gross output is used as seed. It is likely that over the twenty years, more seed has been purchased and less produced on the farms, and there have been reports of increases in the cost of purchased seed.

Seed as a proportion of costs of production (*sebestoimost'*) for grain and potatoes in 1970 is shown by republic in Table 9.14.

Data on seeding rates derived from cost data are conjectural because we do not know how much seed is purchased off the farm or the price paid for purchased seed. Evidence suggests that substantial seed is produced on the farms. One of the problems frequently discussed in the agronomical literature is the inadequate quantity of high quality seed from specialized seed farms. In the United States, where the seed industry is well developed, in 1969 60 percent of the wheat seed nationwide was used on farms where it was produced. In North Dakota, the proportion was lower, 45 percent. There was little change in the proportion of seed produced off farms where it was used over the period from 1964 to 1974.[19] Thus, the technology of wheat seed production, unlike that of corn, makes on-farm production of seed an acceptable alterna-

TABLE 9.14

Seed as a Proportion of Costs of Production[a]
(USSR, 1970)

	State Farms		Collective Farms	
	Grain	Potatoes	Grain	Potatoes
RSFSR	.22	.37	.20	.34
Ukraine	.13	.46	.16	.44
Lithuania	.14	.27	.15	.27
Latvia	.18	.30	.18	.30
Estonia	.16	.26	.16	.26
Georgia	.16	.33	.23	.34
Azerbaidzhan	.16	.36	.19	.41
Armenia	.17	.35	.19	.36
Uzbekistan	.16	.51	.15	.52
Kirgizia	.16	.44	.17	.49
Tadzhikistan	.14	.48	.19	.46
Turkmenia	.11	---	.14	---
Kazakhstan	.21	.42	.18	.41
Belorussia	.22	.30	.21	.29
Moldavia	.21	.51	.19	.51

Source: Sel'skoe khoziaistvo SSSR (Moscow, 1971), pp. 596, 597, 507, 509.

[a]Costs of production do not include payment for land or interest, and so do not correspond to production costs as accounted elsewhere.

tive to purchase of seed for many American farmers. In the Soviet Union, where the seed industry is more backward, it is likely that grain seed is produced off the farm primarily for provision of new varieties.

The recommended seeding norms for Soviet small grains are in general much higher than seeding rates used in the United States. In addition, according to many reports, farms often exceed recommended seeding norms in an effort to attain higher yields. In the journal *Zernovoe khoziaistvo* (Grain Farming) in 1980, A.I. Zholobov, director of the Main Administration of Grain Culture and General Questions of Crop Production in the Ministry of Agriculture, wrote:

It is necessary to leave behind the routinized (without regard for the condition of the field, moisture presence, timing of sowing, biological condition of the seed) approach to seeding norms, and the attempt to compensate for deficiencies in the preparation of the soil, and quality of the seeding with higher seeding rates. This leads to the irrational use of valuable seeding material, when the optimal density of productive stalks can be achieved with a lesser expenditure of seed.[20]

The combination of high recommended seeding norms and actual seeding norms that may exceed recommendations suggests that the use of seed implied by the cost figures is probably on the high side, but not too far wrong.

The average U.S. seeding rate for wheat was 79 kilos per hectare in 1980. For oats, the rate was 93 kilos per hectare; for barley, 91; and for rye, 100. There was some regional variation in seeding rates. In Montana, the rate for oats was only 64 kilos per hectare.[21] Recommended seeding rates for various parts of the Soviet Union are contained in agronomical discussions in the journal, *Zernovoe khoziaistvo*. The rates are usually given in million kernels per hectare. In addition, there are occasional references to the weight of first class seed. If it is assumed that the seeding rates are given for first class seed, the rates in millions of kernels per hectare can be converted to kilograms and compared to American seeding rates. First class wheat seed is said to weigh 42 to 45 kilograms per million kernels. First class barley seed is said to weigh 44 to 45 kilograms per million kernels. Data on rye rates imply that first class rye seed weighs 20 to 25 kilograms per million kernels, but this seems quite low. Data from *Zernovoe khoziaistvo* in 1980 on recommended seeding rates for different crops in different areas are shown in Table 9.15.

There is large variation in the recommended seeding rates. The lowest rates appear to be for Kazakhstan. In the Kustanai region, seeding rates on fallowed land are higher than on continuously cultivated land, but in the Volga region, the recommendation is apparently reversed. These recommended seeding rates on occupied fallow land are higher than on land previously kept in clean fallow.

In Bashkiria in 1980, 712,800 tons of seed were sown to 3.0 million hectares of grain, or 238 kilos of seed per hectare.[22] About 60 percent of the grain area in Bashkiria is sown to wheat, and the remainder to barley and rye. Virtually none of the grain is irrigated, and annual precipitation ranges from 350 mm in the southern black soil area of the autonomous republic to about 500 mm in

TABLE 9.15

Recommended Seeding Rates, USSR

Crop	Location	Rate (Million Kernels)	Rate (Kilos)	Yield (Centners)
Wheat	Kustanai (Kazakh)	2.5–3.2	105–134	
	Clean fallow	3.2	134	
	Prior cultivated	2.5	105	
Buckwheat	Bashkiria (Volga)	3.5–4.0	70–80	7.6
Grain	Belorussia		220–240	
Oats	Kazakhstan		30–50	
Spring Wheat	Kazakhstan	2.5	105	
Winter Wheat	Zavolga (irr.)	5.5	231	
Spring Wheat	Saratov	5–6,	210–252,	
		4–4.5	168–189	
Winter Wheat	Moldavia (irr.)		180	
Winter Rye	Volga region			
	Clean fallow	3.5–5.5		
	Occupied fallow	(10% higher)		
Winter Rye	Bashkiria (Chulpan)	1.5–2.0	30–50	
Rye	Central Black soil	5–5.5		
Buckwheat	Khar'kov (Ukraine)		80	
Winter Wheat	Lower Volga			
	Clean fallow	5	210	
	Occupied fallow	6	252	
Wheat	Krasnodar (N. Caucasus)	4.5–5	189–210	
Winter Wheat	Kherson (Ukraine)	4.5	189	
Winter Wheat	Urals (Kazakh)	3.5	147	
Barley	Western Siberia	5–5.5	210–231	
Spring Wheat	Western Siberia	6–6.5	252–273	
Oats	Western Siberia	5–5.5		
Buckwheat	Western Siberia	2	50	
Buckwheat	Belorussia (Iskra variety)	4.5	163	11.6
	Belorussia (Iskra variety)	2.5	85	11.4
	Belorussia (Iskra variety)	2.5	85	11.6
	Belorussia (Iskra variety)	1.5	51	11.3
	Belorussia (Iubileinaia 2)	4.5	103	13.0
Winter Wheat	Nikolaev (Ukraine, irr.)	5.5–6.5	231–273	32.1
Winter Wheat	Volgograd obl.			
	Early August sowing	3–3.5	126–147	
	Late September sowing	6	252	
	Usual norm	5–5.5	210–231	
Winter Wheat	Orlov (Central Russia)	4–4.5	168–189	
Winter Rye	Orlov (Central Russia)	5.5–6.0		
Winter Rye	Riazan' (Central Russia)	5.5–6.0		
Winter Wheat	Riazan' (Central Russia)	6.0–6.5	252–273	
Barley	Riazan' (Central Russia)	5.5–7.2	242–302	

Source: All data are from Zernovoe khoziaistvo, 1980, various issues.

the northern wooded steppe zone. The average grain yield during the tenth plan period was 17.2 centners per hectare. Thus, in this area, about 14 percent of the bunker yield of grain was used for seed. If the seed was of first class quality, the seeding rate was about 5.7 million kernels per hectare and was higher if the seed was less than of first class. According to another source, the recommended seeding norm for spring wheat in Bashkiria is 5.5 million kernels per hectare.[23] Thus, in Bashkiria in 1980, the actual seeding rate appears to have been quite close to the recommended norm.

What, in sum, does the evidence on seeding rates suggest? According to the cost data, as much as 20 percent of the grain crop and 30 percent of the potato crop is used for seed. The recommended norms suggest that about 200 kilograms per hectare is the average seeding rate for small grains. With average yields of about 15 centners per hectare, seed amounts to 13 percent of the crop, according to this calculation. However, some of the planted area must be seeded more than once, because of winter kill or calamities of nature or judgment. For this reason, it seems likely that between 15 percent and 20 percent of the grain crop is used for seed.

What accounts for these apparently high seeding rates? If the norms are given for the first class seed, then poor quality seed cannot be a reason for high recommended rates, unless first class seed is, itself, of poor quality. Poor quality of seed resulting from inadequate facilities for handling, storing, and treating seeds is not infrequently mentioned. In reference to the Central NonBlack Soil Zone, a commentator in *Zernovoe khoziaistvo* in 1980 wrote:

> The question of establishing on the farms carry-over stocks of seeds for winter sowing on all acreage demands immediate solution. Now only 10 percent of the acreage of these crops is sown with treated seeds, and the remainder is sown with newly harvested seeds. This leads to extension of the seeding period, splitting of shoots, and development of root rot and smut.[24]

Delay of the sowing season may explain, in part, the high seeding rates. In an experiment in Volgograd oblast, researchers reported that if winter wheat could be sown in early August, the seeding rate could be reduced from 5 to 5.5 million kernels per hectare to 3 to 3.5 million. If planting is delayed in this area until late September, the recommended seeding rate is as high as 6 million kernels per hectare.[25]

In reference to grain vetch, a correspondent reported to *Zernovoe khoziaistvo* in 1981 that to expand the area of this crop on his farm, they had to reduce the seeding rate, since they did not have enough seed. In recent years the seeding rate on this farm has been increased 20 to 25 percent and has resulted in yield increases of 5 to 10 percent. With lower seeding rates, according to this correspondent, weeds pose a greater problem, and the need for chemical weed controlling agents is increased.[26]

Thus, the quality of the seed and agronomic practices such as the timing of sowing and availability of fertilizer and chemical weed controls probably explain much of the high seeding rates for the small grains. The puzzle about the high Soviet seeding rates is that it is unclear that they contribute much to higher yields. In a discussion of the effects of seeding rates on cereal yields, W.H. van Dobben says the following:

> Cereals have a great capacity in compensating for low plant density by increasing the number of tillers and grains per ear. Montgomery (1912) observed that difference in seed rates between 60 and 140 kg./ha. had little effect on the yield of winter wheat. A decrease from 340 to 65 plants/m2 gave a loss in grain yield of only 5 percent in one of his experiments with oats.
>
> However, the optimal spacing of any crop greatly depends on soil fertility. . . . The effect of seed rate is appreciable when little nitrogen is available but disappears with a better supply.[27]

In a figure accompanying van Dobben's discussion, the yields of oats under different applications of nitrogen and with seeding rates of 70 kilos per hectare and 140 kilos per hectare are compared. With a low application of nitrogen, the higher seeding rate results in a significantly higher yield than does the low seeding rate. With higher applications of nitrogen, the yields for the different seeding rates approach each other, as shown in Table 9.16.

Table 9.16 may provide a clue to both the high seeding rates and the relatively low fertilizer responsiveness of grains now in the USSR. The high seeding rates may have been advantageous when little fertilizer was available and high yields were sought at almost any cost. However, if these data are correct, then seed and fertilizer are substitutes over the range of fertilizer application now used in the Soviet Union, and yields comparable to those currently obtained could be achieved with considerably less seed.

If, as seems likely, Soviet seeding rates are on the order of 200 kilograms per hectare, and if they could be reduced to about 100 kilograms, then this would yield a savings of 12 million tons of grain on a total grain area of about 120 million hectares. Even if yields did not fall, reduction of seeding rates alone could not save enough grain to eliminate entirely the imports of recent years, but 12 million tons is a significant quantity.

With observed Soviet seeding rates, the policy of discouraging the use of clean fallow becomes even more costly. The area planted to grains in the dry parts of the Russian Republic and Kazakhstan is about 62 million hectares. If seeding rates in these areas are 1.5 to 2 centners per hectare, then expansion of fallow from about 10 percent to 30 percent would save 1.9 to 2.5 million tons of grain per year. The seed saving is seldom included in Soviet calculations of the advantages of increased use of fallow.

TABLE 9.16

Seeding Rates and Yield with Different Nitrogen

Nitrogen (kg/ha)	20	40	50	60
Seeding rate = 140 kg/ha: Yield	3100	3600	3800	3600
Seeding rate = 70 kg/ha: Yield	2000	2500	3000	3500

Source: F. L. Milthorpe and J. D. Ivins, The Growth of Cereals and Grasses (London, 1966); W. H. van Dobben, "Systems of Management of Cereals for Improved Yield and Quality," pp. 320, 321.

WILL THE FOOD PROGRAM
RAISE PRODUCTIVITY?

The inquiry into the relative productivity of Soviet agriculture indicates that agriculture in the USSR suffers from two handicaps, one climatic and the other economic. The country does not have a large area of well endowed land comparable to the American corn belt. However, Soviet climate and soil are well suited for the kinds of agriculture practiced in parts of North America outside the corn belt. The organization of Soviet agriculture and the quality of inputs used in production reduce productivity per unit input to about half of that obtained in comparable parts of North America. Soviet agriculture differs most from North American in the use and productivity of labor.

Without better information on comparative input quality, any division of the productivity difference into that contributed by economic organization and that due to poor input quality is only conjectural. In a more fundamental sense, the quality of inputs available to agriculture is closely related to the institutional structure of the Soviet economy. The quality of purchased inputs depends on the economic relations between farms and the suppliers of inputs. The age and sex composition of the Soviet agricultural work force differs considerably from that in North America, as the next chapter will discuss more fully. The composition of the labor force is itself a product of economic factors and of the interplay between economics and demography. Thus, even if more detailed information on the quality of inputs in Soviet agriculture were available, and if much of the productivity difference could be attributed to poor quality inputs, this would not exonerate the institutional structure from responsibility for poor productivity.

In theoretical analysis, a productivity gap indicates that more output could be produced from inputs currently in use or that the observed level of output could be produced with fewer inputs. In practice, if an economy is to undertake reforms to improve productivity, the two interpretations imply different remedial strategies. Steps to increase output from inputs already in place will not necessarily be the same as those to reduce the resources needed to attain existing output levels. Soviet leaders have clearly stated that they would like to achieve both increased output and reduced costs.

The steps they plan to take to achieve these goals in the 1980s are outlined in the Food Program presented in May of 1982. It is not clear how long the Food Program will outlive Brezhnev, but it is still instructive to examine its content in relation to the potential for productivity increase.

The Program presents a clearer statement of what needs to be done than what will be done. Brezhnev reiterated the known shortcomings in machinery and fertilizer quality, plant breeding, seed availability, and livestock productivity. He noted that relations between farms and suppliers of inputs must improve and that farms must be given more autonomy in their operations. He also put great emphasis on the importance of reducing losses in procurement, storage, transport, and processing of food: "More and more often, we're running into situations in which it's not production, but storage and processing of output and getting it to consumers that's the bottleneck." This is a dimension of Soviet agricultural efficiency that has not been included in the discussion above, and one that should be added to the measured gap in gross or net productivity. Reduction in transport and processing losses figures so prominently in recent Soviet discussions of food problems as to create the impression that inefficiency in production would be tolerable if losses at other stages in the food chain could be reduced.

The remedial actions proposed in the Food Program are essentially twofold: allocation of more money to agriculture, and minor administrative changes. Purchase prices for agricultural products will be raised as of January 1, 1983. Special price markups will be instituted for farms in poor financial shape. The price increases will cost 16 billion rubles annually, in addition to the already large subsidies discussed by D. Gale Johnson in Part I of this volume. Another 16 billion rubles annually will be spent on rural development and road construction, but much of this expense appears already to have been included in the announced Eleventh and Twelfth Five-Year Plan projections for the 1980s. Debts will be written off for financially weak farms, and poor collective farms will receive state funds for capital construction.

The role of agro-industrial associations in agricultural administration will increase, particularly at the district or lowest administrative level. Agro-industrial associations are not new and have been tried on an experimental basis in several republics in recent years. Now they are to be the major administrative innovation to ensure that existing and additional resources allocated to agriculture result in greater output at lower cost.

The district agro-industrial association is to include state farms, collective farms, interfarm enterprises, and other agricultural enterprises, as well as organizations that provide services to agriculture and are connected with processing. The associations are not to be independent of local government. The highest management agency of the district agro-industrial association is the association council, which is formed by the district Soviet, the organ of local government. The chairman of the association council is the first vice-chairman of the district Soviet executive committee.

The agro-industrial association has the right to present draft plans for state purchases to the district Soviet for confirmation. It can distribute centrally allocated agricultural inputs among farms and has some power to redistribute assets already in place. The association can assign tasks to member units in the district and can establish rates of compensation for services rendered by one enterprise to another. It has some power to determine bonuses for farm managers on member farms.

Nothing in the discussion of the agro-industrial associations to date suggests that they constitute an institutional reform sufficient to address the problems that Brezhnev outlined. They may improve communications between and among agricultural enterprises at the local level, but much more is wrong. It does not appear that farms will have greater autonomy in operations or in access to purchased inputs. Input suppliers are to be rewarded according to the output indicators of the farms they serve. This addresses the problem of poor relations between farms and suppliers but is unlikely to compensate for lack of binding contracts and incentives. If a farm fails to meet its procurement plan because feed shipments are not delivered on time, will penalties be charged not only to feed suppliers but also to fertilizer suppliers and to the machine repair stations that serve the same farm? The implication is that they will.

If the Food Program is carried out, it probably will result in some output increase. It is unlikely, however, that the Plan will affect productivity much or reduce costs of production. The Program seems skewed toward provision of additional resources and quite short on changes that will assure a higher return to these resources than past investments have earned. The Food Program is in essence an extraordinary statement of the price that current Soviet leaders are willing to pay in order to improve domestic food availability without committing themselves to major institutional reforms.

CHAPTER TEN

Labor Productivity
and the Labor Market

The last chapter showed Soviet agriculture was about half as productive per unit input as agriculture in comparable parts of North America, with the most significant difference in input use in the labor intensity of production. Agriculture in the less labor intensive areas of the USSR uses about ten times as much labor as comparable parts of North America, as data in Table 9.8 indicate.

Some argue that Soviet agriculture serves as employer of last resort in an economy highly committed to full employment: if Soviet agriculture fulfills the dual purpose of producing food and providing employment for the marginally employable, then labor productivity data are not comparable in the USSR and North America.

Does this argument have any validity? The rural work force in the 1970s grew faster than demand for labor in several Central Asian republics, particularly Uzbekistan. Collective farms in these areas were encouraged to take on some unemployed young people among their member families. A commentator discussing excess labor supply in Uzbekistan in 1981 noted, "Often students living in rural areas with manpower surpluses are urged to return as a group to work on their native collective farms, even though these farms may not have enough work for the personnel they already have."[1] However, the view of Soviet agriculture as a "work-fare" program is not consistent with increasing complaints of labor shortage in agriculture. The increased use of temporary workers during peak season is a symptom of the labor shortage. Temporary workers are used in Central Asia in the same areas where rural underemployment is said to be a problem. The labor shortage is reported chronic, not just seasonal, in parts of Central Russia where migration out of the countryside has been greatest. Furthermore, there is no need that agriculture absorb excess labor in most parts of the USSR outside of Central Asia, because demand for workers in industry and construction is high.

The reasons for the high labor intensity must therefore rest in the organization of agricultural production itself and in the links between agriculture and sectors supplying inputs. The USSR does not lag appreciably behind comparable areas of North America in tractor, combine, and truck power, according to evidence presented in chapter 9. Yet many unskilled workers, most of them middle-aged women, do manual field work. If these workers were not needed in the fields, they could help develop the rural service sector, the backwardness of which is one reason people leave the countryside. The need for unskilled manual labor arises because the machinery mix is inadequate and because the reliability of machines is low. A better mix of machinery would provide what the Soviets refer to as "complex mechanization," instead of the current partial mechanization that necessitates supplementary manual labor for much weeding and harvesting. Farms are stymied in attempts to implement fuller mechanization by difficulties in procuring attachments for basic farm equipment and in keeping the machinery in good repair.

If attention to quality and mix of machinery eliminated the need for the large unskilled manual labor force, would labor productivity rise to North American levels? Most unskilled manual laborers in agriculture are middle-aged or elderly women, although many young women work in positions of higher skill and responsibility, particularly in livestock production. If the labor force is divided by sex, and all women excluded, many highly productive young women will be overlooked, but the remaining workers will for the most part be men under the age of 60, since few men in the older cohorts survived World War II. Most men employed in agriculture have positions of some responsibility and at least minimal training. The data in Table 10.1 show that even if the Soviet labor force is restricted to men, most of whom are younger than 60 years of age, the number of hectares of cultivated land per worker in the USSR is still much lower than in comparable parts of the U.S. Therefore, the mix and quality of machinery does not fully explain the high labor intensity of Soviet agriculture.

A third possible explanation for the low productivity of Soviet labor relative to American is that Soviet workers are less well educated and trained than their North American counterparts. Unfortunately, we do not have data comprehensive enough to allow a full and accurate comparison of the quantity and quality of educa-

TABLE 10.1

Cultivated Land per Worker, USSR and U.S.

USSR, 1970 Hectares/Male Worker		U.S., 1969 Hectares/Worker	
USSR	16.74	Minnesota	43.76
RSFSR	22.30	North Dakota	186.03
Ukraine	11.33	South Dakota	100.26
Lithuania	11.01	Nebraska	74.08
Latvia	14.41	Montana	148.45
Estonia	14.04	Colorado	66.65
Georgia	2.40	New Mexico	29.84
Azerbaidzhan	5.06	Arizona	16.25
Armenia	4.31	Utah	23.29
Uzbekistan	4.44	Nevada	52.81
Kirghizia	6.81		
Tadzhikstan	3.88		
Turkmenia	4.51		
Kazakhstan	41.91		
Belorussia	9.14		
Moldavia	4.45		

Sources: *Itogi vsesoiuznoi perepisi naseleniia, 1970 goda*, Vol. V, pp. 194–294; *Narodnoe khozyaystvo SSSR, 1970*, p. 291; *1969 Census of Agriculture*, U.S. Department of Commerce, April 1979, Vol. II, p. 22; *Agricultural Statistics, 1970*, U.S. Department of Agriculture, p. 441.

tion that agricultural workers receive in the USSR and North America. Many Soviet agricultural workers who are considered to have specialized training have been taught to drive and make simple repairs on tractors and other machinery, skills that do not require specialized instruction in North America. According to the 1970 census, Soviet agricultural workers had on average 6.2 years of schooling, and this includes the relatively poorly educated older generation still employed in agriculture. Young people in the countryside between the ages of 16 and 19 had on average 9.2 years of schooling. The education data from the 1979 census have not yet been published, but it is likely that schooling of the rural population has increased since 1970. Thus, many relatively well educated young people are employed on Soviet farms, together with the poorly educated older generation. Despite incomplete data, it seems that differences in the education of the work force may explain some of the gap in Soviet and North American agricultural labor productivity, but not all.

A fourth explanation for the high intensity and low productivity of Soviet agricultural labor lies in the complex of regulations governing the labor market and wages, although it is difficult to give a quantitative assessment of the importance of institutional factors. The institutional environment affects the flow of labor from agriculture to nonagricultural employment, the allocation of workers among farms, and the effectiveness with which farm workers use their talents and energies.

The labor market should perform several functions in a country in which demand for labor is increasing in industry and in which the agricultural population is still sizeable. It should ensure that opportunities in agriculture change rapidly enough to keep pace with the increased attractiveness of non-agricultural jobs, so that some competent people find it worthwhile to remain in farming. It should provide enough flexibility in the allocation of workers among farms to avoid large inequalities in marginal products of labor among farms as workers leave farms and rural areas at differential rates.

Even the best labor markets cannot accomplish these objectives without supportive functioning of other markets. The Soviet agricultural labor market, however, is poorly organized to meet these objectives. The link between pay and performance is weak, and worker incentives are correspondingly poor. Regulations on the use of hired labor inhibit optimal distribution of workers among farms. Disequilibria in the labor distribution are exacerbated by the migration from agriculture, because resources besides labor are relatively immobile and because pay is poorly correlated with real productivity.

Soviet agricultural labor rules have arisen from two reinforcing sources: production ideology and political suspicion of the peasantry as a class. Soviet production ideology idealizes the factory as the model work place. Centralized organization of atomized workers, each of whom specializes in one part of the production process, is assumed to confer significant economies of scale in all economic activities. Historically, Soviet leaders believed that agricultural producers would not respond as the leadership required if they made their own production and marketing decisions under centrally administered prices. Both suspicion of the peasantry as a class and belief in large returns to scale in agriculture encouraged a form of agricultural organization on both state and collective farms that treats workers as if they worked on an assembly line.

Agriculture is inherently risky. Weather and natural conditions remain variable, even when price instability is removed, as it largely is by Soviet price policies. The achievement of consistently good performance requires sequential decisions about the timing of work and the ability to implement decisions.

Recent discussions of the value of education in agricultural production have forcefully argued that education allows workers to recognize and respond appropriately to change and disequilibria.[2] Systematic limits on the scope within which workers can make decisions and reap rewards for correct ones reduce the benefits obtainable from a better educated labor force. If the frustrations of working in agriculture are greater than those in other sectors, young people will opt for nonagricultural training, even if the material rewards are comparable. Some recent changes in the organization of agricultural labor suggest recognition of these problems at different levels of the Soviet leadership, but the discussion of these problems over the Food Program suggests that the changes will not go far enough.

AGRICULTURAL LABOR LAW

Soviet labor law is a source of distortions in the agricultural labor market. Agricultural labor law differs for state farms, collective farms, and the private sector. Differences between collective and state farms were more pronounced in the early 1960s than in 1982, but significant distinctions remain. Workers on state farms are wage earning employees of the state, and the general body of labor law pertaining to other state enterprises governs the conditions of their employment. Collective farm members are formally joint owners of the productive assets of the farm, with the exception of the land, which the state leases to the collective at no charge. If a member chooses to leave the farm, however, he or she receives no compensation for loss of the nominal share of asset ownership.

Labor laws relevant to collective farm members are contained in the farm charters, which are based on the 1969 Model Charter of the Collective Farm. This Charter states that all work on the farm is to be done by members, if possible. The farm can hire workers from outside only if no available worker among the membership can do the work. Collective farm members have first claim to available work on the farm, and, correspondingly, the farm has first claim on the labor of members. Employers on off-farm projects, for example in construction, are required to have release papers from the collective farm before employing one of its members in temporary work, and the release states the time period for which the worker can be employed off the farm.[3] If there is low paid work to be done on the farm, the management may retain workers instead of giving them releases for more highly paid work off the farm, and farm members are not guaranteed work during slack seasons. Still, off-farm slack season work in construction is fairly common in regions where the weather is sufficiently mild: in 1978 a directive on the conditions for hiring and paying these workers was issued.[4] State machinery maintenance stations can hire state and collective farm drivers in slack season, if the farms release them for temporary work.

Collective farm members, unlike other Soviet citizens, did not have the right to an internal passport until an August, 1974 decree of the Council of Ministers specified that as of July, 1975, all Soviet citizens over the age of sixteen had the right and obligation to have one. Without passports they could not legally leave the farms and obtain housing and work in a new place. (Exceptions are members of the armed forces, who give up their passports for the duration of their service, and Soviet citizens resident abroad with special passports for foreign travel who return temporarily to the USSR.) Under the new passport law, all citizens were to receive new passports, and rural residents living without passports were among the first to receive the new documents.[5] Distribution of passports began January 1, 1976, and was to be completed in 1981.

State farm workers are not bound by the membership relationship that defines the collective farm worker's place on the farm. They are hired by mutual agreement between the worker and the farm administration. Prospective employees must present both an internal passport and work book, the record of past employment. State farms can use full-time and temporary hired workers and are subject in hiring only to the limitations of the wage fund. It is easier to fire a worker from a state farm than to terminate the membership of a collective farm member.

Not all people who work full time on collective farms are members. An increasing number of specialists are hired from outside the membership and choose not to become members. They can negotiate advantages of membership in their contracts and can retain greater job mobility and better state social security benefits by not joining. Data on land use on collective farms show that in 1979 8.5 percent of the collective land used for private plots was worked by non-members, presumably the hired specialists. (In 1965 the corresponding figure was 5.8 percent.[6]) Since most hired specialist families have two working members, nonmembers constitute a minimum of 8.5 percent of the collective farm work force.

Both collective and state farm workers have rights to work private plots and to raise a limited number of livestock for private sale. The size of the plots varies according to the availability of land but cannot legally exceed 0.5 hectares per family. This provision may not be strictly enforced in villages where migration has left unused private plots that cannot easily be incorporated into the collective lands. It is illegal to hire labor for private work. All work on private plots must be done by family members.

In 1981 the rules on the number of livestock that a family could keep privately were changed. In addition to the still restricted number of private livestock raised for private sale or home consumption, families can now contract with the farm to raise collective animals for resale to the farm. The change in the rules on private livestock raised expectations that the Food Program would further loosen restrictions on private agriculture, but the text of the Program devotes little space to private agriculture. Farms are encouraged to aid members and employees in their private production, but no specific provisions strengthen encouragement.

Agriculture draws labor at peak seasons from off-farm sources, in addition to the regular work force. The state conscripts students and nonagricultural workers employed in state enterprises and sends them to farms to augment the regular farm work force, primarily during the harvest. Use of temporary workers has increased in the 1970s, and they contributed between 5 percent and 10 percent of the total agricultural labor input in 1979.[7] Temporary draft labor is recognized as a costly expedient, and its continued increase shows that the costs of distortions inhibiting optimal use of the regular labor force rise as labor migrates out of agriculture.

The increased use of temporary workers on collective as well as state farms suggests that restrictions on the use of hired labor serve primarily to reduce farm initiative in solving peak season labor needs. These laws restrict the local labor market and contribute to the need to requisition temporary workers from outside agriculture. They change the source of supply of hired labor but do not eliminate it.

The increased use of temporary workers from outside agriculture reflects the absorption into formal employment of farm family members who in the past worked primarily in the household economy and joined the agricultural labor force on a seasonal basis. During the 1960s most of these people took jobs outside the household. The only substantial group of able-bodied adults now formally outside the labor force are women in Central Asia and parts of the Caucasus. Most of the absorption, however, had taken place by 1970, and the use of temporary workers from outside agriculture increased even more between 1970 and 1979 than in the 1960s. This suggests that something more than a renaming of the seasonal work force is taking place.

Farms pay temporary workers provided by the state less than they pay their own employees for peak time work, but the productivity of nonagricultural workers is reported to be so low that farms probably employ them mainly out of necessity. Farms pay bonus wages to regular employees for peak time work, such as during the harvest, and temporary workers do not receive these bonuses. They are paid the regular state farm wage rate for work done, but the state provides additional payment by maintaining a proportion of their wages at their regular place of employment during their absence. Temporary machine operators receive regular wages during the days of travel to farm work and 75 percent of their pay for days on the farm. Temporary manual laborers retain 50 percent of their regular wages. Temporary workers can be given bonuses at the farm's discretion, and the new Food Program contains provision for higher bonus payments in kind for temporary harvest workers.

WAGES AND THE TARIFF SYSTEM

Wages in agriculture, as in the rest of the Soviet economy, are regulated by the norm and tariff system, which classifies all work into job categories and assigns a rank on the tariff scale, with a corresponding daily pay rate. The worker who completes the daily norm for that job in a seven-hour workday earns the tariff rate. Jobs requiring skill are classified in higher ranks, and unskilled jobs in lower ranks.

Prior to 1966, collective farm workers were not included in the tariff wage system.[8] Under the old collective farm wage system, work was divided into jobs with daily norms, but fulfilling the norm did not directly entitle the worker to a daily wage. Instead, each job was denominated in work points. At the end of the year, after the farm met all nonlabor production expenses, obligations to the state, and obligatory investment quotas, it divided the residual income among workers according to the number of work points accumulated over the year.

The residual income comprising the wage fund was usually so small that the level of wage payments was very low, and farm members found it both necessary and advantageous to spend much time on their private plots. The uncertainty of the value of a workday discouraged participation in collective work. In addition, inter-farm differences in the value of the workday resulted in different earnings for the same work on neighboring farms.

Efforts to regularize collective farm wages began soon after Stalin's death and continued through the Khrushchev years. In 1953 some collective farms began to give quarterly advances on annual wages. Changes in this direction continued until 1958, when Khrushchev recommended that a uniform money wage tariff for all farms paid regularly throughout the year replace the workday. The goal of these reforms was to raise and monetize wages enough to stimulate increased labor supply from collective farm members.

The Brezhnev administration inherited problems in implementing Khrushchev's wage reforms. In 1966 the new administration recommended that collective farms adopt the tariff and norm system of the state farms.

Collective farms were supposed to implement the recommendation to the extent that their resources allowed, and five-year loans were available for those that could not pay at the minimum rate. Under the new regulations, wages and payments into the state social security system were to have first claim on farm income net expenditures on nonlabor production inputs. The 1966 recommendation was legally strengthened by the provision incorporated into the 1969 revision of the collective farm Model Charter that collective farms must pay a guaranteed wage to members for work in the collective sector. The assembly of members of each farm was to determine the level of the wage.

Many farms did not have the resources to pay wages at state farm levels. Even though farm indebtedness is periodically forgiven, the loans did not allow all collective farms to pay according to tariff rates. The position of the poor collective farms was further complicated by increases in tariff rates in conjunction with increases in the state minimum wage from 45 rubles per month in 1959 to 60 rubles in 1968 and 70 rubles in 1974. Farms that cannot even now meet the prevailing tariff rates can scale down the tariff to correspond to a minimum wage of 60 or even 45-rubles. In 1979 some farms in Belorussia and the Russian Republic were still paying according to the tariff based on the 45 ruble minimum, but their number was said to be decreasing.[9] According to an article published in 1982 in *Ekonomika sel'skogo khoziaistva*, a leading journal of agricultural economics, prosperous collective farms are now encouraged to pay according to a tariff based on a minimum wage of 80 rubles. The writer of the article suggested that the tariff should not formally be changed until all collective farms are able to pay according to the 70-ruble tariff.[10] The tariff based on the 70-ruble minimum wage is the goal for most collective farms now and is shown in Table 10.2.

The tariff lists separate rates for manual labor and work with machines. Each division is further divided into time and piece rates. Jobs for which a daily norm can be established are considered piece rate jobs, and most work is of this sort. The time rate is applied only if a daily norm cannot be set. The rates for machine operators are divided into geographic zones of the country, with higher pay for harsher climates and places where the work year is shorter.

Tariffs are not uniform over all republics. Since not all farms pay according to the same tariff, the system does not provide the geographic uniformity of wages that it implies. However, the tariff does serve as a minimum below which farms should not fall and according to which they can judge their relative positions.

Even on the poorest farms that pay according to one of the lower tariffs, wages may be higher than tariff rates, because a complicated system of bonuses and extra payments operates in conjunction with the tariff system. The bonus system now in use on many

TABLE 10.2

Agricultural Wage Tariff Based on the 70 Ruble Minimum

(Rubles per 7 Hour Day)

Ranks	I	II	III	IV	V	VI
			MANUAL LABOR			
Time Rates	2.76	2.95	3.15	3.43	3.80	4.34
Piece Rates	2.95	3.15	3.37	3.67	4.06	4.65
			MECHANIZED LABOR			
Time Rates						
zone I	2.99	3.36	3.78	4.26	4.78	5.38
zone II	3.36	3.78	4.26	4.78	5.38	6.06
zone III	3.64	4.09	4.60	5.18	5.82	6.55
Piece Rates.						
zone I	3.23	3.64	4.09	4.60	5.18	5.82
zone II	3.64	4.09	4.60	5.18	5.82	6.55
zone III	3.93	4.43	4.98	5.60	6.30	7.08

Sources: Spravochnik po oplate truda v kolkhozakh Belorusskoi SSR (Minsk, 1977), p. 7, and Spravochnik po oplate truda v kolkhozakh (Moscow, 1973), p. 22.

farms was introduced in 1962. Workers receive tariff rates for work performed and bonuses according to the degree of enterprise plan fulfillment. No productivity bonus is paid if production is less than 80 percent of plan. The bonus rises to 25 percent of base tariff rates as production ranges from 80 percent to 100 percent of plan. Extra bonuses are paid for above plan production. There are supplementary and ad hoc bonuses in addition to the standard bonus system, and the number of these seems to have proliferated in the 1970s.

The wage system reflects conflicting goals of wage policy. The tariff is supposed to provide order and fairness and to assure that workers receive equal pay for equal work. However, the uniformity conflicts with the special needs and means of different farms and the changing demand and supply of workers of different skills. The bonus system allows farms to deviate considerably from the standardization of the tariff. Wages for comparable work on state farms differ less than on collective farms because state farm workers are more mobile. On collective farms, the membership relation of workers to the farm and restrictions on the use of hired labor result in wage disequilibria that persist over time.

Because of the multitude of bonuses and special payments, the importance of the tariff system should not be exaggerated. Actual wages diverge considerably from tariff rates, primarily because of differential bonuses. Between 1959 and 1974, tariff rates for manual labor in rank III on the piece rate scale increased 57 percent, from 2.15 rubles to 3.37. Tariff rates for machine work in zone II rank III on the piece rate scale increased 21 percent, from 3.80 to 4.60 rubles. Reported average daily wages on collective farms rose over the same period from 1.40 rubles to 4.54, and on state farms from 2.31 to 5.51 rubles. The increase in reported average wages was thus much greater than that in tariff rates. Reported average wages on state and collective farms in the fifteen republics are shown in Table 10.3. and Table 10.4.

Several developments in addition to increases in tariff rates contributed to higher average agricultural wages. The lowest paid agricultural workers are middle-aged and elderly unskilled women. As they retire and are replaced by better trained young people, sectoral averages increase. The improved skill composition of the agricultural work force in general has contributed to higher wages. The adoption of the tariff system on collective farms and state financing to support it boosted wages in the collective farm sector. Furthermore, many collective farms have been reorganized as state farms. The pace of reorganization was greatest in the 1960s, but reorganizations continue. Low wage collective farms become state farms with lower than average wages, but in most cases wages increase with the reorganization.

Increases in tariff rates cannot explain all the reported increase in average wages, even after one considers the changed skill composition of the work force and the reorganization of collective farms. Rough data on the changing occupational structure of the work force and the increased tariff rates suggest that the two together explain only about half of the reported wage increase. The unexplained portion is due in part to the greater importance of bonus payments, particularly since 1965.

Some bonuses are mandated as part of the tariff system and are proportional to tariff rates. Bonuses in this category are those for harvest work or for seniority on the same farm. For this reason, the bonuses are not entirely independent of the tariff system. However, the ad hoc bonuses for work on particular crops and the

TABLE 10.3

Collective Farm Average Daily Wages

(Rubles, Money and Kind)

	USSR	Rus	Ukr	Lit	Lat	Est	Gru	Aze
1960	1.40	1.46	1.19	1.03	1.51	2.15	1.52	1.65
1965	2.65	2.54	2.69	2.82	2.83	3.46	2.38	2.63
1970	3.90	3.95	3.58	4.78	4.74	6.41	3.83	3.87
1975	4.54	4.70	4.11	NA	5.92	NA	4.95	NA
1978	5.22	5.36	4.86	NA	6.59	NA	NA	NA
1979	5.35	NA	4.89	NA	6.95	9.84	NA	NA

	Arm	Uzb	Kir	Tad	Tur	Kaz	Bel	Mol
1960	NA	1.55	NA	NA	NA	NA	NA	1.49
1965	3.29	3.29	3.27	3.21	NA	NA	NA	2.99
1970	4.43	4.24	3.72	4.17	6.03	4.82	3.34	3.63
1975	4.60	NA	NA	4.53	5.43	NA	NA	NA
1978	NA	NA	NA	4.99	NA	NA	NA	NA
1979	NA	5.41	NA	NA	NA	NA	NA	NA

Sources: Narodnoe khoziaistvo, republics for various years; R. Tabaldiev, Khoziaistvennyi raschet i material'noe stimulirovanie v kolkhozakh (Frunze: Ilim, 1972).

TABLE 10.4

State Farm Average Daily Wages

(Rubles, Money and Kind)

	USSR	Rus	Ukr	Lit	Lat	Est	Gru	Aze
1960	2.31	NA	NA	1.92	NA	2.46	NA	2.21
1965	3.21	3.25	3.09	2.88	3.18	3.39	NA	2.59
1970	4.43	4.51	4.11	4.73	5.07	5.27	3.13	3.63
1975	5.51	5.78	4.92	NA	6.14	NA	NA	NA
1978	6.23	6.51	5.62	NA	7.04	NA	NA	NA
1979	6.36	NA	5.63	NA	7.13	NA	NA	NA

	Arm	Uzb	Kir	Tad	Tur	Kaz	Bel	Mol
1960	2.04	NA	NA	NA	NA	2.76	NA	2.24
1965	2.84	2.91	2.96	3.23	NA	3.65	NA	2.87
1970	4.12	4.23	3.66	3.84	NA	4.81	NA	3.55
1978	NA	NA	NA	4.95	NA	6.37	NA	NA
1979	NA	NA	NA	NA	NA	NA	NA	NA

Sources: See Table 10.3.

newly instituted bonuses for skill categories, such as Tobacco Expert in Moldavia and Irrigation Expert I or II Class in Uzbekistan, offer flexibility for solvent farms to reward good workers and attract needed ones.

Increased flexibility of farms in influencing wages has economic benefits, but the resulting wage inequalities among farms occasion the kind of criticism directed toward the old collective farm work point system. The author of a discussion in 1982 of collective farm wages complained that differences in net receipts per man-day among collective farms result in different wage levels for the same work.[11] This was one of the complaints that led to adoption of the tariff system on collective farms in 1966.

The growing discrepancy between tariff rates and actual wages on many farms and complaints about irregularities in the wage system suggest that an overhaul of the system may come soon. A number of modifications of the tariff system have been tried in recent years. One has been singled out for discussion in conjunction with the Food Program and will probably be encouraged in the future. It is called the job rate plus bonus system and applies primarily to machine operators. Under this system, the work unit is the team or brigade, the size of which varies with local conditions. A job rate plus bonus brigade recently praised in *Ekonomicheskaia gazeta* consisted of fourteen tractor drivers assigned an area of land and told what to grow.[12] Team members receive monthly wage advances, and a bonus rate is set per unit of final output. The team receives the lump sum bonus after harvest and divides it among members according to a system the team devises that takes into account the work time and skill level of team members.

The job rate plus bonus system is quite like the collective farm wage system used during Khrushchev's time, but on a small scale. In Khrushchev's wage system, collective farm workers received periodic advances, and the final division was made according to work points at the end of the year. The small scale of the new brigades and teams probably increases work incentives and improves organization within the team, but some complain that it does not improve overall farm performance. If only one brigade is set up in the new way on a farm, it probably attracts the best workers. Also, it is not clear how land is assigned to the brigade. A problem that press accounts of the brigade system acknowledge is the lack of incentive for the special brigades to cooperate with each other or to participate in general farm tasks. Moreover, the collective farm chairman has the power to draft brigade members for tasks outside the brigade. Thus, the brigade system is not the solution to problems of labor organization and pay.

The two major problems with the norm and tariff system are that it is costly to administer and does not promote labor productivity. The cost of monitoring the quantity and quality of work done is high. Workers who maintain exceptionally high standards may receive bonuses and prizes in the "socialist competition" program, but in general there is little monetary difference between a job poorly done and one competently fulfilled. Each farm is supposed to employ a personnel economist to oversee wages, but many farms do not. The question and answer column of the agricultural economics journal, *Ekonomika sel'skogo khoziaistva*, contains many questions from farm workers and managers about proper determination of wages in particular cases. The complexity of the norm and tariff system probably taxes the understanding and patience of Soviet farm managers and workers as much as our system of support prices and set asides occupies American farmers. However, Soviet farm managers must contend not only with the wage system but also with the whole complex of output and input directions from above.

More important, the tariff system provides little room for decision making on the part of workers. Instructions pass from farm managers to brigade leaders to workers, and workers are expected to follow orders. In the new job rate plus bonus brigades, workers have greater incentive to work well, and the small size of the brigade gives members more say in how the work should be done. However, the brigade cannot determine what it will produce, nor can it independently order inputs. Workers in the new brigades have incentives to be more productive, but they lack authority in important areas to act on the incentives.

PRODUCTIVITY AND WAGES

Low labor productivity was one of the symptoms of agricultural distress that led to the decision of the Brezhnev administration in 1965 to invest heavily in agriculture. Agricultural wages lagged so much behind levels in the rest of the economy that it was clear in the early and mid-1960s that a period of catching up was necessary. During this period, wages were expected to increase faster than productivity. It was expected, however, that the investments of the 1960s would be yielding returns by the 1970s and that labor productivity and wages would increase together, with productivity leading wages.

That this has not happened has caused considerable concern. Productivity improvement lagged considerably behind wage increases throughout the 1970s, according to Soviet measures, which calculate average gross product per worker or per day. According to this measure, labor productivity in agriculture lagged not only behind wage increases, but also behind productivity increase in industry. Capital investment in both industry and agriculture (excluding animal inventories) roughly tripled between 1965 and 1979. Gross average productivity per worker in agriculture increased 69 percent between 1965 and 1979, while the corresponding increase in industry was 101 percent, according to official Soviet data.[13] According to the production function estimations in chapter 9, agricultural productivity net of input increases declined in the northern republics between 1960 and 1979.

The disproportion in productivity growth between agriculture and industry brings two basic tenets of current wage policy into conflict. Wage increases are not supposed to outstrip productivity increases. At the same time, a substantial gap between agricultural and industrial wages violates standards of fairness and harkens back to Stalinist exploitation of agriculture. The wage gap also makes it difficult for farms to compete with industry for skilled workers. The wage gap can be closed either by administrative measures that raise agricultural wages even when productivity lags or by increasing productivity.

OUTMIGRATION AND THE LABOR MARKET

The gap in productivity and wages between agriculture and industry is not unique to the Soviet Union. A differential between agricultural and industrial wages attracts needed workers to industry and stimulates improvements in labor productivity in many countries where industrialization and technological change are taking place. The key to maintaining rough equilibrium between agricultural and nonagricultural wages and productivity is geographic and occupational mobility.

Stalin's decision to keep investment in agriculture at minimal levels and to use institutional barriers to mobility to regulate the outflow of labor from agriculture resulted in severe disequilibria in productivity and wages between agriculture and the rest of the economy. In the post-Stalin era, however, migration out of agriculture has been roughly comparable to that in the U.S. and Europe in similar periods of development. Between the Soviet censuses of 1959 and 1970, migration from rural areas and from agriculture proceeded at between 2 percent and 3 percent annually, as Table 10.5 shows.

The data in Table 10.5 were calculated from the censuses of 1959 and 1970, which provide an age breakdown of both rural and urban population. Using these data, and applying age-specific death rates figured at the national level, it is possible to estimate the proportion of the rural population that has migrated during the intercensal period. The resulting migration rates are net and understate gross migration. For example, in the Russian Republic, the number of rural residents between the ages of 16 and 55 in 1970 was 69 percent that of rural people aged 5 to 44 in 1959. After subtracting the estimated number of deaths, the data indicate that 27 percent of the rural people in this age group migrated, either to Russian cities or to other republics in the eleven-year period. A simple annual rate of migration was calculated by dividing the total proportion of the age group that migrated by 11. The annual rates of physical migration are shown in Table 10.5.

Occupational migration was similarly calculated. In 1959, 65.28 percent of employed rural people in the Russian Republic worked in agriculture. In 1970, the figure was 55.74 percent. The potential agricultural work force was assumed to be 65.28 percent of those aged 5 to 44 in 1959. The actual agricultural work force in 1970 was assumed to be 55.74 percent of those aged 16 to 55. The difference between the surviving potential agricultural work force of 1959 and the assumed actual work force of 1970 was identified as the occupational migrants. Simple annual rates of occupational migration for the republics are shown in Table 10.5

Migration has been shown in studies conducted in many parts of the world to depend on relative earning opportunities, availability of jobs, and factors that affect the costs of migration, such as education, distance, and family size. Of several measures of relative

TABLE 10.5

Migration and Related Data for Soviet Republics

Intercensal Period 1959–70

	1[a]	2[b]	3[c]	4[d]	5[e]
RSFSR	2.41	3.35	1.79	2.71	8.5
Ukraine	1.78	2.65	2.06	1.37	5.0
Lithuania	2.09	3.01	1.95	1.07	6.1
Latvia	.99	2.45	1.69	2.21	9.2
Estonia	1.17	2.71	1.37	2.84	10.4
Georgia	1.57	2.51	2.68	1.07	4.1
Azerbaidzhan	1.66	2.53	2.18	1.16	4.9
Armenia	2.02	3.06	1.88	1.35	10.5
Uzbekistan	1.05	2.02	1.55	.84	4.7
Kirgizia	.90	2.44	1.64	1.14	7.0
Tadzhikstan	1.43	2.20	1.99	.71	4.0
Turkmenia	1.02	1.85	NA	1.22	5.6
Kazakhstan	1.16	2.25	1.18	2.27	12.5
Belorussia	2.47	3.41	2.14	.80	4.7
Moldavia	1.38	2.15	2.00	48	3.1

Sources: Itogi vsesoiuznoi perepisi naselenia 1970 godu, and Narodnoe
khoziaistvo, various republics and years.

[a]Annual rate of physical outmigration from rural areas, 1959–1970,
percent.

[b]Annual rate of occupational migration out of agriculture, 1959–1970,
percent.

[c]Ratio of average nonagricultural wages to agricultural wages, 1965.

[d]Ratio of nonagricultural labor force to agricultural labor force,
1959.

[e]Nonagricultural jobs created annually per 100 agricultural workers,
1959–1970.

earnings opportunities in the USSR, the one that correlated most
closely with occupational migration was the simple ratio of wages
shown in Table 10.5 in column 3. This ratio excludes rural earnings from private plots. It is surprising that income from private
plots can be excluded from the relative earnings ratio, since even
in 1979, according to official data, collective farm households received 27 percent of their total income from this source.[14]

The explanation for the apparent lack of importance in the decision to migrate of earnings from private agriculture is twofold.
Some of those counted as occupational migrants took jobs in rural

areas off farms but remained members of collective farm house-holds and retained rights to work their private plots. In addition, measures of relative earnings that include private agriculture cover the primary source of nonwage income for rural people but do not include nonwage earnings of urban people, because the latter are not reported and are usually illegal. It is quite likely that urban people receive as much as 27 percent of total earnings from the second or unofficial economy. The simple relative earnings ratio is probably therefore a fairly good reflection of actual opportunities.

Two measures of job opportunities available to migrants are shown in Table 10.5. The first is the ratio of the nonagricultural labor force to the agricultural, both measured in 1965. This is shown as column 4 in Table 10.5. The second reflects the rate of growth in nonagricultural jobs relative to the number of agricultural workers and is shown in column 5. It is calculated as the average number of nonagricultural jobs created annually between 1959 and 1970 per 100 agricultural workers.

The data in Table 10.5 show that occupational migration was higher than physical migration and that the rates of both were sizeable. Migration out of agriculture was highest in the European parts of the country and low in Central Asia. Occupational migration was greatest where the wage ratio most favored non-agricultural work and where the size of the nonagricultural labor force was both large and growing rapidly.

The low migration in Central Asia results from historical factors and current economic policy. Industrialization has not proceeded as far or as fast in Central Asia as in European parts of the country, and the demand for nonagricultural labor is lower. Central Asian farms were less devastated by the war than were those in European republics, and the loss of life was less. The high birthrate and scarcity of nonagricultural jobs has resulted in excess rural population in much of Central Asia. Thus, migration off Central Asian farms can be considered more a response to the push of excess supply in agriculture than the pull of excess demand in industry. Furthermore, many Central Asians who seek nonagricultural jobs are unsuccessful because they speak Russian poorly. Managerial positions in Central Asia are often filled by Russian speakers, and they prefer to hire experienced and skilled Russian-speaking workers over Central Asian former farm workers. Concomitant with the buildup of excess labor supply in the Central Asian countryside is a flow of skilled workers into Central Asian cities from outside the region.

According to the preliminary results of the 1979 census, the number of Central Asians living in the Russian Republic and the Ukraine was not sufficient to list separately. Central Asians are among the 1 percent to 2 percent of people of "other nationalities" living in the Russian Republic and the Ukraine, at most 1.5 million people. Over 3 million Russians lived in Central Asia in 1979. Since the family structure of Russians and Central Asians differs, it is likely that more than two working people of Russian nationality lived in Central Asia for every Central Asian of working age outside the region.[15]

The inflow of industrial workers into central Asia would not diminish the opportunities of rural Central Asians if non-agricultural jobs in the region were increasing fast enough to accommodate both local rural migrants and those from outside Central Asia. The occupational data from the 1979 census are not yet available, but between 1959 and 1970 demand for nonagricultural workers grew faster in the Slavic republics than in the Central Asian. The effect of the labor flow into Central Asia is to exacerbate both the perceived labor deficit in agriculture in the northern parts of the USSR and the surplus in the south.

If the agricultural labor markets of the different regions were linked, one would expect the perceived labor shortage in the north and the surplus in the south to result in high wages in the north and low wages in the south. Table 10.6 shows that in 1970 the reverse was true. Wages were higher in Central Asia than in much of the European USSR. These reported average wages are not adjusted for differences in the skill composition of the labor force across republics, but the skill composition of the work force should be correlated with average productivity per day. According to data in Table 10.6, productivity is lower in the Central Asian republics than in the Slavic areas. Both wages and productivity are high in the Baltic republics.

When the price advantage that Soviet domestic prices confer to the Central Asian republics is removed from the productivity figures, Central Asian productivity is shown to be even lower relative to the rest of the country. In columns 4 and 6 of Table 10.6,

TABLE 10.6

Average Gross Productivity and Average Wages

In Rubles, 1970

	1 [a]	2 [b]	3 [c]	4 [d]	5 [e]	6 [f]
RSFSR	3.95	4.51	10.70	10.0	12.70	11.87
Ukraine	3.58	4.11	9.38	8.93	11.40	10.86
Lithuania	4.78	4.73	11.79	10.92	13.15	12.18
Latvia	4.74	5.07	13.09	12.35	15.17	14.31
Estonia	6.41	5.27	18.69	17.47	18.83	17.60
Georgia	3.83	3.13	5.77	5.39	6.67	6.23
Azerbaidzhan	3.87	3.63	5.01	4.14	6.13	5.07
Armenia	4.43	4.12	6.76	6.32	6.32	5.91
Uzbekistan	4.24	4.23	7.28	5.02	8.17	5.63
Kirgizia	3.72	3.66	9.06	7.43	8.08	6.62
Tadzhikstan	4.17	3.84	7.26	5.30	9.86	7.20
Turkmenia	6.03	NA	8.80	5.75	10.83	7.08
Kazakhstan	4.82	4.81	12.39	11.06	13.38	11.95
Belorussia	3.34	NA	8.56	7.93	9.71	8.99
Moldavia	3.63	3.55	9.06	8.47	8.62	8.06

Sources: See Tables 10.3, 10.4; and Sel'skoe khoziaistvo SSSR
(Moscow: Statistika, 1971), pp. 430, 431, 493, 589.

[a] Collective farm average daily wage, rubles, 1970.

[b] State farm average daily wage, rubles, 1970.

[c] Collective farm average gross product per day, 1970, in 1965 constant
Soviet domestic relative prices.

[d] Collective farm average gross product per day, 1970, in 1965 constant
prices converted to American relative prices using ratios in Table 9.4.

[e] State farm average gross product per day, 1970, in 1965 constant Soviet
domestic relative prices.

[f] State farm average gross product per day, 1970, in 1965 constant prices
converted to American relative prices using ratios in Table 9.4.

average productivity data have been converted from Soviet
domestic prices to American relative prices using the ratios shown
in Table 9.4. Collective farm wages in Uzbekistan are 85 percent
of gross average productivity when the Central Asian price bonus
is removed from the productivity data. On collective farms in
Turkmenia, wages are about equal to gross average productivity,
when gross product is figured in American relative prices.

When the use and payment of labor satisfy profit-maximizing
conditions in a market economy, the prevailing wage is equal to

the value of the contribution of the marginal worker. If the production process can be described by a log linear production function of the form estimated in the productivity comparisons in chapter 9, the marginal product of labor is equal to the average product
multiplied by the measured elasticity of output with respect to
labor. If the Soviet planning system resulted in efficient allocation
of resources, the use of labor and the prevailing wage would
mimic the optimal solution under market conditions. The wage
should be related to average productivity by a factor approximately equal to the measured elasticity of output with respect to
labor found in the production function estimates. In the function
estimated for the Soviet south alone, the coefficient of labor was
about .6. (See Table 9.11, equation 9). This coefficient is probably
artificially high because two of the remaining coefficients in the
equation are negative, but it is still not high enough to suggest that
the high wages in Central Asia are consistent with efficient resource allocation.

The high Central Asian agricultural wages probably result from
the interplay of ethnic politics, but recognition of the peculiarity
of Central Asian agricultural wages is seldom included in discussions of the low geographic and occupational mobility of Central Asians. Their reluctance to leave the countryside and their
region is attributed to language and cultural barriers that raise the
costs of migration, but little attention is given to wage policies that
reduce the benefits. In view of the movement of guest workers
across national borders in Europe, the linguistic and cultural barriers that Central Asians face within the USSR do not seem
sufficient to explain their relative immobility. The data in Table
10.5 show that the ethnic and cultural factors that affect migration
are superimposed on a structure of benefits and opportunities for
migration that encouraged outflow of labor from agriculture in
European Russia and discouraged it in Central Asia between 1959
and 1970.

Average productivity in the northern republics is higher than in
the south, but wages still absorb a third to one-half of average
gross product. In the estimation of the production function for the
Soviet northern republics alone, the coefficient of labor is essentially zero. (See equation 8 in Table 9.11). This is too low to reflect
the true contribution of labor to output, but it offers no evidence to

justify wages that are one-third to one-half of average product. Productivity appears too low relative to wages in both the northern and southern republics.

The poor distribution of the outmigration from agriculture has added in recent years to the persistent problem of low labor productivity. Both the economics literature and literary portrayals of life in the countryside present the outflow of labor from agriculture in the major grain and livestock producing regions as a major impediment to increased production.

Rapid migration from the countryside in market economies has allowed labor productivity and wages in agriculture to adjust to increased industrial productivity. It has also had negative effects on rural communities that migrants leave behind, but those most adversely affected are in the commercial and service sectors, rather than farming. It is tempting to consider the reports of the harm the exodus from the countryside causes in the northern parts of the USSR as the counterpart to similar comments that accompanied the migration in the U.S., and to dismiss as misplaced the complaints that the migration is detrimental to the farming as well as the nonfarming rural community. However, the rigidity of nonlabor resources in Soviet agriculture makes it likely that the outmigration may in fact be exacerbating productivity problems.

If labor is leaving agriculture rapidly, other resources must be sufficiently mobile to reestablish an equilibrium consistent with efficient resource use. In the U.S., this has meant consolidation of land in larger farms and more sophisticated equipment. Because resources are relatively mobile, a competent farmer can remain in agriculture even if his nonfarm opportunities are very good.

In the Soviet Union, a young person on a collective or state farm can look forward to a standard-sized private plot and the wage level for his or her work that the farm can offer. If it is a poor farm, the wage is probably low and is sustained by subsidies and loans from the state. The gap between urban and farm wages is greatest for poor farms, and people with opportunities to leave do so. Those who stay gain little from the higher land to labor ratio: even if the marginal product of labor increases, it is likely to result in reduced indebtedness to the state, with little change in wages. There is no market for land, so competent farmers cannot consolidate holdings. As skilled workers leave poor farms, the marginal physical product of remaining skilled workers increases, but the ability of the farm to pay these workers falls. Farms where wages are lower than for alternative nonagricultural work have no mechanism whereby a very good farmer can do well in agriculture. Young people on such farms try to leave before it is too late.

On the more prosperous farms, wages and living conditions may compare favorably with urban alternatives. These farms can pick and choose among applicants and may admit skilled young people from poorer farms. It is quite likely that the person who moves from a poor farm to a prosperous one has a higher physical marginal product on the poor farm but is paid a higher wage on the prosperous farm.

The plight of the poor farms is worsened by the fact that the young and better trained workers leave. Additional machinery could substitute for the loss of labor power, but the young migrants take with them the skills needed to run the machinery. Thus, in numbers of workers, it appears that the Soviet Union has excess labor in agriculture, even in the northern republics. At the same time, the distribution of workers and the skill composition of the work force is consistent with a labor shortage in important regions of the country. It is a labor shortage created by the wage and price system and the institutional rigidity of Soviet agriculture.

Rates of outmigration from agriculture seen recently in the Soviet Union are not higher than those in America or Europe during comparable periods of development or in parts of the Third World today. However, the flight of young skilled people from agriculture in whole regions of the country has contributed to production problems. The low productivity and problems of recent years should not be attributed to the migration of labor from agriculture, since the problems are fundamentally related to the rules and regulations governing agricultural production. However, it is likely that the migration has worsened already severe disequilibria. For this reason, serious Soviet discussions of the migration and labor shortage should not be dismissed as an attempt to hide economic problems.

APPENDIX

Data and Sources

Data used in this study are taken from official sources. For the Soviet Union, the main sources are the annual national statistical yearbook, *Narodnoe khoziaistvo SSSR*, the statistical yearbooks of the fifteen republics, and the agricultural yearbook, *Sel'skoe khoziaistvo SSSR* (Moscow: Ts.S.U., 1971). For the United States, the main sources are the annual of the Department of Agriculture, *Agricultural Statistics,* the *Statistical Bulletins* of the USDA, and the censuses of agriculture. For Canada, the main sources are the publications of Statistics Canada, in particular, *Agricultural Statistics for Canada,* and the *Handbook of Agricultural Statistics.* For Finland, the main source is the annual *Statistical Yearbook of Finland (Suomen Tilastollinen Vuosikirja).*

Land is defined to include cultivated land and fallow and to exclude natural pastures and grazing lands. For the Soviet Union, land includes seeded area plus fallow, which together compose *ploshchad' pashni,* plus land devoted to perennial plants, such as orchards. Cropland that is grazed is included. For Finland, land is defined as arable land. Meadow and improved pasture are excluded, but hayfields and cropland grazed are included. For the United States, land includes cropland harvested, used only for pasture, in cover crops, on which crops failed, and cultivated summer fallow. Idle cropland, woodland, rangeland, and pasture are excluded. For Canada, land includes planted area plus summer fallow. Land area in all sample units is expressed in thousand hectares.

Labor for the USSR includes days worked in agriculture in collective farms, state farms, and the private sector. Days worked in agriculture on collective and state farms in 1970 are shown in *Sel'skoe khoziaistvo SSSR,* pages 430–31. The same source gives indices of gross productivity and product per day worked for each of the republics for the period 1960–1970. These data allow construction of a series for 1960–70 of days worked in agriculture on collective and state farms. For the period 1971–79, *Narodnoe khoziaistvo SSSR* and the republic statistical yearbooks give data on the total wage bill and average daily wages on collective farms. These data together allow construction of a series of total days worked on collective farms in both agricultural and nonagricultural tasks. I assumed that 90 percent of the days worked on collective farms were in agriculture. Data on state farms for the period 1970–79 include the average annual number of workers, average monthly wages, and average daily wages. These data permit calculation of the days worked per month per worker and, with the average annual number of workers, the total days worked on state farms. The total days worked in socialized agriculture is the sum of days worked in agriculture on state and collective farms.

The national and republic statistical yearbooks give data on direct labor inputs per unit output of different products in the collective farm sector, plus the private sector output of major agricultural products. To calculate days worked in the private sector, I assumed that labor input per unit output in the private sector in 1960 was equal to that in the collective farm sector and that labor productivity improved 1 percent per year between 1960 and 1979. The resulting series of days worked in the private sector showed high correlation with annual fluctuations in output due primarily to weather. The deviations from trend in each republic were subtracted, and the detrended series served as days worked in the private sector. The total labor input in Soviet agriculture is the sum of days worked in socialized and private agriculture.

American agricultural employment data are reported by state in *Agricultural Statistics*. In addition, the Department of Agriculture calculates labor input per unit output of different products by agricultural region and reports the results in the series of *Statistical Bulletins*. The juxtaposition of the two labor series for several sample years, assuming the same seven-hour standard work day used for official Soviet accounting, implied 168 days worked per worker in the Lake States, 208 days in the Mountain States, and 212 days in the Northern Plains States. I used 200 days per year for Minnesota, 208 for the Mountain States, and 212 for the Northern Plains States to derive total days worked in agriculture in the American states.

Canadian agricultural labor data are reported for Ontario and the Prairie Provinces for 1960–74 in *The Labor Force*, published by

Statistics Canada (December 1974, vol. 30, No. 12, Table 40, p. 67). Later years of the same publication give the breakdown for the Prairie Provinces by province, and the earlier data for Prairie Provinces were disaggregated in the same proportions as are indicated in the later years. The Canadian data on people employed were converted to days worked by assuming 212 days per person, as was the case in the Northern Plains of the United States.

The Finnish statistical yearbook reports days worked in agriculture by farm family members and hired workers. All labor data are expressed in thousands of days worked.

The machinery variable is a sum of tractors, combines, cars, and trucks weighted by horsepower. Data on machines on farms in the USSR are available in *Narodnoe khoziaistvo,* and in the republic statistical yearbooks. Machines on farms in the United States during census years are reported in the Censuses of Agriculture. The years between censuses were interpolated. *Agricultural Statistics for Canada* report data on machines on farms in Canada during census years. The years between censuses were interpolated. The FAO *Production Yearbook* gives annual data on the number of tractors on farms in Finland. The 1973 *Finnish Statistical Yearbook* gives a complete report of machines on Finnish farms in 1969. The proportion of cars, trucks, and combines on Finnish farms relative to tractors was assumed constant over the twenty years. Comparative data on horsepower of American and Soviet machines are given in *USSR and the United States: Price Ratios for Machinery, 1967 Rubles—1972 Dollars,* National Foreign Assessment Center, September 1980, ER 80–10410.

Fertilizer use in thousands of metric tons active ingredients for the Soviet republics is reported in *Narodnoe khoziaistvo.* Data for the United States are reported in *Agricultural Statistics.* Data for Canada are reported in *Fertilizer Trade,* published by Statistics Canada. Data for Finland are reported by the FAO.

Animal inventories for the USSR are reported in *Narodnoe khoziaistvo,* the republic yearbooks, and *Sel'skoe khoziaistvo SSSR.* The figure used is as of January 1, when available. When only the December figure is reported, it is used for the following year. In the United States, animal inventories are reported as of January 1 in *Agricultural Statistics.* In Canada, the inventory is on December 1 and is reported in *Handbook of Agricultural Statistics, Agricultural Statistics for Canada,* and *Livestock and Animal*

Products Statistics. The December figure was used for the following year. In Finland, the animal inventory is on June 15 and is reported in the statistical yearbook. Animals were aggregated with the following weights: 0.8 for cattle, 0.2 for hogs, 0.1 for sheep and goats, and .01 for poultry.

The climate variable for the non-Soviet sample is Buringh, van Heemst, and Staring's PDM, the measure of potential dry matter, modified by the limiting factor of soil or moisture condition.[1] The Buringh, van Heemst, and Staring data are calculated for soil regions that do not respect political boundaries. Measures for the republics, states, provinces, and country in the sample were obtained by transferring the soil zones to political maps, and calculating a weighted average of the modified PDM for each political unit. The weights for aggregation were the proportion of the total cultivated area of the republic or state contained in each soil zone within its boundaries.

Irrigation is included in this calculation as if it were a gift of nature: irrigated land is not distinguished from naturally well watered land. The costs of irrigation depend on the natural endowment of surface and subsurface water, and, in this sense, the potential for irrigation in a region is closely linked to the natural resource endowment.

The climate variable is constructed to capture differences in agroclimatological conditions in cross section within the sample, and it is constant in time series.

Buringh, van Heemst, and Staring caution that their data may not be accurate for the USSR, and calculation of the climate variable as described above for the Soviet republics shows that, in fact, their data cannot be used for the Soviet part of the sample. The Buringh, van Heemst, and Staring data show a very high level of solar energy in Soviet Central Asia and the Caucasus, and their factor of water reduction for these regions does not appear to reflect correctly the severe moisture deficit. As a result, nonirrigated areas of the Caucasus and Central Asia appear from their data better endowed than the Ukraine or Moldavia. The calculations for the United States, Canada, and Finland do not appear flawed in this way. The Buringh, van Heemst, and Staring data not only defy common sense, but also are statistically inadequate in estimation of the Soviet sample alone. Better natural conditions should contribute positively to agricultural output, but the sign on the coefficient of the climate variable constructed with these data is negative. Use of this variable in a joint estimation for the Soviet and non-Soviet samples would burden the Soviet part of the sample with a spurious handicap.

Evaluation of the natural agricultural environment in the USSR is not a new endeavor, since these evaluations are used in determining output plans and in evaluating results. There is, therefore, a substantial Soviet literature on agroclimatological indices. The basic work most frequently cited by later authors is that of D. I. Shashko.[2] Few of these studies, unfortunately, provide nationwide indices of the kind needed for the present study. Curiously, a Soviet biologist has ranked the Soviet republics using a methodology similar to that of Buringh, van Heemst, and Staring, and reports results quite like theirs.[3] The author cites Buringh, van Heemst, and Staring without comment. As long as the calculated potential yield is not properly adjusted for the water deficit, the difference between actual yields and calculated potential yields increases as one moves to the southeast away from the Baltic republics. The biologist who conducted the study is from the far northwest, Estonia.

A work that is far from ideal but usable for the purposes of this study is that of V. V. Egorov, who creates an index similar to that of Buringh, van Heemst, and Staring, but in different units.[4] The Egorov index seems reasonable, but on careful examination, cannot be reproduced from the data included in the study. The index for each republic is a weighted average of the different zones within the republic, but the data for the zones are not always consistent with the composite index. The most serious problem with Egorov's index is that Turkmenia has twice the ranking of Uzbekistan. When the index for Uzbekistan is recalculated from the constituent zones in the republic, the difference between Uzbekistan and Turkmenia is reduced, but still quite large. Some of this difference is accounted for by the fact that Uzbekistan has an area of rain-fed agriculture in the mountainous parts of the republic, whereas cultivated nongrazing land in Turkmenia is virtually all irrigated.

If Buringh, van Heemst, and Staring's variable is considered acceptable for the non-Soviet parts of the sample, and Egorov's (ad-

justed) for the Soviet republics, the problem of merging the two
into one climate variable valid for all thirty sample areas still remains. To do this, I assumed that Buringh, van Heemst, and Staring are correct in their ranking of the Ukraine relative to the non-
Soviet sample, and that Egorov is correct in his ranking of the
other Soviet republics relative to the Ukraine. With these assump-
tions, the two indices can be merged into one. The resulting climate variable for the thirty geographic units is shown in Table 9.1.

Output is expressed in thousands of wheat equivalent units.
Wheat relative prices for the USSR and the United States are
shown in the text in Table 9.3. Total output for each area in each
year is aggregated first using Soviet wheat relative prices, then
using American wheat relative prices. The square root of the
product of the two is used as the output variable. Soviet small
grains are discounted 11 percent to account for differential measures of moisture and trash.

CONCLUSION

Soviet Agriculture
and the Soviet Economy

D. GALE JOHNSON

Karen Brooks and I have analyzed the productivity and efficiency of Soviet agriculture, given the natural resources it possesses. Soviet officials make frequent references to the climatic limitations that influence agricultural performance, and many Western observers accept the view that climatic conditions are a major determinant of the poor performance of Soviet agriculture. In Parts I and II we have attempted to isolate the effects of natural and climatic conditions, on the one hand, and policy factors, on the other hand, upon the productivity and efficiency of Soviet agriculture. We conclude that climatic factors fail to explain a significant part of the poor performance and present many examples of the adverse effects of particular policies upon either the level of output or the costs of production. However, we do not argue that climatic factors and other natural conditions are unimportant. One conclusion that emerges from our studies is that Soviet planners and bureaucrats have not been sufficiently flexible and imaginative to adjust to the great variability of natural conditions that confronts Soviet agriculture. Such variability exists across both space and time.

Our work indicates that there are very great differences in the productivity of Soviet agriculture as one looks at different farm products and geographic areas, similar to differences in other agricultures but hardly to the same degree. Part I shows that the average level of grain yields in the USSR is comparable to the yields in climatically similar areas in North America, if adjustment is made for the difference in the amount of clean fallow. But the analysis shows that minimizing clean fallow in the USSR results in high year-to-year variations in yields and significantly higher costs of production than would prevail under other farm management practices. It also shows that yields of cotton and sunflower compare favorably to yields in North America, though in recent years Soviet success in sunflower production has been severely damaged by a series of policy decisions. But Part I also shows that yields and productivity of other crop products, in particular the feed and forage crops, lag far behind what is achieved in climatically similar areas. Yet the poor output level of the feed crops has made it necessary to import enormous amounts of grain during the 1970s. Had the yields of feed crops been comparable to those in climatically analogous areas, much less imported grain would have been needed.

Part II supports the startling result that the resources devoted to agriculture in the Soviet Union produce approximately half as much as the same bundle of resources would produce in climatically similar areas in North America. This means that to produce a unit of output—a ruble's worth of farm products—requires much more land, labor, and capital in the Soviet Union than would be required to produce the same unit of output in North America in the analogous areas. This result should not be interpreted to mean that if only the Soviet Union would abandon socialized agriculture, farm output could be doubled from the currently utilized resources. It is more meaningful to interpret productivity comparisons to mean that recombining resources, providing resources of nonfarm origin of the same quality as those provided in the comparison areas, and carrying out farming operations in a timely and appropriate manner could lower the costs of production substantially, by perhaps as much as a half. If all of the negative policy factors that we have noted, as well as many others, were eliminated, improvements in the utilization of resources would clearly result in a combination of greater output and lower production costs.

Part II also shows that a large part of the difference in productivity of agriculture between Soviet and North American agriculture is in the average productivity or output per worker and not in yield per unit of land. The differences in land productivity are minor compared to the labor productivity differences. As presented in Table 9.8, average product of labor in the United States is almost everywhere ten times that in the Soviet Union and in some cases is as much as twenty to thirty times greater. The regression results in Part II indicate that for all resources, productivity in the United States is approximately double that in the Soviet Union. The much greater difference in output per unit of labor, our measure of labor productivity, is due to the use of much larger amounts of labor on farms in the Soviet Union than in climatically comparable areas.

An important though probably unintended consequence of the management of Soviet agriculture over the past two decades has been the small decline in the absolute amount of labor used in agriculture. Between 1960 and 1979 the total labor input in the socialized sector declined less than 10 percent; for the same period of time farm employment in the United States declined by 46 percent and in Canada by more than a third.[1] The continuing high level of agricultural employment in the Soviet Union, in spite of the very high rate of investment, is particularly relevant, given the current and anticipated slow growth of the national labor force. Improvements in the utilization of agricultural resources could result in the release of millions of workers for nonfarm activities.

The low productivity of labor in Soviet agriculture and the slow rate at which labor is being displaced by machinery, buildings, and equipment was the reason for the emphasis on the labor market in Part II. Substantial narrowing of the productivity gap between Soviet agriculture and its Western counterparts will require great improvements in the utilization of labor. This will require not only more appropriate wage policies and increased investment in human capital in rural areas but also major changes in the management and supervision of farm labor, as well as achievement of a much closer relationship between individual productivity and pay or reward.

Put even more briefly, we have concluded that the output and productivity of Soviet agriculture can be significantly increased if the appropriate policy reforms are undertaken. While climatic factors do impose limitations upon the potential level of farm production, our work has shown that output could be substantially increased on the basis of known farming practices and that production costs could be much lower. The climatic conditions faced by Canadian agriculture are not superior, on the average, to those prevailing in the Soviet Union, yet Canada has one of the world's lowest-cost agricultures.

MAJOR NEGATIVE POLICY FACTORS

Agricultural production in the USSR is much less than it could be, and production costs are higher than they need be. Our work has identified many of the policy factors that have been important in creating the present difficulties. Several are worthy of note in a brief summary. Three major areas may account for most of the shortcomings of Soviet agriculture. These are excessive centralization of the planning, control, and management of agriculture, inappropriate price policies, and defective incentive systems for farm managers and workers and for enterprises that supply inputs to agriculture and that market, transport, and process farm products.

These factors are interrelated, and what appears improvement in one may not have a significant positive result. To some degree, the excessive detail of planning and of planning indicators imposed upon farms is a necessary consequence of various features of the prices for farm inputs and products. Prices are set by the planners; the established prices do not result in equality of demand and supply. Some prices for farm products are quite profitable; other prices are very unprofitable. If farms were not directed to produce particular products, the farms in total would produce more of some products than could be sold at those prices, while the output of other products would be curtailed and the supply would fall far short of demand. Planners are thus faced with the necessity of either reforming the price system, a task of enormous complexity, or intervening in the production decisions of individual farms. So far, the planners have continued to intervene rather than accept the need to realign prices to approach more nearly those that would prevail in the market.[2]

But it is not only the output of individual farms that must be planned in great detail but also inputs such as machinery, building materials, fertilizer, insecticides, and protein feeds. If farms were permitted to purchase the most profitable amounts of these inputs, demand would greatly exceed supply in some cases and fall short in others. Given that prices generally remain unchanged for several years, some device must be found for allocating available supplies among the farms. Thus, farms have little to say about matters that are of great importance to them, and those who do make allocations of such inputs are incompetent to do so adequately.

The policy of fixed nominal prices of most food products, especially livestock products, has great potential for long-run harm to agriculture. As we have noted more than once, the cost of making up the difference between what is paid to the farms and what is charged to consumers has grown rapidly. For 1983 the food subsidy bill will exceed 50 billion rubles or perhaps as much as 8 or 9 percent of gross national product. This policy decision has deleterious consequences. The fixed prices for livestock products, especially meat, have encouraged the growth of demand for such products at a much more rapid rate than supply has or could have been expected to grow. The enormous costs of demand's exceeding supply at the prevailing prices have been noted—inordinate amounts of time spent in shopping and the need to create alternative and duplicate marketing and rationing systems for many ordinary products. Consequently, the output produced is made available to consumers in a costly manner, either because of time wasted in searching for meat in the stores or because of the duplication of marketing facilities when the meat is distributed by employers and trade unions.

The current system of planning and management fails to provide appropriate incentives for those who participate directly in agricultural production or who provide goods and services to the farms. With the current system of payment for farm work, the farm worker sees little or no relationship between his or her work and the pay received. Consequently, there is little incentive to do any particular job well, to work hard, or to work long hours during busy seasons of the year. The many criteria used to judge the performance of directors of collective and state farms are often inconsistent with achieving a high level of output at low cost. The plans include guidelines for the number of livestock held as well as the planned level of livestock output. But if the planned number of livestock is larger than the available feed supply can feed, meeting this goal or criterion is counterproductive and results in lower output. Even gross output is not an appropriate criterion for a low-cost agriculture; rewarding directors and farm managers for exceeding a gross output objective results in high costs of production and wastage of resources.

Nor are those who work for enterprises related to agriculture properly motivated to carry out their functions in a manner that would contribute most to agricultural productivity. The enormous wastes of fertilizer and of farm output during marketing, transportation, processing, and retailing are not due solely to lack of facilities but also to a failure to make it in the workers' interest to take more care. But, of course, the lack of facilities such as appropriate freight cars and refrigeration or inadequate canning capacity is due to the low priority given the food and service sector.

BUT NOT ALL IS NEGATIVE

While there is much to criticize in the performance of the Soviet agricultural system, it has some positive elements. Russia has had famines, some invoking enormous loss in life and great suffering, throughout its history. There have been three since the Communists took control—the early 1920s, the early 1930s, and 1947.[3] Each of the famines could have been avoided had different policies been followed. But an important accomplishment of the past three decades has been that the threat of famine no longer exists in the USSR. The level of grain production is now great enough so that the requirements for grain for food, industrial uses, and seed can be met from even a very poor grain crop. In addition, the substantial inventory of livestock serves as an important reserve in case of dire need. There is now no doubt, based on the evidence of the enormous grain imports of recent years, that the capacity exists to bring into the Soviet Union the amounts of grain that are required to prevent a substantial reduction in livestock production. The present level of production of grain and other food products is such that only an unimaginable disaster would cause a famine in the USSR even if no food came from the outside.

For a considerable period of time it was possible for Soviet officials to point with some pride to the achievements in the production of several products, such as cotton, sugar beets, and sunflowers. While the latter two appear to have registered declines in yields and production in recent years, the USSR has achieved and maintained self-sufficiency and a significant net export position in cotton, even with its relatively unfavorable climatic conditions.

While many details are lacking, the high growth rate in the production of poultry and eggs achieved over the past fifteen years represents a positive achievement. Although feed productivity in poultry production is apparently substantially below that achieved in Western Europe and North America, the current meat situation in the USSR would be much bleaker had it not been for the success in increasing poultry meat production. The growth of poultry and egg production occurred primarily in special state enterprises outside the ordinary state and collective farms and is similar to what has occurred in other situations where a high priority has been assigned. But history has shown that at any time only a small part of agriculture receives the priority, attention, and intelligent direction required to achieve significant success.

AGRICULTURE AND THE SOVIET ECONOMY

Soviet agriculture is a significant negative factor in the Soviet economy. As has been shown, nearly a third of national investment has been allocated to agriculture, including social as well as productive investments, and its supporting industrial sectors. Even with this enormous investment, the growth of agricultural output has been disappointing during the 1970s. Meat products have disappeared from the stores in most urban areas, and an alternative distribution system, with rationing, has been instituted. Meat is available in most areas at the collective farm markets, but at two to three times the state store prices.

Soviet officials have long emphasized achieving a level of per capita meat consumption similar to consumption in Western Europe. While there was considerable success in increasing meat consumption during the 1960s and early 1970s, in the years between 1975 and 1982 per capita consumption did not increase. This was true even though the USSR was the world's largest grain importer during this period, in some years importing a fifth of its total grain supply. It had been a significant net exporter of grain at the beginning of the 1970s.

Food and other agricultural products now constitute a major claimant for the foreign exchange earnings of the Soviet economy. In 1981 the USSR imported $16 billion more in agricultural products than were exported. In 1969–71 the excess of agricultural imports over exports was only $0.7 billion.[4] Most of the imports of agricultural products require payment in convertible currencies. Consequently, the shortcomings of Soviet agriculture constitute a significant claim not only against domestic resources but also against valuable foreign exchange.

Perhaps the most important strain that agriculture places upon the Soviet economy is the fiscal drain of the enormous food subsidies. Beginning in 1983 these subsidies will require a large fraction of the income of the Soviet government. The annual per capita cost of the subsidies will be about 195 rubles or somewhat more than a month's wage for an industrial worker. This is greater than the combined per capita expenditures for health and education. In 1976 the estimated per capita expenditures upon health and education together were 115 rubles.[5] Health and education expenditures in 1983 are unlikely to be more than 135 rubles.

It is true that the food subsidies represent income transfers within the economy and do not directly involve the use of real resources. But as recent Polish experience has shown, a time may come when the fiscal burden of subsidies becomes so great that these burdens are no longer consistent with a viable political and economic system. The subsidies create great distortions in the economy, since paying for the subsidies requires taxes upon other sectors of the economy. Soviets pay the food subsidies through higher prices for such consumer products as textiles, radios, television sets, and other consumer durables. While consumers and workers must and do pay the full bill for their food, the policy of fixed nominal prices and subsidies carries with it significant inefficiencies. In addition to the costs imposed upon consumers because demand exceeds supply, the high cost of food subsidies causes the Soviet planners to delay increasing prices paid to farms to cover rising costs of production. Thus, the subsidies serve as a barrier to expansion of agricultural production by delaying output price adjustments.

How significant are the shortcomings of Soviet agriculture for the economy as a whole? The slow growth and high cost of agriculture has clearly been a drag on the growth of per capita real earnings in the Soviet economy. Our analysis of the potential growth of agricultural production during the 1980s indicates that agriculture will remain a negative factor in the overall growth of the Soviet economy. But I do not believe that agriculture's poor performance will become a dominant factor in either the domestic or the foreign policies of the USSR. It is hard to believe that Soviet agriculture can impose significantly higher costs upon the Soviet system than it has during 1979–1982. During those years the Soviet system absorbed the effects of four poor grain crops as well as exceedingly low outputs of other products during some of the years. The negative impacts of the poor crops were absorbed in the face of the U.S. grain embargo imposed in January 1980, which had some modest impact upon the supplies of grain available to the Soviet Union for 1979–1980. While there is considerable dispute about the amount of grain denied to the Soviet Union, even if the upper probable limit of 6 million tons is accepted, the net reduction in total grain supplies would have been no more than 3 percent. The main impact of the embargo may have been to increase the cost of grain imports in 1980 because of higher prices paid for grain from Argentina and the added costs of transportation for the greater distances involved. One estimate of the added cost was $1 billion.[6]

One interpretation of the conservative nature of the Food Program announced in May 1982 is that the Soviet leadership has decided that the costs of limited performance and inefficiencies of the present agricultural system represent bearable costs. They apparently rejected alternative possibilities and arrangements, including radical changes in the planning and management of agriculture. Thus, the present quite unsatisfactory situation presents fewer dangers and costs than would major changes in policies, such as significant decentralization of agriculture management and a major reform of prices. It is hardly reasonable to assume that the current leadership did not give thought and consideration to the costs of continuing along the current path in agriculture versus the costs and benefits of alternative paths.

It is reasonable to assume that the USSR will continue to be a major importer of agricultural products during the 1980s. In Chapter 8 I have projected annual grain imports in the range of 25 million to 40 million tons for the rest of the 1980s. Other agricultural imports, including meat, sugar, fats and oils, tobacco, and fruits and vegetables, are likely to remain at recent high levels. Our emphasis upon grain imports may give the misleading impression that the cost of grain imports accounted for most of the cost of agricultural imports. In fact, in 1980 grain and products accounted for only about a third of the nearly $17 million import bill.[7] But the policies that have resulted in rapidly growing grain imports have had similar effects upon the growth of demand and domestic supply and thus upon the need to increase imports.

Some believe that a grain embargo could be an effective policy instrument for influencing Soviet behavior. A grain embargo will not be effective for at least two reasons. The first is that Soviet grain imports at 45 million tons constitute only a fifth of world grain imports. The United States exported almost exactly half of the grain that entered world trade in 1981/82.[8] Consequently, even if all U.S. grain exports were kept from the USSR, over 110 million tons would remain available from other sources. The second is that our recent experience shows that we cannot obtain sufficient support from other grain exporters to prevent the USSR from importing about as much grain as it is willing to pay for.

While I believe that the costs that agriculture imposes upon the Soviet economy are bearable and will be so for the 1980s, I do not want to leave the impression that the costs are without significance. The high level of investment in agriculture, the very large number of workers permanently in agriculture, and the great seasonal movement of urban workers to the farms to help with planting and harvesting do represent significant costs. If these costs could be substantially reduced, the range of viable alternatives available to the Soviet leadership would certainly expand. More resources would be available for a wide range of objectives, ranging from higher real incomes for Soviet citizens to greater military expenditures or to increased interventions of a political nature in various parts of the world.

Notes

Chapter 1

1. *The USSR in Figures: 1980* (Moscow: Statistika Publishers, 1981), pp. 126–29 in Russian language edition. All measures herein are metric.

2. Until 1981 the bonus was determined by the level of planned procurements. This policy apparently resulted in significant favoritism; a modest procurement goal was a valuable asset. Starting in 1981 the bonus for collective farms has been for sales in excess of deliveries for 1976–80.

3. I. Lukinov, *Economic Bases of Planned Price Control in the Agro-Industrial Complex of the USSR* (paper presented at the Sixth U.S.-Soviet Economic Symposium, June 7–11, 1981, Alma-Ata), p. 5.

4. G. Lisichk, "The Peasant Farmyard as an Ally of Communal Production," in *Literaturnaya gazeta*, December 17, 1980. Translated in *Current Digest of the Soviet Press*, XXXIII, No. 4 (February 25, 1980). The chairman of the May Day Collective Farm describes the advantages of the approach: "On the collective farm's livestock sections we use 12 to 13 centners of feed units per centner of added weight. But for the animals raised in cooperative arrangements with collective farmers, we use just 4 centners. We gain space for animals in the communal livestock sections, and this space isn't cheap." The collective farm chairman was not without some self-interest in the matter. He, his wife, son, and daughter-in-law raised 20 pigs in one year on 0.15 hectares of land and earned 3,000 rubles, and he indicated that he could increase his income to 5,000 rubles by increasing the number of pigs raised to 35. An article translated in the same issue of the *Current Digest of the Soviet Press* that consisted of questions and answers on private livestock stated that for the RSFSR it was anticipated that 8 million pigs and 300 million young fowl would be produced in this manner in a year. It was noted that the feed would be supplied by the farms. It also indicated that credit of up to 3,000 rubles for up to 50 percent of the cost of constructing facilities on the private plots for raising livestock to be sold to the farms was to be made available. The number of livestock permitted to families appears quite substantial, if the above example is realistic.

5. David W. Schoonover, "Soviet Agricultural Policies," in Joint Economic Committee, U.S. Congress, *Soviet Economy in Time of Change*, Joint Committee Print, 96th Congress, 1st Session, 1979, Vol. 2, pp. 87–115, provides an excellent review of Soviet agricultural policies, including the planning and management of agriculture.

6. "Planning Soviet Agriculture: Current Problems," in International Association of Agricultural Economics, *Papers and Reports; Fourteenth International Conference of Agricultural Economists*, August 23-September 2, 1970, p. 49.

7. *Pravda*, November 17, 1981. Translated in *The Current Digest of the Soviet Press*, XXXIII, No. 46 (December 1982), p. 4.

8. Boris Mozhayev, "From Remarks at the Round Table: The Easier You Go, the Farther You'll Get," *Literaturnoye obozreniye*, No. 5, May 1981, pp. 11–14. Translated in *The Current Digest of the Soviet Press*, XXXIII, No. 38 (October 21, 1981), p. 15.

9. Ibid., translated, p. 16.

Chapter 2

1. Douglas B. Diamond and W. Lee Davis, "Comparative Growth in Output and Productivity in U.S. and U.S.S.R. Agriculture," in *Soviet Economy in a Time of Change*, Joint Economic Committee, 1979, Vol. 2, p. 50, and U.S.D.A., ERS, *World Indices of Agricultural and Food Production*, Stat. Bul. 669, July 1981.

2. U.S. Department of Agriculture, ERS, *USSR: Review of Agriculture in 1981 and Outlook for 1982*, Supp. 1 to WAS-27, May 1982, p. 19.

3. U.S.D.A., ESCS, *USSR Agricultural Situation: Review of 1978 and Outlook for 1979*, Supplement 1 to WAS-18, p. 15. Procurement prices in 1977 for live animals (primarily beef and pork) averaged 1,570 rubles per ton (71 rubles per hundred weight); eggs, 0.83 rubles per dozen; grain, 107 rubles per ton. In 1979 milk prices were 277 rubles per ton (12.5 rubles per hundred weight).

4. In fact, per capita grain consumption may have declined between 1975 and 1980 by 2 kilograms or by 1.4 percent. Between 1970 and 1975 the decline was 8 kilograms or 5 percent, a rather more reasonable rate of decline. See *The USSR in Figures: 1980*, p. 182 (Russian edition).

5. The Tenth Plan had an ambitious goal for delivery of fertilizer to agriculture, with a planned increase of 52 percent. Actual deliveries fell short of this, increasing by 31 percent. Machinery deliveries increased significantly during the plan period, not quite at the rate originally planned. However, high scrappage rates held the growth in machinery inventories to a very modest rate. Fertilizer deliveries during the Tenth Plan averaged 18.1 million tons in terms of nutrient weight and 13.8 million tons during the Ninth Plan.

6. Diamond and Davis, "Comparative Growth in Output and Productivity in U.S. and U.S.S.R. Agriculture," p. 50.

7. David M. Schoonover, "Soviet Agricultural Policies," esp. pp. 94–98 and Werner G. Hahn, *The Politics of Soviet Agriculture, 1960–70* (Baltimore: The Johns Hopkins University Press, 1972), pp. 5–161.

8. Jerzy F. Karcz, "Seven Years on the Farm: Retrospect and Prospects," in *New Directions in the Soviet Economy*, Joint Economic Committee, 1966, p. 414. This article provides an excellent summary and analysis of Soviet agriculture for 1959–65.

Chapter 3

1. Diamond and Davis, "Comparative Growth in Output and Productivity in U.S. and USSR Agriculture," p. 50.

2. *The USSR in Figures: 1979 and 1980*, for data on stocks of farm machinery and deliveries in 1980.

3. U.S.D.A., Supplement 1 to WAS-27, p. 33.

4. *Sel'skaya Zhizn'*, February 12, 1981. The new soybean price is 350 rubles, about $500, per ton. The farm price of soybeans in the United States in mid-1980 was about $270 per ton.

5. These two new forms of price increases involve substantial budgetary costs. The previous bonus system provided payments averaging 3 to 3.5 billion dollars; presumably about this amount was added to the base procurement prices. The new bonus system has been estimated to increase farm incomes by 4 billion rubles. The two changes here in prices paid to farms will result in an increase in agricultural price subsidies of as much as 7.5 billion rubles in 1981 compared to 1980. Thus, total agricultural output price subsidies were as much as 35 billion rubles in 1981.

There will be further price increases for most farm products effective on January 1, 1983.

6. *Moscow News*, an English language weekly (No. 23, 1981), carried a full page article on the meat and milk situation in the USSR by Lev Voskresensky. The article starts with the following provocative question: "Why is the USSR having difficulties with meat and dairy products production?" His main argument was that demand was growing too fast, though he does not note the near absence of any per capita supply growth after 1975. But he makes two interesting points. One is that a significant part of the meat supply goes around the state food stores: therefore, the supply in the stores is not an adequate indication of the meat supply. He notes the expansion of the public catering network and that many enterprises "also have food order systems." Thus some workers can purchase food at their place of work: "Of course, certain people are bypassed by these channels of food distribution." (p. 12).

Another factor the author notes is that prices are not a barrier to increased demand. After noting that meat and milk and other subsidies cost 26 billion rubles (the figure for 1980 is 30 billion rubles of which all but 1.5 billion rubles was for food products) he wrote: "Economists can argue endlessly and make as many declarations as they please about the expediency of the current system of subsidized low prices, but the pricing policy is not going to change. Keeping strictly to this policy, the state travels from the premise that the growing demand for livestock produce is a justifiable phenomenon."

In my visit to Alma Ata and Tashkent in June 1981, I found meat plentiful in the collective farm markets at prices double or more than in the state store: 6 rubles for lamb, 4 rubles for beef and 4 rubles for pork per kilogram. But I saw no fresh meat in the several food stores that I visited, except for about ten hog heads. When sausage was available, there were lengthy queues.

7. Egg production per capita in 1976 in the USSR was approximately 75 percent of the U.S. level. See *Consumption in the USSR: An International Comparison*, Joint Economic Committee, 1981, p. 20.

8. Recent output levels and the 1985 goals are given in U.S. Department of Agriculture, Economics and Statistics Service, *Agricultural Situation: USSR; Review of 1980 and Outlook for 1981*, Supplement 1 to WAS-24, April 1981, p. 5. The 1985 goal for hay is 48 percent greater than 1980 output; for silage 61 percent. The goal for haylage calls for only 13 percent increase, but this source of feed is much less important than either hay or silage.

Chapter 4

1. *Izvestiya,* September 18, 1981, p. 2. Translated in *The Current Digest of the Soviet Press,* XXXIII, No. 38 (October 21, 1981), p. 19.

2. L. M. Johnson, "Economic Analysis of Crop Rotations in Western Canada," *Canadian Farm Economics* 13, No. 5 (October 1978), 9–24. The results that I have reported are for ten-year average yields and prices. Slightly different results were obtained when 1977 prices were used. With 1977 prices a rotation of fallow and two years of grain crops provided a net return of approximately 10 percent more than a two-year rotation of fallow and a grain crop. The reason for the difference in results was that grain prices relative to input prices were higher in 1977 than on the average for the decade.

3. I. N. Listopadov, "Crop Structure-Soil Fertility—Grain Production," *Zernovoye khozyaystvo,* No. 6 (1980), p. 17.

4. S. I. Gilevich, "Crop Rotation—The Basis for Guaranteed Yields," *Zernovoye khozyaystvo,* No. 6 (1980), pp. 19–20.

5. N. Gryzlov, "Developing the Food Program is a Key Task for the Soviets: Bryansk Potatoes," *Izvestiya,* July 3, 1981, p. 2. Translated in *The Current Digest of the Soviet Press,* XXXIII, No. 27 (August 5, 1981), p. 18.

6. See Part II, Chapter 9, for a further discussion of why seeding rates have been so high.

7. Academician V. Tikhonov, "The Development of Agriculture's Interbranch Ties," *Pravda,* August 4, 1978. Translated in *The Current Digest of the Soviet Press,* XXX, No. 31 (August 30, 1978), pp. 7–8. The period was apparently the decade from 1966 to 1976.

8. F. Chernetsky, "Spinning its Wheels," *Izvestiya,* (January 5, 1982). Translated in *The Current Digest of the Soviet Press,* XXXIV, No. 1 (February 3, 1982), p. 11.

9. V. Avdevich, "Manage Diligently: The Land Won't Write It Off," *Sovietskaya Rossiya,* May 30, 1981. Translated in *The Current Digest of the Soviet Press,* XXXIII, No. 28 (August 12, 1981), p. 13.

10. I. Totsky, "Giants Without Gear," *Pravda,* January 7, 1982. Translated in *The Current Digest of the Soviet Press,* XXXIV, No. 1 (February 3, 1982), p. 12.

11. V. Tikhonov, "Conversation on a Timely Topic: The Food Problem," *Sotsialisticheskaya industriya,* April 9, 1982, p. 3. Translated in *The Current Digest of the Soviet Press,* XXXIV, No. 18 (June 2, 1982), p. 11.

12. Diamond and Davis, "Comparative Growth in Output and Productivity in U.S. and U.S.S.R. Agriculture," pp. 40–42. The dollar value of USSR investment in agriculture is based on the use of purchasing power parities for agricultural machinery and equipment and construction. The resulting value of the investment ruble is about $2.90.

Chapter 5

1. Food and Agriculture Organization, *Production Yearbook, 1980.* Rome: FAO, 1981.

2. Ibid.

3. "Animal Husbandry is a Shock Front," *Pravda,* November 23, 1981, p. 2. Translated in *The Current Digest of the Soviet Press,* XXXIII, No. 47 (December 23, 1981), p. 25.

4. *Moscow News,* No. 23, 1981, p. 12.

5. D. Gale Johnson, "Soviet Agriculture Revisited," *American Journal of Agricultural Economics,* 53, No. 2 (May 1971), p. 262.

6. *Consumption in the USSR: An International Comparison,* Joint Economic Committee, 1981, pp. 23–24. The expenditures on alcohol, other beverages, and tobacco in the USSR account for 12 percent of total consumption expenditures compared to 4 percent in the United States.

7. Data on per capita disposable income are from M. Elizabeth Denton, "Soviet Consumer Policy: Trends and Prospects," in *Soviet Economy in Time of Change,* Joint Economic Committee, 1979, Vol. 1, p. 775. For livestock output, see David W. Carey and Joseph F. Havelka, "Soviet Agriculture: Progress and Problems," ibid., Vol. 2, p. 86. Population data are from official Soviet sources. The 1981 per capita disposable income is estimated by the writer and is intended only as a rough approximation.

8. V. Tolstov, "This Can Serve as a Model: Advance Order," *Trud,* January 8, 1982. Translated in *The Current Digest of The Soviet Press,* XXXIV, No. 2 (February 10, 1982), p. 1.

Chapter 6

1. U.S. Department of Agriculture, ESCS, *USSR Agricultural Situation: Review of 1979 and Outlook for 1980,* Supplement 1 to WAS-21, April 1980, p. 9.

2. In Part II, Karen Brooks presents comparative data on yield and production variability for grains. These data indicate substantially greater year-to-year yield variability in the USSR than in Canada.

3. *USSR: The Impact of Recent Climate Change on Grain Production* ER 76–10577 U, October 1976. This study was extended and updated in *USSR: Long-term Outlook for Grain Imports,* Central Intelligence Agency, ER 79–10057, January 1979.

4. J. A. Dyer, J. Girt and S. C. Lok, "Economic Benefits to N.S. Feed Grain Producers from Timeliness Improvements in Spring Field Operations," *Canadian Farm Economics,* 16, No. 1 (1981), 6–11.

Chapter 7

1. Speech by Comrade L. I. Brezhnev at the Plenary Session of the CPSU Central Committee on November 16, 1981. *Pravda* and *Izvestiya,* November 17, 1981, pp. 1–2. Translated in *The Current Digest of the Soviet Press,* XXXIII, No. 46 (December 16, 1981), p. 4.

2. "On the USSR Food Program for the Period up to 1990 and Measures for its Implementation—Report by Comrade L. I. Brezhnev" *Pravda,* May 25, 1982, pp. 1–2, *Izvestiya,* pp. 1–3. Translated in *The Current Digest of the Soviet Press,* XXXIV, No. 21 (June 23, 1982), p. 7.

3. Carl E. Wadekin, *Agrarian Policies in Communist Europe* (Totowa, New Jersey: Allan Held, Osmun, c. 1982), pp. 53–54.

4. "On Instances of Gross Violations and Distortions in the Practice of Planning Collective Farm and State Farm Production" *Pravda* and *Izvestiya,* March 24, 1964, p. 3. Translated in *The Current Digest of the Soviet Press,* XVI, No. 12 (April 15, 1964), p. 10.

5. Ibid., XVII, No. 11 (1965), p. 4.

6. Ibid, XVII, No. 12 (1965), p. 10.

Chapter 8

1. Michael D. Zahn, "Soviet Livestock Feed in Perspective," in *Soviet Economy in a Time of Change,* Joint Economic Committee, 1979, Vol. 2, p. 184.

2. Ibid., pp. 182–84.

3. The 17 percent increase is for 1985 compared to 1978–80, and livestock output is weighted by 1970 ruble prices.

4. This comparison was for 1985 with 1978–80. It is reasonable to assume that use of these feeds during 1978–80 differed little from 1976–80.

5. I have drawn heavily upon Zahn, "Soviet Livestock Feed in Perspective" in this chapter. He recognizes, as do I, that Soviet data on feed production and use are inadequate. In particular, estimates of the feed units derived from pasture represent a residual. Zahn's estimates, as well as Soviet data, indicate that the absolute amount of feed derived from pasture has hardly increased over the past two decades. Is this a reasonable result? The result is consistent with what we know about the low priority given to pastures and to meadow hays and the absence of any significant upward trend in the yield of meadow hays.

6. U.S.D.A., *USSR: Agricultural Situation, Review of 1979 and Outlook for 1980,* Supplement 1 to WAS-21, April 1980, pp. 35–37.

7. I have not seen a specific grain production goal for 1990. The announcement of the Food Program stated that by 1990 the yield of grain crops should be increased by 6 to 7 centners per hectare, bringing the yields to 12 to 22 centners per hectare. However, it said nothing about the grain area. If the grain area remained at the recent level of 127 million hectares, the midpoint of the yield range would give a production of 273 million tons. This is too high for the production goal for the entire plan period. One implication is that the area of clean fallow is to be increased and the grain area reduced to about 121 million hectares. A grain goal of 260 million tons for 1990 seems a reasonable interpretation of the information provided.

8. These projections are based on the linear yield trend presented in Table 6.8. If a log linear trend is used, the projected outputs are somewhat higher, namely 226 million tons for 1981–86.

9. After I made the above estimates, I received a copy of "Climate and Grain Production in the Soviet Union" by Russell A. Ambroziak and David W. Carey (*Soviet Economy in the 1980s: Problems and Prospects,* Joint Economic Committee, 1982). Their grain output projections are even more pessimistic than mine. With average climate the 1981–85 output projection is 212 million tons (1985, 215 million tons); their high estimate is 230 million tons and the low estimate 183 million tons.

10. "On the USSR Food Program for the Period Up to 1990 and Measures for its Implementation—Report by Comrade L. I. Brezhnev" *Pravda,* May 25, 1982, pp. 1–2, *Izvestiya,* pp. 1–3. Translated in *The Current Digest of the Soviet Press,* XXXIV, No. 21 (June 23, 1982), p. 6.

11. "The USSR Food Program for the Period up to 1990" *Pravda* and *Izvestiya,* May 27, 1982, p. 104. Translated in *The Current Digest of the Soviet Press,* XXXIV, No. 22 (June 30, 1982), p. 11.

12. "Present-day Problems of Restructuring the Countryside," *Voprosy ekonomiki,* No. 5, May 1978. Translated in *The Current Digest of the Soviet Press,* XXX, No. 30 (1978), p. 6. The translation states that "a total of 900 to

1,000 km. of paved roads" must be built, but this is a misprint. The text states that each farm must build 16 to 20 kilometers of paved roads; at the time there were approximately 48,000 collective and state farms.

13. "The USSR Food Program for the Period up to 1990" *Pravda* and *Izvestiya*, May 27, 1982, p. 104. Translated in *The Current Digest of the Soviet Press*, XXXIV, No. 22 (June 30, 1982), p. 11.

14. "On the USSR Food Program for the Period Up to 1990 and Measures for its Implementation—Report by Comrade L. I. Brezhnev" *Pravda*, May 25, 1982, p. 102, *Izvestiya*, pp. 1–3. Translated in *The Current Digest of the Soviet Press*, XXXIV, No. 21 (June 23, 1982), p. 7.

15. "The USSR Food Program for the Period Up to 1990" *Pravda* and *Izvestiya*, May 27, 1982, pp. 1–4. Translated in *The Current Digest of the Soviet Press*, XXXIV, No. 22 (June 30, 1982). p. 12.

16. Y. U. Mezhberg, "Present-Day Problems of Restructuring the Countryside," *Voprosy ekonomiki*, No. 5 May 1978, pp. 78–88. Translated in *The Current Digest of the Soviet Press*, XXX, No. 30, (1978).

17. Boris Mozhayev, "From Remarks at the Round Table: The Easier You Go, the Farther You'll Get," *Literaturnoye obozreniye*, No. 5, May 1981, pp. 11–14. Translated in *The Current Digest of the Soviet Press*, XXXIII, No. 38 (October 21, 1981), p. 16.

NOTES TO PART II

Chapter 9

1. A. M. Emel'ianov, *Ekonomika sel'skogo khoziaistva na sovremennom etape* (Moscow: Moscow State University, 1980), p. 256.

2. D. Gale Johnson, "The Derivation of Crop Analogues for the Soviet Union," mimeo, University of Chicago, 1950.

3. V. G. Pozdniakov, "Ispol'zovanie opyta v proizvodstve zerna," *Zernovoe khoziaistvo*, No. 4 (1980), pp. 38–40.

4. J. H. Chang, "Potential Photosynthesis and Crop Productivity," *Annals of the Association of American Geographers*, 60 (1970), p. 97.

5. See, for example, J. H. Chang, "A Climatological Consideration of the Transference of Agricultural Technology," in *Agricultural Meteorology*, 25, No. 1 (September, 1981), pp. 1–13; and F. Hashemi, G. W. Smith, and M. T. Habibian, "Inadequacy of Climatological Classification Systems in Agroclimatic Analogue Evaluations—Suggested Alternatives," in *Agricultural Meteorology*, 24, No. 3 (July 1981), pp. 157–173.

6. P. Buringh, H. D. J. van Heemst, G. J. Staring, "Computation of the Absolute Maximum Food Production of the World," Agricultural University, Wageningen, January, 1975, in H. Linnemann, Jerrie DeHoogh, Michiel A. Keyzer, and H. D. J. van Heemst, *Model of International Relations in Agriculture*, Contributions to Economic Analysis 124 (Amsterdam: North Holland, 1979). The measure was used by Mundlak and Hellinghausen in cross-country estimation of agricultural production functions, and it performed acceptably in that context. See Yair Mundlak and Rene Hellinghausen, "The Intercountry Agricultural Production Function—Another View," *American Journal of Agricultural Economics*, 64 (November 1982).

7. V. V. Egorov, "Prirodno-selskokhoziaistvennoe raionirovanie zemel'-nogo fonda SSSR," *Nauchnye trudy VASKhNIL*, (Moscow: Kolos, 1975).

8. Yujiro Hayami and Vernon Ruttan, *Agricultural Development: An International Perspective* (Baltimore: Johns Hopkins University Press, 1971).

9. *Handbook of Economic Statistics, 1980* (Washington: National Foreign Assessment Center, CIA), p. 189.

10. *Narodnoe khoziaistvo SSSR*, 1979.

11. *Narodnoe khoziaistvo SSSR*, 1979, p. 312.

12. Ye. L. Manevich, "The Rational Utilization of Manpower," in *Voprosy ekonomiki*, No. 9 (September 1981), pp. 55–66. Abstract in *The Current Digest of the Soviet Press*, XXXIV, No. 8 (March 24, 1982), p. 5.

13. V. G. Glinianyi, *Ispol'zovanie rabochego vremeni v rastenievodstve* (Moscow: 1978), p. 15.

14. Stephen Rapawy, *Estimates and Projections of the Labor Force and Civilian Employment in the USSR 1950 to 1990*, Foreign Economic Report No. 10 (U.S. Department of Commerce, September 1976).

15. *FAO Fertilizer Yearbook*, 1979, Vol. 29 (Rome: Food and Agriculture Organization of the United Nations, 1980), Table 11.

16. *Vestnik statistiki*, No. 3, 1981, p. 78.

17. A high degree of collinearity among independent variables reduces the confidence with which effects can be attributed to any one of the variables separately. Multicollinearity can be expected in this sample primarily in the time series dimension. All the estimations reported below have been cleaned of multicollinearity through a procedure developed by Yair Mundlak. The procedure requires extraction of the principal components of the cross-product matrix formed from observations on the n independent variables, and retention of the k less than or equal to n components that together contribute at a specified statistical level to the explanation of the dependent variable. The technique is developed in Yair Mundlak, "On the Concept of Non-Significant Functions and its Implications for Regression Analysis," in *Journal of Econometrics*, 16, No. 1 (1981), 139–149. When multicollinearity is not a serious problem (with seriousness defined in the specification of the statistical level of the test), all the principal components of the original matrix are retained, and the estimation is equivalent to the ordinary least square estimation.

The geographic units in the samples differ greatly in size, and heteroscedasticity is a problem that could potentially affect the standard errors of the estimated coefficients. Since the standard errors are important in determining which principal components are retained, heteroscedasticity can also affect the magnitude of the estimated coefficients.

In order to correct for heteroscedasticity, the dependent variable was expressed as output per hectare. Land was retained among the independent variables, and the estimated coefficients were thus not constrained to sum to unity. In the estimation with output per hectare as the independent variable, all coefficients except that of land are equal to those that would have resulted if output had been used as the dependent variable, and heteroscedasticity had not been a problem. The estimated coefficient for land in the first case differs from that in the second by unity. In the results reported as equations 1, 2, and 3 in Table 9.10, the coefficient of land and the t statistic have been adjusted to equal what would have been obtained had the dependent variable been output and had heteroscedasticity not been a problem.

The equations were first corrected for heteroscedasticity, and then the principal components procedure to correct for multicollinearity was applied.

18. Douglas B. Diamond and W. Lee Davis, "Comparative Growth in Output and Productivity in U.S. and U.S.S.R. Agriculture," in *Soviet Economy in a Time of Change*, Joint Economic Committee, 1979, Vol. 2, p. 32.

19. *Field Crops: Production, Farm Use, Sales, and Value by States*, USDA Crop Reporting Board, Statistical Bulletin No. 597, April 1978.

20. A. I. Zholobov, "Zernovoe pole: itogi, problemy, zadachi," *Zernovoe khoziaistvo*, No. 1 (1980), p. 4.

21. *Agricultural Statistics*, 1980.

22. *Zernovoe khoziaistvo*, No. 2 (1981), pp. 5, 10.

23. K. Sh. Bagamanov, *Problemy ustoichivogo razvitiia i povysheniia effektivnosti zernogo proizvodstva* (Moscow: 1977), p. 109.

24. S. S. Sdobnikov, "Vozmozhnosti uvelicheniia proizvodstva zerna," *Zernovoe khoziaistvo*, No. 10 (1980), p. 5.

25. V. N. Molchanov, "V Volgogradskoi oblasti," *Zernovoe khoziaistvo*, No. 9 (1980), p. 29.

26. *Zernovoe khoziaistvo*, No. 1 (1981), p. 29.

27. W. H. van Dobben, "Systems of Management of Cereals for Improved Yield and Quality," in Frederick Milthorpe and J. D. Ivins, eds., *The Growth of Cereals and Grasses* (London: Butterworths, 1966), p. 320.

Chapter 10

1. G. A. Shister, "Sources of Replenishment for Uzbekistan's Working Class at the Stage of Developed Socialism," in *Istoriia SSSR*, No. 6 (November-December 1981). Abstract in *The Current Digest of the Soviet Press*, XXXIV, No. 8 (March 24, 1982), p. 8.

2. See, for example, T. W. Schultz, "The Value of the Ability to Deal with Disequilibria," *Journal of Economic Literature* 13 (1975), pp. 872–76; and Finis Welch, "Education in Production," *Journal of Political Economy* 78 (1970), pp. 32–59.

3. "Typovoi dogovor na vypolnenie kolkhoznikami-otkhodnikami i drugimi grazhdanami rabot po stroitel'stvu ob'ektov v sel'skoi mestnosti," *Ekonomika sel'skogo khoziaistva*, No. 10 (1978), p. 124.

4. Ibid.

5. B. T. Shmilin, *Molotkastyi, serpastyi* (Moscow: 1979).

6. *Narodnoe khoziaistvo SSSR 1979*, p. 237; and 1965, p. 277.

7. See chapter 9, p. 137.

8. Lazar Volin, *A Century of Russian Agriculture* (Cambridge, Mass.: Harvard University Press, 1970).

9. *Ekonomika i organizatsiia sel'skokhoziaistvennogo proizvodstva* (Moscow: Mysl', 1979), p. 343.

10. N. Shal'nev, "Puti sovershenstvovaniia raspredeleniia po trudu v kolkhozakh," *Ekonomika sel'skogo khoziaistva*, No. 5 (1982), p. 74.

11. Ibid., p. 72.

12. N. Dudorov, "The Harvest Determines the Pay," *Ekonomicheskaia gazeta*, No. 22 (May 1982), p. 18. Abstract in *The Current Digest of the Soviet Press*, XXXIV, No. 24 (July 14, 1982), p. 9.

13. *Narodnoe khoziaistvo SSSR*, 1979, pp. 148, 307.

14. Ibid., p. 411.
15. *Vestnik statistiki,* No. 2 (1980), pp. 11–30.

Appendix

1. P. Buringh, H. D. J. van Heemst, G. J. Staring, "Computation of the Absolute Maximum Food Production of the World," Agricultural University, Wageningen, January 1975, in H. Linnemann, Jerrie DeHoogh, Michiel A. Keyzer, and H. D. J. van Heemst, *Model of International Relations in Agriculture,* Contributions to Economic Analysis 124 (Amsterdam: North Holland, 1979).
2. D. I. Shashko, *Agroklimaticheskoe raionirovanie SSSR* (Moscow: Kolos, 1967).
3. Kh. G. Tooming, "Na kakoi uroven' urozhaia orientirovat'sia pri programmirovanii urozhaia," in I. S. Shatilov and M. K. Kaiumov, *Nauchnye osnovy programmirovaniia urozhaia sel'skokhoziaistvennykh kul'tur* (Moscow: Kolos, 1978), pp. 10–17.
4. V. V. Egorov, "Prirodno-sel'skokhoziaistvennoe raionirovanie zemel'nogo fonda SSSR," *Nauchnye trudy VASKhNIL* (Moscow: Kolos, 1975).

NOTES TO CONCLUSION

1. Calculated from D. Gale Johnson, "International Trade and Agricultural Labor Markets: Farm Policy as Quasi-Adjustment Policy," *American Journal of Agricultural Economics,* Vol. 64, No. 2 (May 1982), p. 359.
2. For an informed and perceptive discussion of the numerous abortive efforts to reform the Soviet economic system, see Gertrude E. Schroeder, "The Soviet Economy on a Treadmill of 'Reforms,' " in the *Soviet Economy in a Time of Change,* Joint Economic Committee, 1979, Vol. 2, pp. 312–40. Schroeder summarizes the minimal effects of what were intended to be significant reforms: "A decade of reforming the reforms has not altered the nature of the Soviet economic system in any essential respect. It remains one of rigid, highly centralized planning of production, formal rationing of nearly all producer goods, centrally-fixed prices, and incentives geared to meeting plans. Since these characteristics of the system contain the roots of its difficulties in using resources efficiently and gearing production to customers' wants, it is no surprise that the problems have defied solution" (pp. 336–37).
3. "Famine," in *Encyclopedia Britannica,* 1962 edition, vol. 9, p. 63.
4. Food and Agricultural Organization of the United Nations, *Trade Yearbook,* 1980, and U.S.D.A., ERS, *USSR: Review of Agriculture in 1981 and Outlook for 1982,* Supp. 1 to WAS-27, May 1982, pp. 11–14.
5. *Consumption in the USSR: An International Comparison,* Joint Economic Committee, 1981, p. 20.
6. Testimony, Frank E. Doe, *Allocation of Resources in the Soviet Union and China—1981,* Joint Economic Committee, 1981, p. 168.
7. U.S.D.A., ERS, *USSR: Review of Agriculture in 1981 and Outlook for 1982,* p. 14.
8. U.S. Department of Agriculture, FAS, *Foreign Agriculture Circular: Grains,* FG-26-82, August 16, 1982, pp. 26–29.